RENEWALS 458-4574
DATE DUE

	APR 24 2008		
GAYLORD			PRINTED IN U.S.A.

The Char

D0038754

*For Geoff Armstrong for his part in building the CIPD and
for Duncan Brown for giving me scope.
And for the next generation who will help people learn at work
throughout the world. Over to you.*

The Changing World of the Trainer

Emerging Good Practice

Martyn Sloman

ELSEVIER

AMSTERDAM • BOSTON • HEIDELBERG • LONDON • NEW YORK • OXFORD
PARIS • SAN DIEGO • SAN FRANCISCO • SINGAPORE • SYDNEY • TOKYO
Butterworth-Heinemann is an imprint of Elsevier

Butterworth-Heinemann is an imprint of Elsevier
Linacre House, Jordan Hill, Oxford OX2 8DP, UK
30 Corporate Drive, Suite 400, Burlington, MA 01803, USA

First edition 2007

Copyright © 2007. Published by Elsevier Ltd. All rights reserved

No part of this publication may be reproduced, stored in a retrieval system or transmitted in any
form or by any means electronic, mechanical, photocopying, recording or otherwise without
the prior written permission of the publisher

Permissions may be sought directly from Elsevier's Science & Technology Rights
Department in Oxford, UK: phone (+44) (0) 1865 843830; fax (+44) (0) 1865 853333;
email: permissions@elsevier.com. Alternatively you can submit your request online
by visiting the Elsevier web site at http://elsevier.com/locate/permissions, and selecting
Obtaining permission to use Elsevier material

Notice
No responsibility is assumed by the publisher for any injury and/or damage to persons or property
as a matter of products liability, negligence or otherwise, or from any use or operation of any
methods, products, instructions or ideas contained in the material herein.

British Library Cataloguing in Publication Data
A catalogue record for this book is available from the British Library

Library of Congress Cataloguing in Publication Data
A catalogue record for this book is available from the Library of Congress

ISBN-13: 978-0-7506-8053-0
ISBN-10: 0-7506-8053-9

For information on all Butterworth-Heinemann publications
visit our web site at http://books.elsevier.com

Typeset by Charon Tec Ltd (A Macmillan Company), Chennai, India
www.charontec.com
Printed and bound in The Netherlands

07 08 09 10 11   10 9 8 7 6 5 4 3 2 1

Library
University of Texas
at San Antonio

Working together to grow
libraries in developing countries

www.elsevier.com | www.bookaid.org | www.sabre.org

ELSEVIER   BOOK AID
            International   Sabre Foundation

Contents

Series Preface

Contemporary organizations are increasingly operating in a context that is service-led and knowledge-driven. The volatility of the external context and the rapid pace of change increasingly demand innovative approaches to maximize organizational performance. People are increasingly recognized as the key element in organizational capability and the need for effective and appropriate people development is more important than ever before. The responsibility for effective people development is shared between senior managers, training professionals, line managers and individual employees but the challenges facing today's organizations provide an ideal opportunity for the training function to demonstrate its ability to add value at a strategic level. To take advantage of this opportunity it is necessary to not only recognize the changes that are required but also to be able to implement them effectively.

Whilst much has been written about people development generally and training interventions specifically, real life examples of what works and what doesn't are often not context-specific. Trainers and managers can often face an overwhelming pressure to follow trends or apply quick fixes to a range of people development issues and it can be difficult to determine what to change and how to change it in order to make a difference. We have therefore developed this series to bridge the gap between theory and implementation by providing workable solutions to complex people management issues and by sharing organizational experiences. The books within this series draw on live examples of strategic HR in practice and offer practical insights, tools and frameworks that will help to transform the individual and functional delivery of HR within a variety of organizational contexts.

The Changing World of the Trainer is a valuable addition to the series as it shows the pivotal contribution that people development can make to organizational performance. The central premise of the book is that the context in which learning, training and development is delivered has changed radically from the time when the systematic training model was dominant. The book makes a strong case for the need for people developers (or trainers) to recognize that new competitive models demand a different approach to the acquisition of knowledge and skills to serve the organization. In this new approach the emphasis shifts from training to learning and the function of people development becomes learner- rather than trainer-centred.

This book is written for everyone who has responsibility for planning and delivering interventions to enhance the skills and knowledge of the workforce. Drawing on a wealth of experience, the author creates a vision of learning and development in which the benefits to individuals and organizations are evident. Although under-pinned by theory and academic research, the book is essentially practical and eminently readable. The reader is guided through each of the nine propositions, which are clearly explained and illustrated with case studies from a vast range of organizations from private, public and not-for-profit sectors. The use of different organizations serves to emphasize the need to make interventions context-specific; learning and development is definitely a case where one size does not fit all. This is further supported by the use of check-lists at the end of ear- lier chapters to help practitioners identify key issues in their own organization. The book is also truly international with case studies from organizations in 19 countries across Europe, India, the USA and Canada, China, South Africa and the Middle East. Furthermore, the final section of the book considers the extent to which the emergent approach to learning and development has become a model with global relevance. This book provides inspiration and practical advice to any- one involved in people development who aims to increase their value to and influ- ence in their organization.

Julie Beardwell
Associate Dean & Head of HRM
Leeds Business School

Linda Holbeche
Director of Leadership & Organisational
Development
The Work Foundation

Other books in *The HR Series* include:

Organization Design: The Collaborative Approach by Naomi Stanford

Transforming HR: Creating Value through People by Martin Reddington, Mark Williamson and Mark Withers

HR – The Business Partner: Shaping a New Direction by Barbara Kenton and Jane Yarnall

Preface and acknowledgements

This book is written for practitioners. It is hoped that it will be of value to those who are planning and delivering interventions in organizations that are intended to enhance the knowledge and skills of the workforce. A decade ago these people would have been designated as trainers. Today, however, roles have been blurred and many different players in organizations are involved in the process of learning, training and development. 'Trainers' (to use the term for the time being) operate across a wider canvas and are developing new approaches and require new skills. A new vocabulary is emerging to describe their activities. They are joined in their efforts to increase the knowledge and skills of the workforce by management developers, organization developers and now by talent managers.

Moreover, this change of role is occurring throughout the world. Trainers are facing similar challenges and problems, whatever their nationality. This makes it an exciting time for the profession: we have a unique opportunity to make a significant contribution to the organization and to the individual, irrespective of our location. It is a good time to ask where we are coming from, what are our objectives and to share information on how to get there.

For 20 years I made my living as a trainer and training manager. I worked in both public and private sector organizations and in management consultancy. Not only did I enjoy the job greatly, but I acquired a considerable respect for my fellow professionals. Almost without exception, they believed that what they were doing was worthwhile and brought their full capabilities to bear on the task in hand and, in the spirit of the profession, strove to extend those capabilities.

Some six years ago, I was fortunate to be able to join the staff of the Chartered Institute of Personnel and Development. This gave me the time and scope to research the issues that had emerged during my previous employment. It also brought me into contact with a wide range of people management and development specialists, both in the UK and overseas. Many of them have contributed to my thinking and ideas – far more than those whom I have explicitly mentioned in the text. However, it is a pleasure to be able to thank some of the many people who have assisted and supported my work.

First of all, my appreciation to my colleagues at the Chartered Institute of Personnel and Development (CIPD), especially my bosses Geoff Armstrong and Duncan Brown. They gave me the essential resources of time and budget and supported the project from the outset. All my colleagues within the research function supplied some insights or input at critical stages, but particular thanks are due to Victoria Winkler, Eileen Arney, Jessica Jarvis, Barbara Salmon, Annie Bland and Charlotte Richardson.

The following people acted as critical readers: Deepali Prashantham, Gill Rudge, Sandra Smith, Carmel Kostos and Alison Walker. Toni Borsattino undertook extensive analysis of the information provided by participants at the various input meetings held across the world. The members of CIPD's Learning Training and Development Panel were an invaluable source of good advice. Two members of the panel, Janice Caplan and Jennifer Taylor, provided many ideas and their contribution was particularly valued. Jennifer Taylor prepared the list of practical questions which have been included at the end of the chapters in the earlier parts of the book.

From the ASTD, Brenda Sugrue, Ray Rivera and Tony O' Driscoll were of great assistance as was Graham O' Connell of the UK's National School of Government. To ensure that the work retained its international perspective, a global steering group was consulted at various stages. My thanks to its membership: Adrian Morgan and Carmel Kostos (Australia); Andrzej Wozniakowski (Poland); Carmel McNaught (Hong Kong); Doug Watt (Canada); Frances Wilson (UK); Gary Willmott and Son Joo Gog (Singapore); Norman Jardine (Belgium); Paul Sudnik (UK/Poland); Tony Ren (China); Prim Kumar (China); and Lois Webster (USA).

Lois Webster and Prim Kumar were crucial in ensuring access to organizations in China; my appreciation to them and Prim's colleagues and my friends in the Alphasta consultancy, Beijing, China.

Much of the energy which drove this project came as a result of the interviews with those responsible for the initiatives described in the case studies. In my view, as will become evident, these are the people who are defining the future of my chosen profession. It is in good hands. I have acknowledged them by name throughout, but there is insufficient space to list the large number of people who facilitated the introductions. I hope that no one will be offended at what can only be a general note of appreciation. One organization was especially supportive, so special thanks to all who helped at the Hilton Group.

Finally, on a domestic note, my thanks to my wife Anne. She readily accepted the need for extensive travel, early morning and late evening telephone calls to finalize overseas case studies and extensive periods writing in our Norfolk home. The same is true of our cat, Poppy, who is the subject of the cameo that begins the text proper.

PART 1

Introduction

1

The central premise

Fifteen years ago, we extended our family with the addition of a cat. My wife comes from rural Norfolk, in the East of England, and the cat was born in her home village of Little Snoring. The cat, then a tiny kitten, had lived in a barn; faced with a cat flap in a terraced house in London, she did not know what to do. She looked quizzically at me, my wife and my sons. After an interval my elder son said: 'OK Dad, what are you going to do now? Are you going to bring back a flip chart from work and draw a diagram? Are you going to go through yourself to demonstrate? Or are you going to borrow the firm's video camera, push the cat through the flap, play the recording and ask the cat what three things it could have done better?'

Nothing it seems to me better captured the trainer mind-set at the time. We could design and deliver effective training in classroom situations. We could deploy a range of alternatives. We were committed, positive, helpful and innovative, but we were often a bit peripheral. Our basic models were trainer-centred rather than learner-centred. We concentrated on what we could deliver rather than what the learner might need.

At that time, the dominant model for training, learning and development in organizations was known as Instructional Systems Design (ISD). This had its origins in work undertaken in the US military. Taught extensively in North American Universities and Colleges, it crossed the Atlantic to the UK in the late 1960s where it became known as the systematic training model. Given this pedigree, ISD, or systematic training, has influenced the thinking of trainers throughout the world – indeed, for many it defined their job.

Essentially, the ISD/systematic training model sees the actions necessary to improve individual and team skills (and by implication the skills available to the organization) as a series of sequential steps or interventions. These steps are: identify training needs, design training, deliver training and evaluate the training.

It would be surprising if any model that was developed in the last century could still command the same central position in the trainers' thinking. The argument advanced throughout this book is that the context in which learning, training and development must be delivered has changed radically. We are operating in an economy that is service-led and knowledge-driven. Different business models apply and these require a different approach to the promotion and development of workforce skills.

In this book, we will consider the consequences of the new context in which we operate. The core argument will be that new competitive models demand a different approach to the acquisition of knowledge and skills to serve the organization. Importantly, and this will be considered in this introductory chapter, the emphasis has shifted from training to learning and the role of the trainer becomes learner- rather than trainer-centred. This necessitates a different set of relationships with managers across the organization – we will describe this as a partnership model. Although the interventions must depend on the nature of the business, the role of the trainer (or people developer, which will be our preferred term) has become one of supporting, accelerating and directing learning interventions that meet organizational needs and are appropriate to the learner and the context.

The book will proceed as follows. In Part one we will discuss in turn our central premise, the new context in which we are operating and the consequences for delivery practice. In this first chapter, we will present the case for becoming learner- rather than trainer-centred in our approach. The chapters which make up Part two (Chapters 2 through to 4) explain this further by considering why this change is necessary and what has brought it about. In Part three, Chapters 5 through to 10 consider aspects of the trainers' job. Our traditional, well-established approaches must be considered in a new light and refined to take account of different circumstances – this does not mean that all previous practices should be abandoned. Indeed, the tone of the book is optimistic. Provided we are willing to embrace change and adapt, we can expect a considerable increase in our value to and influence in the organization.

The final part of the book takes us into some different territory. In Part four (Chapters 11 through to 15), we will ask whether the emergent approach to training and people development has become a global model. This is not only a fascinating and challenging question in itself, but is of critical importance for the future progress of the world economy.

The conclusion that will be presented in this final part is that the underlying model is the same throughout the world. Those involved in learning, training and development are intervening to develop the knowledge and skills of the workforce to allow the organization to deliver high value products and more efficient services. That is what we are about, wherever we are. However, we are operating in some very different circumstances and therefore need to intervene in different ways. In particular, the prior receptiveness of the learner, what we will call labour legacy, must be a major factor in the nature of the interventions that are likely to be effective in promoting learning.

Throughout the book, we will present case studies drawn from a whole range of organizations. They are intended both to highlight aspects of the challenges facing those responsible for training and learning and the approaches that they are adopting to meet those challenges. They highlight good practice but are not intended to define best practice. As will be seen, the form of activity or intervention adopted is often very specific to the context of the organization.

The arguments developed in this book draw much of their inspiration from this case material. They have also been influenced by the insights assembled during a series of international seminar sessions involving those involved in people development in a variety of different countries. No claim is made that large numbers of people who contributed to the case studies or at meetings are in any way representative of the whole community of trainers. Those who agreed to be interviewed, attended meetings or contributed to polls and discussion sites were a self-selected group who were interested in the challenges facing their profession. They are likely to be better at their job than the profession as a whole.

Any current investigation of the international pattern of learning and training must rely heavily on the case study technique. In educational research this has been developed into something known as 'narrative enquiry'. This involves undertaking transcribed conversations with informed or relevant parties, going 'where the story leads', undertaking analysis and drawing conclusions. At this stage, there is little alternative to this approach – it would be quite impossible, for example, to have undertaken a robust international survey of global learning and development practice. It would be nice to have a sound body of well-researched, academically-sound, information in many of the areas we discuss, but neither the information base nor the shared vocabulary of understanding is available at present. Academic researchers are asked to excuse this deficiency and take comfort in the fact that there is a huge task awaiting their attention.

However, and this will be argued more powerfully in the last sections of this book, it is important to begin a debate and share information among practitioners on the problems that we face. In this way we can hope to advance together. We cannot wait for precise information before beginning the discussion.

Some propositions

The arguments advanced in the first three parts of the book will be developed around nine propositions. These are presented in Table 1.1 and set out the context in which knowledge and skill acquisition takes place in the modern organization.

These propositions were developed in the second half of 2005 by an expert panel of practitioners assembled by the Chartered Institute of Personnel and Development (CIPD). A larger number of propositions were presented to the panel and those that did not gain support were eliminated and those that were deemed ambiguous were redrafted. In November 2005, the nine propositions were placed on the CIPD

Table 1.1 Summary propositions and scores

1. A shift is taking place from training, an instructor-led content-based intervention, to learning, which is a self-directed work-based process, leading to increased adaptive capacity.	7.28
2. Effective individual learning is critical if employees are to acquire the knowledge and skills needed to support the organization's business objectives and delivery targets.	8.98
3. A review of training and development interventions must ensure that the learning achieved is aligned with business activity.	8.84
4. Many different HR roles are involved in the people development effort and the boundaries between organizational development, management development and training are becoming increasingly blurred.	7.41
5. Those in senior management need to be aware of the implications of the shift from training to learning and give their full support to the new processes and practices that must be implemented in the organization.	8.91
6. The delivery of effective people development practices requires a considerable increase in commitment and enhanced skills from all managers, particularly first-line managers.	8.85
7. While off-the-job classroom-based training still has a place, it no longer occupies the central role in training provision as other forms of intervention are becoming more important.	6.74
8. Technology is becoming an important enabler in people development, but there are many conceptual and practical issues to be resolved surrounding its implementation.	7.88
9. It is important to demonstrate the value to be derived from people development activities, but traditional hierarchical training evaluation may not be the most appropriate method.	7.68

The right-hand column gives the average score recorded by over 1000 participants. They were asked to rate their agreement on a scale of 0–10, where 0 was 'strongly disagree' and 10 was 'strongly agree'.

website and members involved in training and development (and interested non-members) were invited to indicate the extent to which they agreed or disagreed with the statements.

Just over 1000 people completed this poll from November 2005 to May 2006. As is evident from the Table, all the propositions secured a significant measure of agreement. Looking at the results in a little more detail, however, offers some useful advance insights on the issues that will be considered in the chapters that follow. It is helpful to divide the propositions into three groups.

The propositions that command the highest support are numbers 2, 3, 5 and 6. These can all be said be to related to the role of training in the business. The message here is positive – learning, training and development are now important drivers of organizational success, but we need to involve all parties to leverage our activities. Two propositions form the middle section in terms of agreement and both concern current problems or 'work-in-progress' for the profession. These are propositions 8, on technology and 9, on evaluation. These cover important technical questions and indicate areas where we need to improve our practice.

The three propositions that received the lowest scores – though, even here, a high measure of agreement was recorded – were numbers 1, 4 and 7. All three relate to the trainer's role and the shift from the traditional classroom model. One interpretation is that many respondents see a move to a more varied approach to delivery and a shift to a more interventionist 'organizational development' type role as being desirable if they are to do their jobs effectively. However, such a transition takes time. In their organizations, they may be progressing slowly and may, indeed, be meeting some resistance. It will be seen that this interpretation is consistent with the pattern that emerges in many of the case studies – particularly those drawn from less advanced economies.

Because these nine statements command general agreement it does not mean that they are mere truisms. One of the major arguments that will be developed throughout this book is that broadly similar considerations apply in some very different situations. Essentially, we are all trying to move in the same direction and facing the same barriers and constraints. This point will be illustrated further in Chapter 5 when we will consider some barriers to progress.

Training to learning

In the first three parts of the book, a discussion against the background of the propositions will be used to develop a new framework. Irrespective of the organization, the trainer must consider needs, delivery and effectiveness. However, the interventions that lead to more effective learning do not simply lie in the domain of the trainer. Moreover, they are ongoing activities not a sequential process. The trainer will therefore no longer be concentrating on a series of discrete activities which follow from projects or events that they have introduced or been asked to manage. As will be seen, their role is much wider and this is, in part, a consequence of the shift in focus from training to learning, which is the first proposition to be considered in this book.

Proposition 1   A shift is taking place from training, an instructor-led content-based intervention, to learning, which is a self-directed work-based process, leading to increased adaptive capacity.

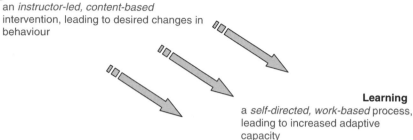

Training
    an *instructor-led, content-based*
    intervention, leading to desired changes in
    behaviour

Learning
a *self-directed, work-based* process,
leading to increased adaptive
capacity

Figure 1.1 The shift from training to learning [2, p. 26–7]

In 2002 and 2004, the Chartered Institute of Personnel and Development com-missioned Cambridge Programme for Industry to produce two research reports. The first, 'How do people learn?' looked at how people do and can learn at work. The report's authors introduced and analysed a number of different theoretical stances (or learning pedagogy) [1]. The second report 'Helping people learn' looked at the practical steps that could and should be taken to encourage individual and team learning [2].

Helping people learn offered precise definitions of the terms training and learn-ing and these are set out in Figure 1.1 [2].

Jake Reynolds, the author of 'Helping people learn', argued that a shift from training to learning is both inevitable and desirable. He characterized this shift in the following terms: 'The progressive movement from the delivery of content to the development of learning capabilities is a people development strategy' [2, p. 27]. Although they may not articulate it as clearly, it will be shown that this is exactly what many trainers are trying to achieve.

In the next chapter, it will be argued that this shift of emphasis from training to learning is a consequence of the changing competitive business model. However, at this stage, it is important to recognize that training and learning describe different activities. Critically, learning lies in the domain of the learner. Only learners can learn: they can be made to sit in the training room or in front of a screen, but they cannot be made to learn. Therefore, an effective strategy to promote learning must consider the wider context and issues of management, motivation and preparedness.

The shift from training to learning will happen in any event but, if it is not man-aged effectively, it will be a haphazard process. Employees will learn bad practices as well as good practices. They will rapidly learn from their peers the extent to which an organization will tolerate substandard performance, for example, but this does not feature as a topic in training intervention! Therefore, trainers need to develop a strategy to manage the shift from training to learning. Such a strategy will give rise to a set of activities or interventions.

The next case studies presented in this book illustrate such strategies – they were developed for organizations facing some very different challenges.

The European Commission is one of the larger organizations considered in this book. It is certainly the most multinational (Case study 1.1). The Head of Training inherited a situation where staff were under trained. Having introduced a range of training courses, his challenge is now to move to the next stage where the emphasis is on learning.

Case study 1.1 From training to learning in the European Commission

Introduction and background

In 2006, some 28 000 staff were employed at the European Commission with the largest number based in Brussels, a heavy concentration in Luxembourg and the remainder across various sites in Europe and beyond. Following the accession of ten new members in 2004 (from Eastern Europe, the Baltic States and Cyprus and Malta), there are now 25 members and 21 official languages. Staff are drawn in representative proportions from all 25 countries and must be able to communicate in at least two official languages – English and French being the most commonly used. The challenge of training and developing such a diverse group is the subject of a separate case study.

In 2000, major reforms in the internal management of the European Commission were implemented, following the resignation of the Commission in 1999. As a consequence, there was an increased emphasis on good management in general and, in particular, in the importance of people management and development. A number of new personnel policies were introduced, including a new appraisal system. One of the main strands of the reform process was the need for a more coherent strategic framework for human resources. A Commission decision of 7 May 2002 called on the Commission's Directorate-General for Personnel and Administration (DG ADMIN) to:

Ensure overall coherence of training policy and action in the Commission, identify training needs which are in the interest of the Commission as a whole and designate training actions which have a compulsory character or which are essential prerequisites for certain career steps.

It is fair to say that, before the 2000 reforms, a limited amount of training activities were in place and they were insufficiently coordinated.

The central training function and its challenges

Norman Jardine is Head of the Learning and Development Unit in DG ADMIN. He manages a central team of some 50 people and coordinates the activities of additional training staff in the 40 Directorates General which comprise the Commission. The client group of learners range from the most senior specialists through to the wide range of administrative and support staff present in any large organization. He has identified the following as his global challenge. First are the problems and opportunities based in working in a multilingual, multicultural and multinational organization. This is the subject of a separate case study (see Chapter 13, Case study 13.2, p. 237).

The second challenge, to an extent compounded by the first, is the sheer complexity of the organization, the changing agenda and the need to deliver a wide range of initiatives against a date time pressure. There are increasing demands on staff, they travel a lot and can arrive with expectations that working for the Commission will provide them with excellent opportunities and support for career development. As a result, there are many positive drivers for the training and learning from staff themselves.

Norman Jardine faces challenges that many training managers in large organizations would recognize. He has to convince line managers who have a widely different range of prior experience and commitment to training, learning and development and different views of its importance. Withdrawal rates from events due to workload pressure can be high.

In addition, he would like to be in a position to demonstrate more effectively the importance of the training, learning and development effort.

From training to learning

A key element is Norman Jardine's strategy to shift the balance away from training to learning. Initially, following the reforms of the early 2000s, a target average of 10 days training per year per staff member was set. By 2005, this had been achieved, with an average of 11.5 days per person.

This target has had the effect of gaining awareness and respect of the value of training and integration across the Commission. However, in Norman Jardine's view, there is simply too much 'classical' training in place. He wishes to see other forms of learning being supported and a far better relationship between the immediate job task and individual learning. This means:

> *25% less training, much more activity in teams and a sharper focus on the demands of the job.*

He has illustrated his intentions in practical terms.

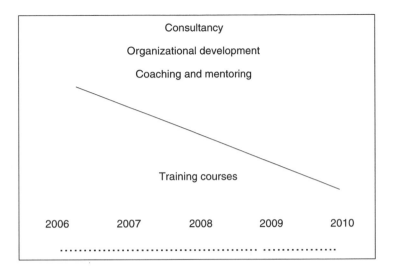

A requirement and consequence will be a different approach, skill set and competencies from trainers themselves. One of his intentions for his own team is to create a set of client managers who can build a better relationship with DG ADMIN's service:

If not, we will be seen as the bureaucrats in the middle who make people do things they don't want to do.

A related challenge is the need to develop better communication channels with the job-holders themselves.

Norman Jardine feels that the shift from training to learning will receive strong support over time since any move to take learning beyond the formal course has been well received when it has been implemented. In his words, part of the reasons for the over-emphasis on formal training has arisen because in the past:

No-one has been brave enough to say we should do things differently.

The case based on Cavendish Farms in Canada (Case study 1.2, Figure 1.2) describes an initiative where participants are self-selecting. The organization here has chosen to support an intervention which signals strong commitment to individual learning and displays a powerful sense of corporate social responsibility and meeting the needs of the local community.

Case study 1.2 The learning centre at Cavendish Farms Corporation, Prince Edward Island

Background and context

Cavendish Farms, 'The Potato Specialists', is a quality producer of frozen potato products; the corporation grows, processes and sells potato products throughout Canada, the USA, the Caribbean, Europe and Asia. Cavendish Farms has three North American production facilities: one in North Dakota, USA and two in Prince Edward Island (PEI), Canada. This case study concerns the introduction and development of a learning centre at the processing plants in New Annan, PEI. Customers of the plant include grocery stores, restaurant chains and well-known fast-food outlets.

Some 850 employees work at this New Annan facility. Approximately 150 are managers, staff and supervisors and the remainder are employees who are directly involved in the various departments which, together, yield the final product. These employees work in diverse areas including storage (80 million pounds of potatoes are stored on site), the farm shop, raw receiving, processing, packaging, shipping, quality assurance, maintenance, stores and waste water treatment. The plants are highly automated, so many of the jobs are concerned with routine processes. However, it is the commitment, knowledge and skills of the employees which contribute to the process efficiency and improvement.

Prince Edward Island is the smallest of the Atlantic Provinces on Canada's east coast. Although it is known for its unspoiled beauty and agricultural industry, approximately half of the Island's 130 000 residents are in urban centres. PEI is a small province with a competitive job market and Cavendish Farms is the Island's largest private sector employer. As such, through its commitment to workplace literacy and life-long learning, it is enhancing the learning opportunities of the employees, their families and the larger community.

The learning centre

As an indication of its commitment to employee learning, Cavendish Farms opened a learning centre in 2003. It consists of a well-equipped classroom, with 10 computer stations, a library, whiteboards and associated educational resources. Importantly, it is staffed by a full-time licensed teacher. One of the initial tasks facing the teacher, Ellyn Lyle, is to undertake an individual assessment of the learner and his or her needs. She has developed a formal assessment tool which establishes baselines in self-perception, prior opinion of schooling, communication skills, vocabulary, reading comprehension, grammar usage and mechanics of writing, and mathematics. In her words though, it really comes down to the following:

The learner and I have a chat. Well-phrased questions help me to determine where that learner currently is (baseline) and where he or she would like to be. Nothing to it – we build the bridge. It may take a few months, or it could take a few years. It's really about commitment. Theirs to themselves and mine to learn with each and every one of them as the individuals they are.

The learning centre is open from 8:00 am–4:00 pm Monday to Friday and typically some eight individuals will be present at any one time. The challenge for the instructor is to provide support, stimulation and facilitation for individuals to help them remain engaged with learning.

The Company has defined the centre objectives as follows:

■ Improve literacy, numeracy and critical thinking skills of employees at all levels.
■ Improve employees' understanding of their contribution to the organization.
■ Provide employees with the skills and competencies necessary to improve their workplace performance and to increase their opportunities for advancement.
■ Provide academic assistance to apprentices and others involved in training and education opportunities.
■ Increase employees' morale and confidence.

Although the emphasis is on individual choice, a range of specific programmes are offered and marketed. Particularly popular courses are those that end with grade 12 English and math credits, General Educational Development (GED) diplomas, professional writing and continuing education (post-secondary facilitation) and those that enhance computer skills. As indicated by the chart in Figure 1.2, there are also several other popular areas of study.

The Company covers the full costs of the centre, supplying the teacher, resources and space. It has also introduced the following cost-sharing policy as an encouragement to individual learning – for every two hours spent in learning, the company pays the individual one hour's regular wage. There is no limit to the number of hours an employee can commit to study. Cavendish Farm has invited family members of employees to participate in the learning centre as well. Although the cost-sharing incentive cannot apply, the materials are still covered and they attend at no personal cost.

What is exciting about the centre, according to the instructor, Ellyn Lyle, is its proximity to the workplace – it is situated at the plant. This removes barriers and creates opportunities. As Ellyn Lyle puts it, 'If I am discussing Pythagoras' theorem, we can go out and look at the angle formed by the jib of a crane'.

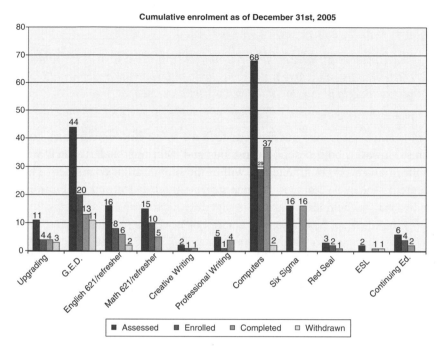

Figure 1.2 Enrolment at the Cavendish Farms learning centre

The basis of participation

The following extract from a company publication outlines the basis on which the centre operates:

- Participation is completely voluntary.
- The environment must be based on confidentiality and respect.
- Classes are scheduled at the learners' convenience.
- Each programme is based on the learner's goals, for his/her satisfaction.
- The instructor is also a learner and engages the employees in the reciprocal nature of teaching and learning.

It can be seen that the emphasis at the centre is on general education for the self-motivated learner but, as Ellyn Lyle stresses, this creates enhanced confidence, which leads to greater commitment and capability. As one 50-year-old female learner states:

> *Returning to school has been a real inspiration. The relaxed and friendly atmosphere makes us look forward to each new day of learning with confidence and renewed spirits.*

Initially, when the centre was created in 2003, the intention was to proceed on a 12-week trial basis period; this has been extended repeatedly. The centre is now an important feature of Cavendish Farms' approach to skill development and, by December 31, 2005, 190 of the 850 management, staff and employees at the New Annan plants had requested and participated in learning at the centre.

At first glance these two cases seem to have more differences than common features. However, both describe conscious and clear approaches which are well-formulated and well communicated within the organization concerned. They are transparent strategies designed to encourage individual learning. Moreover, they show that training and learning are not mutually incompatible; both have their part to play in building up the knowledge and skills needed to move the organization forward. Only in one respect are they competing activities: both require energy, time and resources from the trainer. It is impossible for any individual to spend all of his or her time in the training room and simultaneously plan and deliver interventions which support the individual learners in the workplace.

Adaptive capacity/capability

The second half of Proposition 1 argued that learning led to increased adaptive capacity. This is an important feature of the distinction between training and learning. Indeed, Jake Reynolds, writing in 'Helping People to Learn' went as far as to argue that adaptive capacity is the greatest gift of learning as:

It allows an organization to remain agile in the face of uncertain future conditions, whereas other outcomes of learning, such as new knowledge and skills, tend to have specific applications and a shorter shelf-life [2, p. 5].

and he argued that:

Learning leads to adaptations in the behaviour of employees that, if properly aligned with group and corporate goals, will allow the organisation to deliver greater value to stakeholders [2, p. 4].

There is a danger of allowing vocabulary to obscure what is at heart a very simple concept. Both training and learning contribute to the creation of enhanced knowledge and skills which work to the benefit of the organization. Training – the instructor-led, content-based activity – is more specific and targeted in its ambitions and scope; in some circumstances this can be a strength. However, individual and organizational learning can do far more. By increasing the employee's confidence and self-belief, it can make the individual far more able to learn new techniques and processes. This develops organizational capacity or capability. Either term is acceptable – there is no need to get hung up on semantics. What is important at this stage is to recognize that a workforce who are willing and able to adapt will allow the organization to compete and deliver. Building adaptive capacity is a realization of the Chinese proverb: 'Give a man a fish and you feed him for a day. Teach a man to fish and you feed him for a lifetime'.

In 2005, the Institute of Employment Studies (IES), a research and consultancy centre, produced a report for the Chartered Institute of Personnel and Development and a number of UK Governmental organizations. The report considered a number of aspects of the contributions of skills to business performance and concentrated on the problem of measurement. This last aspect will be further explored in Chapter 10. What is of particular note at this stage is the exploration of the way in which training and development, to use the IES term, had an impact. This introduced the term capability, which was defined in the following terms:

> *Capability is expressed in turn, through the activities of people – the effort they make, the new products or services they create or the quality of what they do. That activity will impact on the amount of work that takes place – the productivity of the workplace, and the satisfaction of consumers or customers of the organisation. And it is productivity and customer satisfaction which are likely to give rise to final outcomes of profit or shareholder value (for private sector companies).* [3, p. 9]

Individual capability, however defined, can be developed through learning and training interventions. The challenge of organizational capability development is much broader:

> *What we do know is that it would appear to be affected by the wide range of HR practices that have been linked in the literature to organisational performance and therefore these practices may help us understand just what it is that underpins capability and what can be used to help organisations monitor and improve their performance. . .*
>
> *However, whereas training and skill development are focused on the growth of capability, the effectiveness of the workforce is also dependent on the way in which it is utilised in practice. The most educated and highly trained people may not do a good job if they are disinterested or de-motivated and therefore this utilisation is dependent on the motivation and engagement of employees. Their attitudes to their organisation, their manager, their colleagues, customers and their job, all affect their performance.* [3, p. 10–11]

This extract extends our understanding of adaptive capacity in a number of important aspects.

Capacity (or capability) is not simply a matter of acquiring or possessing the knowledge and skills to do current and future jobs. It is also about motivation and commitment (often lumped together as 'attitude'): the willingness on the part of the individual to apply the knowledge and skills when given the opportunity, indeed to seek that opportunity. This must necessarily involve a wide range of human resource interventions to develop and reinforce that commitment and motivation. It cannot be done simply through encouraging relevant learning, still less can it be done entirely in the training room.

The useful model of capability development produced by the IES which considers component elements in building capacity is reproduced as Figure 1.3. Called the 4A Model, the elements are defined as follows:

- *Access*: the organization's policy and practice on recruitment and selection. The literature suggests that rigorous recruitment practices, valuing skills at selection and providing an opportunity for internal advancement in the organization, all contribute to performance.
- *Ability*: the skills of the workforce (generally proxied by qualifications), the provision of ongoing training and development opportunities including: on- and off-the-job training; coaching and mentoring; and structured work experience.

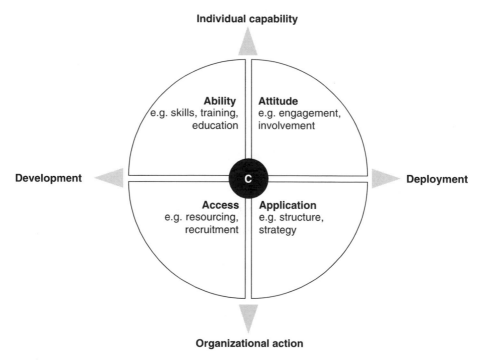

Figure 1.3 The 4A model of capability. Source: IES, 2005 [3, p. 17]

■ *Attitude*: the policies which can enhance employee motivation and engagement, such as performance management systems (including appraisal and one-to-one discussions with line managers), performance related reward, profit or gain sharing practices, family friendly working practices and communication practices.

■ *Application*: the opportunities organizations supply which enable people to apply their skills and enthusiasm in the workplace such as: job design – the scope the job provides for people to make a difference; practices encouraging people to contribute ideas; and fundamentally, the business strategy the organization is pursuing [3, p. 11–12].

What is helpful about this diagram is that it focuses on both individual and organizational aspects of capability and also emphasizes deployment, putting the capability to use, as well as developing that capability.

A new role definition

Irrespective of the organization, today's training professionals must operate in a wider context. They need to develop and deliver their initiatives through the involvement of a wide range of people in the organization. The shift from training to learning demands a new mind-set and new initiatives.

Against this background the following definition of the role of the trainer is offered:

Supporting, accelerating and directing learning interventions that meet organizational needs and are appropriate to the learner and the context.

How this can be achieved will be the subject of Part two of this book. This chapter will end by presenting some research, some questions that practitioners may wish to consider and a plea.

In this book, much of the research will be drawn from British and North American sources, but one of the joys of the project was the discovery that, throughout the world we are facing the same problems. Throughout the world, trainers are embarking on the same complex journey to design and implement more effective interventions to develop knowledge and skills in the organizations. Case study 1.3 therefore highlights some recent research undertaken by Italy's association of trainers and an Italian University. Many of the issues identified in their findings will be considered in later chapters.

Case study 1.3 An Italian perspective on training and learning

In 2006, AIF (Italy's Association of Trainers) and the University of Cà' Foscari, Venice, published the results of a major collaborative study on training strategies and policies in Italian companies [4]. Interviews were undertaken with training and/or human resources managers in 20 companies using a common methodology.

The conclusions demonstrated that training and learning are continuing to grow in importance. They also showed that some organizations are using increasingly sophisticated approaches to ensure that training and learning are meeting both business and individual needs. There were some conflicting responses evident, with indications that practice did not always match awareness. However, the central conclusion was:

Certainly training today, in the twenty sample organisations, has an increasing strategic importance, even compared to the recent past. This strategic importance is not just that training is seen as a way of developing people and their competencies, or evolving the culture of the business, but that it is also seen as a tool for improving competitiveness.

Among the indications that this was the case were:

- training needs analysis is more closely aligned to analysis of business strategy
- the role of the line manager in training and learning is increasing in importance
- training is covering a wider population than before
- training is being decentralized to business units
- the focus has changed from learning how, to doing in a particular context
- there is an increased link between training and work
- there is increasing emphasis on providing solutions that allow for the focus to be meeting the learning needs of the individual.

Specific findings on current Italian practice in these 20 organizations include the following points.

Line managers

Decentralization of training to line managers is happening in phases. In most cases, line managers are responsible for carrying out needs analysis and for requesting training, but the central training function is responsible for planning training and making it happen. Projects are developed and run jointly by the central training function and line managers. In some organizations there is a complete decentralization of training to business units. The loss of the 'big picture' here is seen by some as a drawback.

Individual needs identification

The report identified a number of trends in the way in which individual's needs were identified:

- people are responsible for their own development (it is their own responsibility and up to their initiative to decide which of the programmes being offered are appropriate)
- training programmes are being developed aimed at personal growth and employability and not necessarily connected to the person's role and work objectives
- emphasis is being placed on the needs of the individual, which may be different from those identified by the organization
- customized training solutions are gaining in use.

On-the-job training

- More than 80% of the sample organizations place significant importance on training on-the-job.
- However, this is rarely formalized or institutionalized.
- Training on the job is recognized as a reality, carried out by bosses, colleagues and others; it is often integrated into e-learning interventions, especially for updating operational processes or regulations.

The questions are set out as an Appendix to this chapter. They are drawn from the CIPD research project described in more detail at www.cipd.co.uk/helpingpeoplelearn

The plea concerns the terminology: given this wider set of responsibilities and activities, is the term 'trainer' appropriate? How many of those involved in 'supporting, accelerating and directing learning' spend most of their time acting as training instructors in a classroom? There is now a strong case for using the term 'people development' to describe this broader activity and people development professional or developer for short to describe the individual. These terms will be preferred in later analysis but, on those occasions where other writers or participants in case studies use the term trainer or training, this will be respected.

Appendix

Some practical questions

1. What are the key priorities for the business? List up to four high-profile activities or initiatives that management regards as critical drivers in the fulfilment of business objectives or service delivery targets.

2. How should the drivers you have listed above, be promoted by actions to support and promote individual and team learning?

3. What significant organizational change initiatives are taking place or are planned?

4. What opportunities do these change initiatives create for enhanced individual and team learning and improved learning practice throughout the organization?

5. What resources, time and money, will be required to take the actions suggested by your answers to the above questions?

6. How far is the distinction between training and learning, as illustrated in Figure 1.1 (p. 8), understood by others in your organization?

7. When did you last engage in discussions with your key stakeholders (i.e. your Chief Executive, senior business heads, other personnel professionals not in a training and learning role) on the above questions?

8. Do you have a formal articulated strategy for learning as opposed to a listing of training opportunities? If so, who in your organization is aware of it?

These questions were prepared by Jennifer Taylor based on extracts from the on-line tool on Training to Learning which is available to members through www.cipd.co.uk/helpingpeoplelearn

References

[1]. Caley, L., Mason, R. and Reynolds, J. (2002) How Do People Learn? London: Chartered Institute of Personnel and Development. Available at: http://www.cipd.co.uk/NR/rdonlyres/EE171F3B-A2D1-4A6F-A4A3-2AFBBE164688/0/2438howpeoplrn.pdf
[2]. Reynolds, J. (2004) Helping People to Learn: Strategies for Moving from Training to Learning. London: Chartered Institute of Personnel and Development.
[3]. Tamkin, P. (2005) Measuring the Contribution of Skills to Business Performance. Brighton: Institute for Employment Studies.
[4]. The research 'Indagine sugli Investimenti Formativi nelle Grandi Aziende n Italia – 2005' was undertaken by dell'Associazione Italiana Formatori and by the University 'Cà Foscari' of Venice, under the leadership of Ulderico Capucci. (see www.aifonline.it)

PART 2

The context

2

The New Economy

This chapter considers the business context in which the developer is operating. There is an important point to be made at the outset: training and development are derived activities; they take place as a consequence of business needs, not for their own sake. The aim of the organization can be variously described as driven by the need for profit (private sector), a requirement to deliver a public good or service (national or local government) or to achieve some aim considered worthwhile by a committed group of people (voluntary sector). There are multiple descriptions in between.

The argument advanced by those in human resources is that acquisition of appropriate knowledge and skills by the employees is, in most cases, essential to these aims and, in all cases, desirable. What has been argued in the previous chapter is that this acquisition will increasingly depend on learning rather than training. These ideas are brought together in the next proposition which is reproduced below.

> **Proposition 2** Effective individual learning is critical if employees are to acquire the knowledge and skills needed to support the organization's business objectives and delivery targets.

In the next chapter, some frameworks and models will be presented. They should assist in exploring the links between business objectives and people development.

First, however, we must ask ourselves what sort of jobs are involved in the modern economy? What sort of workforce do we employ? There are some arguments developed by Robert Reich that offer some useful insights. Although they have proved controversial, they have the advantage of clarity of analysis, which assists us in our thinking, and provide some clear guidance.

The Reich Thesis

Robert B. Reich was President Bill Clinton's Labour Secretary and a former Harvard academic. He is a forthright commentator on employment and work. In two significant books, 'The Work of Nations' [1] and 'Reason: Why Liberals will Win the Battle for America' [2], he looks at the nature of work in developed economies.

'The Work of Nations' was published as long ago as 1991 and the underlying thesis has been very influential. Essentially, Reich argues that it is in the interests of developed countries, and the USA in particular, to shift output from high volume to high value goods and services. Customers will pay a premium for such services and they cannot be readily duplicated elsewhere in the world. It will be seen that the desire to produce higher value added goods and services is a feature of virtually every organization featured in a case study in this book.

Where Reich is particularly insightful is when he considers the effect that such global competition has on the job tasks undertaken by those in employment. In 'The Work of Nations', he identified three broad categories of work, which he called routine production services, in-person services and symbolic analytic services.

To quote from 'The Work of Nations':

Routine production services entail the kind of repetitive tasks performed by the old foot soldiers of American capitalisation in the high volume enterprise. They are done over and over – one step in a sequence of steps for producing finished products tradeable in world commerce [1, p. 174].

In person services ... also entail simple and repetitive tasks ... the big difference between in-person servers and routine producers is that these *services must be provided person-to-person and cannot be sold worldwide* [1, p. 176].

Symbolic-analytic services ... include all the problem-solving, problem identifying and strategic-brokering activities. ... Like routine production services (but unlike *in-person services) symbolic-analytic services can be traded worldwide and thus must compete with foreign providers in the American market. But they do not enter world commerce as standardized things. Traded instead are the manipulation of symbols – data, words, oral and visual representations* [1, p. 177].

Reich developed his argument over an extended period – the books cited here were 12 years apart in publication. By 2004, he offered the following argument on the changing pattern of employment.

Every task that's repetitive – anything that can be done more cheaply by automated machinery or computer software or by a person labouring in a poor country – is no longer going to be done by Americans at American wages [2, p. 124].

>   *Look closely at the American economy today and you find the growing cat-*
>   *egories of work. The first involves identifying and solving new problems ... I*
>   *call this 'symbolic analytic' work because most of it has to do with analyzing,*
>   *manipulating and communicating through abstract symbols – numbers,*
>   *shapes, words, ideas. ... Most symbolic analysts work alone or in small teams.*
>   *If they work with others they often have partners and associates rather than*
>   *bosses or supervisors* [2, p. 128].
>
>   *The second growing category of work involves personal service such as the*
>   *nursing and physical therapy. ... Also included in this group are retail sales*
>   *personnel, restaurant and fast-food workers, hotel workers, barbers and hair*
>   *stylists, personal trainers, cab and limo drivers, household domestics, repair-*
>   *ers, plumbers, electricians, custodians, security guards, child-care workers,*
>   *elder-care workers and hospital attendants and orderlies* [2, p. 128–9].

So, in summary, the 'Reich thesis' is that the growth areas in employment in developed economies will consist of symbolic analysts or, to use a more popular expression, 'knowledge workers' and those involved in personal services. Routine production will be outsourced, probably overseas.

Much debate has taken place on the validity and importance of what we have described as the Reich thesis. There are differences of opinion on the extent to which his symbolic analysts and in-person service workers are becoming domin-ant in the developed economy. This has important implications for the public pol-icy debate on the best form of labour market intervention. However, there does not seem to be any question but that routine production services are declining in rela-tive terms in advanced economies.

The change in the pattern of the workforce has profound implications for eco-nomic policy. Improvement of workforce skills is a high priority for many gov-ernments throughout the world, as will be considered in Chapter 13. However, this economic policy aspect does not concern us in the context of our current discus-sion. What matters is how such an analysis can assist us in generating our ideas on learning and development in the organization. It will be argued that such a classi-fication, if not interpreted too precisely, can be of considerable value in assisting the design of a training and learning strategy. This will be demonstrated through case study illustrations. However, to position that discussion, a number of general points need to be made in advance.

The first is that many organizations contain a mixture of all three categories of workers identified by Reich. A modern hospital, for example in any country in the world, will employ knowledge workers/symbolic analysts (the specialist clinicians) or those involved in in-person services (porters and catering staff) and certainly administrative routine production staff (those involved in maintaining records). Is a maintenance engineer at the hospital a symbolic analyst (at a senior level), involved in routine production (at the most junior level) or in-person service (since the work has to be done on site)? Some departments and some jobs involve aspects of all three types of work.

The second general issue concerns the concept of value and its link with competition. The underlying point is simple; greater profitability is achieved through higher value added products which are produced by a workforce with better knowledge and skills. Hence, governments wish to invest in skills and try to move national output higher up the value chain into more sophisticated products. Many of the cases in this book, particularly those that describe private sector initiatives, are underpinned by an implicit desire on the part of the organization to move up the value chain.

A personal experience may illustrate this point. For Welsh Rugby supporters, the most enjoyable match of the season is our game with Ireland. Our good-humoured song for the bars of the stadium is 'I'd rather dig a pit than pave your drive'. The Welsh cultural heritage is based on a now defunct coal industry; the Irish have been stereotyped as building workers who travelled to find jobs. No harm is intended or taken: the two nations have a long-standing mutual affinity. The point of the story is that we, the Welsh, have got it completely wrong but the Irish (as stereotyped) have the right idea. The future lies in the personal services delivered at point of contact where there are opportunities for selling on and introducing higher value added products. Coal is a commodity and will be mined where it is cheapest.

As indicated earlier, the main purpose of introducing the Reich classification was the insight that it gives to the design of a learning and development strategy. The argument here is that each of the three categories makes a different contribution in generating value through the application of their knowledge and skills, their learning and development needs should therefore be considered differently. Again, it must be emphasized that the categories are blurred in practice, but illustrations will assist in making the point. Here we will alter the order of the categories and start with knowledge workers (his symbolic analysts), then go to routine production and then personal services.

Linklaters is one of the leading law firms in the City of London. It has highly motivated staff who seek to increase their knowledge and a global reach. Two different perspectives of the same issues are offered: one from the centre in Case study 2.1 and one from Hong Kong in Case study 2.2.

At the Amcor packaging plant in Radomsko, Poland, the challenge is very different (Case study 2.3). The need is to get the routine production workers to appreciate the importance of the acquisition of knowledge and skills. Only in that way will the plant be able to compete in the future.

Harvey Nichols, the fashion retailer, employs a sophisticated sales force involved in in-person or personal service activity. The intervention that is described in Case study 2.4 is based on peer group reinforcement of best practice.

Case study 2.1 Supporting the global learner at Linklaters

Background

Linklaters is one of the so-called 'magic circle' of law firms. With Head-quarters in the City of London, it has just over 500 partners and 6000 other staff – half of whom are fee-earning lawyers. The firm specializes in highly complex transactions, particularly those involving different national jurisdictions – much of its work is undertaken for financial institutions. As a result, the work is high-value added and rarely straightforward. The firm has 29 offices in 22 countries across the world and these necessarily include the major financial centres. In Asia, for example, it has offices in Tokyo, Japan, in greater China (Hong Kong, Beijing and Shanghai), Singapore and also Bangkok in Thailand.

The underlying challenge

The people employed at Linklaters are well-educated high achievers. They are 'career aggressive' in the sense that they are keen to demonstrate their expertise with both peers and clients and to receive appropriate recognition. Now, and in the future, clients are demanding a wider perspective from their advisers and Linklaters' lawyers must demonstrate, not only that they are experts in law, they must also display awareness of business strategy and an in-depth knowledge of client business – and have the skills to build relationships based on that knowledge.

Learning and development are therefore recognized as critical. Staff need to maintain their expertise and stay at the leading edge, with a precise knowledge of technical changes in the law. For the individual, mastery of knowledge and skills through learning is the gateway to career development. If such people are frustrated in career advancement through lack of development opportunities, they could well decide to leave the firm.

The challenge facing Linklaters' learning and development (L&D) team is therefore not one of engaging the learner. It is one of ensuring that all learners, irrespective of location, have access to learning opportunities that they will value. The firm's European Managing Partner has recently placed great emphasis on ensuring its staff in smaller offices, for example in Lisbon or Bratislava, can readily find access to learning they value. If such learning opportunities are available and the L&D team can make it easily accessible and if it adds value to clients, such learning will be put into practice.

The learning strategy

Off-the-job training events still have an important part to play. Indeed, despite the growth in the other forms of delivery, there has been an increase in training courses. Those events that are designed and delivered by the Global team include a Senior Leadership Programme using Harvard faculty, New Partner Induction, a Career Development Centre for senior associates, programmes for new associates and events with a specific focus like negotiation skills and maximizing profitability. Such events are organized globally and held in different locations in Europe and Asia. However, a whole variety of events are organized by different businesses or locations, beyond those on the actual programme and this is seen as a welcome development, not a threat to the centre.

Geographical and time constraints, however, have meant that there are limitations to what can be achieved through face-to-face exchange. As a result, the Head of Global Learning and Organizational Development, Des Woods, and his team have sought to develop electronic repositories of information and to use technology to distribute material. This has become a central feature of their strategy.

Currently, it is possible to access, through the firm's Intranet, some 200 separate media rich clips or videos which have been created internally and deal with technical or business issues. These are being generated at a rate of two or three a week and the final figure available is likely to exceed 1000. Des Woods sees this as an important way of creating and distributing learning and knowledge and one that is consistent with the firm's culture. He offers the following illustration of its value:

> In one of our smaller European offices, one of our partners visited a client and was asked what he knew about a highly complicated debt instrument. The partner committed to come back with a detailed answer the following day. That evening he was able to access and apply a video clip of a presentation on the subject by another partner in London earlier that year.

Des Woods estimates that up to 400 people in Linklaters will eventually be able to generate learning material and must be encouraged to do so. If they are engaged in this way they cannot, in his words, 'go through the bottleneck of learning and development'. A system must be in place to encourage the growth of such material, which is increasingly including material on wider business as well as technical issues. Web-casts, a synchronous form of e-learning, where participants receive a lecture delivered by subject master expert over their PCs, are also growing in importance. Linklaters have recently purchased new software to extend this facility. The role of Global Learning and Development is therefore twofold. First, to ensure that structures and systems are in place to capture and distribute material; this involves the specification of 'skins' or templates. Secondly, it is to increase awareness of what is available. According to Des Woods:

We really need to understand the market and ensure that valued products are available to meet the need of that market.

The global dimension

It can be seen from the above that the learning and development strategy must recognize the demanding client base: motivated and self-confident learners who are distributed geographically across the world. Structures and systems must be in place to meet their needs. This obviously demands an awareness of different cultural characteristics which could affect the learning offering.

This, Des Woods recognizes, is a critical part of his skill-set, but one he can only gain through experience. He describes the challenge as more subtle and less visible than people expect. The successful web-casts delivered from Hong Kong to audiences in other parts of Asia (described in Case study 2.2) reflected effective local mediation. In each of the offices someone acted as a facilitator and interpreter and used break-out groups during intermissions in the broadcast to develop and consolidate understanding and learning. A global message, central transmission and local mediation and support is, in Des Woods' view, a model that works across all locations.

Different cultural traditions and working patterns can raise issues for learning and development. In Japan, for example, western lawyers will work core, albeit extended, hours at the office. Japanese lawyers, the 'bengoshi', may arrive later but be committed to work very long hours and feel a great sense of guilt about taking any time away from the main focus of their work. They must therefore be instructed to take time to learn by their boss; it must be made compulsory. Generally in Asia, the attitude to learning events, once the individual is participating, is positive and this can make it more difficult to obtain accurate feedback – indeed feedback is best obtained through the participants' boss who will have received a more balanced picture. Another illustration of adjustments that can be made through experience is a recognition that non-UK participants are more likely to read and value pre-course material.

Des Woods recognizes the dangers of generalization and places much emphasis on local mediation, delivered by an aware individual. Given his emphasis in distribution through technology, he feels that there is also much to be done to ensure ease of access – further development of character-readers that manage Asian text are a good example. However, he is optimistic that such developments will be forthcoming and global access will become much easier.

Case study 2.2 Linklaters: a perspective from Hong Kong

In November 2005, Deepa Raval was appointed as Learning and Development Consultant Asia. She was seconded from the Headquarters' learning and development team, initially for a six-month period which was extended to eighteen months. Based in Hong Kong, her main objective was to ensure that base line training was in place across the full range of learning needs to support the firm's global focus on career development. These were: technical training for fee-earners; management and interpersonal skills at all levels; compliance and training to meet the requirements of the legal profession; IT training; and language training.

Building up provision

Generally, there is a high level of commitment from Partners – and the Region's Chief Operating Officer is particularly supportive. Linklaters is a knowledge-intensive organization with people who are committed to updating their skills. However, there are a number of practical problems in ensuring that training and learning provision meets requirements.

First, resources in the Asian offices of Linklaters are tightly managed and time to participate in non-fee-earning activities is at a premium. As Deepa Raval puts it:

> *If it is left to fee-earners to plan and implement training it won't happen. Clients' demands will always come first. They will leave it to the learning and development professional to take the initiative – and this is right given the demands of the business.*

At the outset, technical training was identified as the priority and here the expertise lies in-house. This training is based on the application of the law using the approach developed within the firm. There are specialist Linklaters' courses in such areas as legal drafting, acquisitions, loan agreements, private equity – and a whole range of areas of legal skills and knowledge.

It is important that, where possible, fee-earners learn together as the firm emphasizes shared knowledge across disciplines and offices. Every Linklaters office must have the capacity to transact operations to a consistently high quality across a wide range of jurisdictions. However, given that there are six offices in Asia, it is impossible to achieve the shared learning experience by holding events in one central location. The costs and travel time would be too great.

Technical training using video-conferencing

A particularly attractive solution, which overcomes these problems, involves the use of video conferencing. This approach has been adopted with some success and, once a month, it is used to deliver technical training sessions led by a Linklaters subject matter expert. He or she will present a session using PowerPoint slides in one of the Asian offices and it will be received and considered by learners in the offices across the region. The timing of the events is geared to fit round the peaks and troughs in the fee-earners' working day.

Importantly, there is a live facilitator in each office to support learners and manage the practical exercises and case study exercises. Events are structured to allow participants to share experiences in local break-outs and then report back to the whole group through video-conferencing.

Other training issues

The virtual conferences have proved a success and the immediate feedback from electronic reactionaries has produced good evaluation scores. However, Deepa Raval regards the less formal comments from participants and their Partner bosses as a better indicator of value:

> *People can be generous on evaluation forms – they can be uncomfortable in saying that they don't like something (in some cultures it may be a matter of 'face'). However, if these initiatives do not have an impact they would not be given the support to allow them to continue.*

The region is a full participant in the global partner development programme – including the Senior Leadership Development programme which uses the Harvard faculty and New Partner Induction. A customized version of New Partner Induction was recently held in Asia.

Deepa Raval offers the following comments on the way that cultural differences affect the delivery of training in the region:

> *There are differences and those responsible for the design and delivery of training must accommodate accordingly. It may be a matter of the learner's ability in the English language, it may be culture and it may be a mixture of both. However, delivery must be such that all learners can feel comfortable and thus in a state of mind where they can learn.*

33

In her view, the Tokyo office is probably the one with the most distinctive culture – not least because the client base is mainly Japanese. However, the important thing is to design training initiatives so that all offices receive the same opportunities and are requested to make the same contribution to the learning and development effort.

Case study 2.3 Effective learning in a Polish packaging plant – Amcor, Radomsko

Background and context

Amcor is one of the world's largest packaging companies; it has headquarters in Melbourne and 80% of its revenues are derived from activities outside Australia. It operates in 39 countries and has some 27 000 employees worldwide. Given this geographical spread, Amcor operates a decentralized structure with local managers having significant autonomy and responsibility for performance and growth.

One of Amcor's four key market segments is PET (polyethylene terephthalate) plastic bottles and jars. The plant at Radomsko in Poland (180 km south of Warsaw) is one of a number of production facilities. Raw materials are processed to produce shaped but not finished bottles which are then despatched to soft-drink or food producers. Amcor also has European plants in North Wales, Spain, Belgium, France and Germany and elsewhere outside Europe. The Radomsko factory is a low cost producer, but by no means the lowest in the world.

The Polish factory was established as a greenfield site in 1993 and since then it has passed through several changes of ownership before becoming part of Amcor in 2002. Seventy people are employed at Radomsko, of whom 40 can be described as process operatives (working across four shifts of ten employees). The remaining 30 are managers, supervisors, technicians and sales and administrative staff. The company has explicitly stated its commitment: 'To provide the training and development necessary to realize mutually beneficial individual and company goals'.

However, as the company statement puts it:

> We believe local people are better equipped to cope with their specific issues, whether it be negotiating with customers and suppliers or interfacing with their workforce. They understand the local culture and are quick to react in today's changing environment.

The underlying challenge

Paul Sudnik, Amcor Business Unit Director, Central & Eastern Europe, has held management responsibility for the plant since 2004. He is a professional manager with an engineering and production background and a strong personal commitment to employee development. He sees two major skills objectives: first, the need to create a more favourable attitude to education in general; secondly, the need to nurture 'the skill of care and judgement' among process operatives.

He is anxious to stress many positive aspects of the challenge. First, under a succession of owners, Radomsko, has been a professionally run and well-managed factory. The new machinery which, when installed in 1993 was state of the art, is well-understood by the workforce who have developed and shared the necessary process skills. Secondly, there is a stable and committed workforce; over three-quarters of them have been at the factory since it opened. The relatively remote location leads to a degree of stability, since comparable jobs are rare. Amcor is recognized as a good employer and this generates positive attitudes extending beyond mere compliance to retain the job.

However, Paul Sudnik regards the legacy of the previous attitude to employment in Poland as a barrier. Essentially, he feels that guaranteed employment did not create an individual incentive for the worker to seek to acquire and enhance skills. As a result, the employees are less conscious of the need to take responsibility for their learning and do not see sufficiently the link between enhanced skills and company profitability.

Further, certainly in Poland, there was not the educational structure in place to support the acquisition of skills and the resultant qualifications. At its simplest, the 'night-school tradition' is absent.

The interventions

The current training and learning interventions in place can be grouped into three categories.

First, there is declared support and sponsorship for work-related qualifications. Finance staff are pursuing UK and USA accreditation through examination with full company support. One of the senior production staff is undertaking an MSc. The two human resource staff are undertaking an introductory course. Particular problems arise over the accessibility and suitability of available opportunities in a remote area.

The second intervention concerns language training. All staff are able to participate and, so far, 15 people have taken up the opportunity. It should be remembered that many of the management team already have good business English and do not need this facility. Amcor has commissioned a local language school to come to the factory at times which allow any employee to take classes irrespective of shift.

The third initiative is aimed at the process workers. It links learning and knowledge with production by focusing on Key Performance Indicators (KPIs). Up to 10 KPIs are in place at any one time and are a central part of the way that the Amcor group hold Radomsko to account. All KPIs are reported on each month. At that time, a short seminar is held with a group of supervisors and process operatives to review a chosen and critical KPI. The intention is not simply to look at improvements in that part of the factory's activity. The intention is also to gain an increased awareness of the management practice and underline the employees' part in securing improvements.

Looking forward

The current interventions that are underway must be seen as part of a developing strategy to enhance skills against a tradition in which personal responsibility for learning is not strong.

Looking to the future, the factory is reaching the time when there will need to be a major commitment to investment in more modern plant and equipment. Enhanced skills will be required. This will require a new approach and a new attitude to skills acquisition and sharing. As Paul Sudnik puts it:

> *If Radomsko is to compete in the world economy, all staff will need to recognize the importance of owning personal career paths both inside and outside the company.*

Case study 2.4 Retail learning, vision and values at Harvey Nichols

Background

Harvey Nichols is a well-known retailer of luxury brand goods with a flagship store in Knightsbridge, London and store outlets in Edinburgh, Leeds, Manchester and Birmingham in the UK and international stores in Riyadh, Hong Kong, Dublin and Dubai, with Istanbul opening in autumn 2006. It also owns two up-market restaurants.

A major project began early in 2003 to embed a set of brand values that had been identified as defining business success. These three brand values:

- We provide a feel-good experience
- We are exclusive but accessible
- We provide fashion leadership

reflected the company's approach to customer service. The challenge was to decide how they could be expressed in terms of visible behaviour: the critical question was 'What does it look like when it happens on the shop floor?' Once this had been determined, the development of individual skills could be progressed.

A project team was established to translate these three values into something that would be tangible and of practical value. The project team was made up of the following: staff representatives from each of the individual sites who were considered active customer service champions within the business, a director who acted as the project sponsor and members of the HR team whose role was to steer the project and manage the project plan. The project team members in turn created their own teams within each of their respective sites. In this way, using a mixture of the top-down and bottom-up processes, a set of people values and behaviours were developed. Those associated with the first brand value – we provide a feel-good experience – are set out in the table below.

People values	Behaviours
Eager to engage with customers in order to deliver a great experience	Being welcoming – using eye contact and positive body language
Willing to go the extra mile	Actively helping customers and colleagues
Enthusiastic and positive	Listening to customers and colleagues
People who like people!	Looking for how to say 'yes'
Strong, clear communicator	Encouraging colleagues to work as a team

In addition to the people values and behaviours, a number of illustrative 'customer journeys' were prepared to provide specific examples of expectations, barriers and opportunities.

Rolling out the system

In the summer of 2003, launch events were held at every site, to present the values and the associated behaviours. Directors led these events and actors presented role-plays of desirable (and undesirable) behaviours. Subsequently, the department managers (who could be responsible for anything between six and 24 staff) were charged with ensuring that the values were embedded in the company. All department managers attended a one-day 'train the trainer' course and were provided with the necessary tools for team discussions and exercises. The competencies that underpin the performance review system, and the system itself, were updated to reflect the desirable behaviours identified from the brand values exercise. The new performance review system was introduced to the company in 2005.

The on-going task facing the HR department at Harvey Nichols is to ensure that such behaviours are recognized and reinforced in the context and culture of an up-market retail organization.

Karen McKibbin, the Learning and Development Manager, has explicitly rejected the idea of a generic training course for all sales assistants. A traditional training solution is not considered appropriate. In her view, sales assistants will learn best through immediate feedback and personal reinforcement with support from their managers and peers. Input from the small group of Harvey Nichols specialist advisers (the elite sales people who receive additional recognition for their exceptional capabilities) emphasized that it would be wrong to be over-prescriptive on what makes for good customer service; it involves an elusive ability to 'read the customer'. This can be learned, but may not be trainable.

Against this background, in late autumn 2003, Harvey Nichols introduced the Brand Champion Scheme. This was based on immediate recognition and potential reward for people who demonstrate the values. Importantly, it was the sales assistants' peer group who were given the responsibility for identifying such examples. All staff were issued with voucher cards, which they could complete when they observed exceptional action in accordance with the values. They would hand these vouchers to the person who had demonstrated this behaviour who would then forward them to HR as evidence of eligibility for designation as a Brand Champion. Such a designation earned one-off rewards.

Linking learning with performance

The challenge now is to create learning opportunities for the less proficient. According to Karen McKibbin, these too must be based on immediate peer feedback and manager support. Developing such options is a major current concern for her. Buddying-up staff with a suitable peer is one evident possibility; this is already used in inducting new staff. Harvey Nichols has been actively seeking to extend the number of staff who can act as buddies. Another major thrust is to develop the department manager's ability to question and provide quality feedback in a non-threatening fashion. It is Karen McKibbin's firm view that staff learn on the job and that such learning is inextricably linked with performance.

What these four case studies illustrate is that different groups of workers need to be treated in different ways if they are to acquire the knowledge and the skills that the organization needs. To underline a point that should have now become obvious: people development is no longer simply a matter of offering a menu of training courses – however well designed and capably delivered. The support, acceleration and direction of learning requires a range of activities which must be focused on the learner's needs and their contribution to organizational performance.

In part this requires a consideration of the individual's learning style or preferences. This topic will be considered in Chapter 5. However, another obvious factor is that the 'learner offering' available should reflect the different functions that people are performing in the organization.

Table 2.1 offers a simple categorization based on the analysis that we have drawn from Reich's work and the analysis undertaken in this chapter. In the course of the book we shall return to many of the issues introduced in this Table. Some questions to help practitioners in their organizations are included as an Appendix at the end of this chapter.

Table 2.1 Training learning and development requirements by category of workers

All employees need the skills to operate basic systems (especially technology) and enhance their interpersonal skills to enable them to advance and take more responsibility in the organizations. In addition:

Knowledge workers*	Must proactively manage their own technical/professional skills updating and contribute to knowledge sharing across the organization.
Routine production*	Achieve basic competence in role in shortest possible time. Embrace opportunities to develop job-related skill and contribute to shared improvements in processes.
Personal services*	Achieve basic competence in role in shortest possible time. Learn to 'read' customer needs and transmit these needs through to process improvements.
	Develop skills of customer liaison and emotional resilience. (The ability to be positive with difficult customers and difficult situations.)

*This categorization is based on Reich, R. B. (1991) The Work of Nations [1].

Appendix

Some practical questions

1. Do all your learners have the basic capability to take advantage of the opportunities available? Does this apply at all levels and in all parts of the organization?

2. Are your learners keen to learn and to acquire new knowledge and skills? Are there issues of learner motivation to be addressed at some levels and in some parts of the organization?

3. Have you ensured that your learners have access to opportunities to develop their knowledge and skills?

    (i)   How have you achieved this?

    (ii)   How do you know that you have been effective?

4. What actions do you need to take to capitalize on those who are ready to learn? And to assist those who are not yet prepared?

These questions were prepared by Jennifer Taylor based on extracts from the on-line tool on Training to Learning which is available to members via www.cipd.co.uk/helpingpeoplelearn

References

[1]. Reich, R.B. (1991) The Work of Nations. New York: Vintage Books.
[2]. Reich, R.B. (2004) Reason: Why Liberals will Win the Battle for America. New York: Alfred Knopf.

3

People and the Business

The case studies set out in the previous chapter illustrate how different interventions should be tailored to the circumstances of the organization. This introduces two concepts which are critical to the way that we should approach people development. The first is that of 'intervention': individual and team learning will not happen as an inevitable consequence of day-to-day organizational activity. They require interventions which 'support, accelerate and direct' learning to return to the role definition introduced earlier. As will be seen, such interventions will be undertaken by a wide range of people in the organization and in a variety of different ways.

The second concept is that of 'contingency'. This suggests that the appropriate interventions will depend on the circumstances of the organization; there will not be a best practice which is applicable to all situations. Where these two concepts of interventions and contingency come together is in the need for alignment. A critical role for the people development professional is to ensure that the resources committed to the learning, training and development effort reflect and reinforce business priorities. As the third of our nine propositions states:

> **Proposition 3**   A review of training and development interventions must ensure that the learning achieved is aligned with the business activity.

At first glance, such a proposition may appear self-evident. Certainly no one would argue to the contrary: no one would advocate that training and development interventions should be free-standing activities, floating independently from business needs! However, the challenge here is a complex one. If a Training and Development Department offers a menu of classroom-based training courses, there is a danger that:

■ these could become out of date and fail to reflect the urgent and immediate knowledge and skills required in the business,

- the style of delivery would not match the style (or culture) of other activities that take place across the business,
- quite simply the wrong people could participate. They could be those who volunteer because they are interested (or simply enjoy participating) or have progressive and committed managers.

This may sound unduly negative. Certainly, anyone who is sufficiently interested to read this far into the book would not operate in this way. However, consider the following e-mail received from a manager in a research establishment in Scotland who had heard of the 'helping people learn' project. She herself had assumed an international leadership role of some importance in a prominent voluntary organization and wrote in some frustration.

> *What a pity more organizations don't adopt this perspective on training and learning. Our HRD manager has all the qualifications but she concentrates on organizing courses and feels that if she has done this she has fulfilled her duties. She pays very little attention to the relevance of the course and a lot of attention to the cost, how many she can cram into the room to get her money's worth and in filling up the training section on the performance review form.*

Alignment and learning culture: an Australian perspective

One of the most interesting and accessible reports encountered in the course of the research for this book was produced in 2002 by the National Centre for Vocational Education Research in Australia [1].

The authors Robyn Johnston and Geof Hawke set out to explore how the concept of a learning culture and a commitment to learning was understood by Australian organizations. They presented a valuable series of case studies. In their exploration they offered a wide range of insights. For example, as a counter to the casual approach of simply offering courses (highlighted immediately above) the report suggested:

> *a 'learning culture' is something achieved through a deliberative arrangement designed to maximise productive works in a highly competitive environment where the organisations' systems have to be designed to support the development of employees if productivity goals are to be achieved. In short, the model does not idealise 'learning culture' or 'a commitment to learning' as a desirable ethos that evolves through exhortation of managers alone or the goodwill of employees who are persuaded of its worth, but as a result of various managed organisational changes [1, p. 33].*

Importantly, the researchers emphasized that there is no universal single solution which can be adopted. The research team:

Rejected the frequently unstated assumption that a learning culture is a homogenous [sic] concept which manifests itself uniformly within organisations. The team saw this phenomenon as both socially and contextually constricted. . . [1, p. 4].

In considering the concept of learning culture, the research team highlighted the following key issues.

First, a learning culture does not happen by accident; creating a learning culture is a managed process.

At times these systems/practices involve the implementation of more formal training and development systems. On other occasions, or in other enterprises, the required learning is more informal and is achieved with the establishment of a more communicative environment in which individuals play a more active role in making decisions about their work practice and are provided with more feedback on their own performance [1, p. 31].

Secondly, a learning culture must take full account of the business drivers:

There is evidence that employees in all of the participating organisations require new types of working knowledge. In all cases innovative systems or structures had been established to support or drive the required learning. In addition, in all cases, a more communicative workplace environment is emerging. This requires employees to possess enhanced communication capacities in order to liaise and network with other members of the organisation, or to contribute more actively than previously to the decision-making about the work processes [1, p. 24].

Thirdly, a multiplicity of approach and interventions are required.

A commitment to learning on the part of the organisation was seen as encompassing formal and informal initiatives implemented within the organisations, or behaviours displayed which encourage learners to acquire new skills, to adopt new ways of practice, and to share knowledge on work and work practice [1, p. 9].

In summary, this study indicates that the development and maintenance of a learning culture is a response to organizational needs for enhanced production or service provision rather than a more specific response to policy initiatives related to skill formation. Organizations embark on this pathway as a response to immediate pressures and implement approaches and develop systems which best meet their own needs. It is important to avoid a 'one size fits all' approach – especially one that primarily promotes a training classroom model of employee development.

When this has been achieved it is easy to see that this is the case. This is true of most of the case studies presented in this book – that is why they are chosen. The next three case studies offer some further illustrations.

Wegmans Food Markets (Case study 3.1) is one of the most successful US retailers. One of its key selling points is the superior product knowledge of its staff and training learning and knowledge sharing interventions are designed to reinforce that advantage.

Case study 3.1 Learning and the business at Wegmans Food Markets

Background

Wegmans Food Markets is a major regional supermarket chain and one of the largest private companies in the USA. It was ranked number one in the Fortune Magazine 2005 list of the '100 best companies to work for'. Wegmans employs some 35 000 people and operates 69 stores; these can vary from large stores employing over 600 staff to smaller stores employing just over 200. Originally, Wegmans operated in the North-East of the USA (New York State, New Jersey and Pennsylvania), but its success has led to an expansion southwards in Virginia and Maryland.

The company's branding is 'making great meals easy'. It focuses on all aspects of a successful culinary experience – the serving and setting as well as the preparation and cooking. The emphasis is on the customer experience and, indeed, customer education. Wegmans produces and sends 'Menu' magazine four times a year to over a million recipients; this contains advice on products and preparation and cooking techniques.

The business proposition is based on knowledgeable and committed employees at the store who can interact easily with customers and give them advice and support. Product knowledge and the capacity to communicate and share this knowledge are essential. Employee learning is therefore critical to success. To quote Danny Wegman, the CEO, in a recent interview:

Knowledge drives interest and if you are interested in something you pay more attention to it and it becomes more important to you.

Here, Danny Wegman was talking of customer knowledge. However, a desire to encourage staff to gain job and personal satisfaction by expanding their knowledge and skills lies at the heart of the Company's approach to training and learning.

The place of learning

Yolanda Benitez, Wegmans' Director of Training and Development, emphasizes two related features of learning at Wegmans. First, it must take place close to the workplace and, secondly, wherever possible, be experiential in nature.

Formal classroom training is probably no more than 10 to 15% of the training effort. As Yolanda Benitez puts it:

> *The store itself is the preferred environment in which people learn. They learn from each other, they learn from the suppliers, indeed they learn from the customer. Learning comes from all sorts of different experiences: it happens all the time and in different ways. It is experiential learning that makes the difference.*

The emphasis on store-based learning means that Wegmans must adopt a highly decentralized approach. Learning at the store level is a collaborative effort. Each store has an employee representative (HR generalist) who shares in the responsibility along with the store's management team, under the leadership of the store manager, for ensuring that employee learning takes place. Since most of the learning experience is delivered on-site, the precise mix of activities is determined at the store level. Many exciting initiatives, mainly relating to extending product knowledge, take place and are shared and communicated across the group. In-house cookery and food preparation demonstrations are held on a regular basis and visits to farms and suppliers are common. Such an approach can only work if there is a commitment to create a learning culture and appropriate structures are in place. The place of learning in the organization is set by the company leadership and Danny Wegman expressed it in these terms:

> *For years we believed in making sure that our employees kept on learning things even if it wasn't in performance plans. We ask 'what are you learning this year that will help you improve as a person and as a team member?' We've been doing things like this for so long they're just a way of life. It's education but you don't always realise it.*

Structuring the learning experiences

Learning takes place at the store and is managed locally. In addition, each of the Wegmans divisions has a full-time designated Training Coordinator. However, the structures and templates for training and learning across Wegmans are designed by the training and development team made up of instructional designers, facilitators and leadership trainers. They are responsible for offering, mainly blended, solutions to improve product awareness and soft-skills capabilities – with an inevitable emphasis on customer relationship. Though, as Yolanda Benitez puts it: 'We prefer to talk of knowledge-based service, rather than selling'.

One important mechanism facilitates the progressive acquisition of individual knowledge and skills. This is known as the bubble chart: it is an accessible competencies map which indicates the learning opportunities available through the product 'Universities'. The competency levels are set out as a simplified matrix, which maps the levels of staff progression (employee or team member, team leader, store manager etc) with product knowledge grouped in five job families (for example meat, seafood, cheese).

There is a core group of five courses required of each family with additional courses required of job families at each successive level. There is a group or common set of requirements that apply to all families: these concern health and safety, sanitation requirements and customer service. These are first dealt with at orientation but are reinforced at higher levels as the employee progresses through his or her career. An example of an on-the-job recommended learning activity that supports the product knowledge learning is set out below.

Product knowledge

Pick a product in your department and learn as much as you can about it. It may be a new product or one you are just not familiar with. Taste it or use it, if possible, so you will be able to speak from experience. If it is a food item, learn about how it can be served and what would go well with it. If it is a non-food item, learn about how it is used, or identify other products that are used with it.

The bubble chart is also used in guiding career choice and increasingly for recruitment and broader human resource management.

Yolanda Benitez must ensure that all training materials and tools are relevant and reflect the distinctive Wegmans' learning culture. Her challenge is to understand the business and deliver templates that add value to learning in a busy store environment. Her background in the business is of considerable assistance in this role. She must also strive to ensure that all employees have access to information, particularly the 'learnings' set out in the bubble. The information should be clear to them and offer a gateway to real development opportunities.

At Wegmans, the intention is that learning is fully integrated with the day-to-day activity. This, in Yolanda Benitez's words, 'is a model that works for us'. Each store reports on a regular basis against a series of indicators. People development is one of these and, at present, the Training and Development team are working to develop and refine an appropriate metric to capture learning rather than the far less significant course-based activity. However, the place of learning and training was best expressed by Danny Wegman, the CEO.

> *We don't have a formula for measuring that, but we ask ourselves, Are we being successful as a company? Are we getting good feedback from our people on the various courses that we're offering? Do they feel they (the courses) are relevant to their success as individuals and as part of the company. . . . Because everything is a learning event for our employees, it's very hard to capture all that. It's just part of doing business. It's the right thing to do for our people so we don't necessarily track it as an expense.*

Adapted from an article that appeared in Training and Development, September 2005 by Bingham, T. and Galagan, P. with permission from the ASTD.

Infosys, in Bengaluru India (Case study 3.2) is an IT services company which is moving up the value chain into broader consultancy services. Again, knowledge sharing is critical and the place of the taught course is carefully considered.

Case study 3.2 Matching training interventions with organizational needs at Infosys

Background: the growth of the company

Infosys is one of the fastest growing and most successful IT services companies in the world. Founded by seven professionals in 1981, it relocated to Bengaluru the following year. It is a global player in the knowledge economy with headquarters in India.

The original founders, all of whom had a technical, engineering or scientific background, established the company when India was a controlled economy. They were unable to obtain permission to import a computer and began by selling their services to local organizations, often foreign owned, who possessed the necessary hardware. They then entered an arrangement with a US-owned software house and moved through a phase of gradual growth. Their reputation, as is the case with a number of Indian software houses, was established at Y2K. This was the time when the systems and packages throughout the world needed an overhaul and India had the ability to deliver reliably and quickly.

Infosys was listed on the US NASDAQ exchange for high-tech stocks in 1999 and is now a $1 billion turnover company. Its growth was assisted by a

cautious, conservative attitude at the time of the dot.com bubble. It has traditionally been focused on IT services but is moving towards higher value added
services by providing business solutions. Infosys has always been strong on
application development and maintenance, particularly of legacy software systems. It is rated at the highest level five of the CMM (Capability Maturity Model
from SEI of Carnegie Mellon University, USA) for the software industry.

In the words of the Head of Education and Research at Infosys,
Dr M.P. Ravindra:

> *Our aim is to become a provider of business solutions leveraging technol-*
> *ogy to compete with any consultancy in the world. This ambition is built*
> *on the vast pool of talent available in India, but demands a commitment*
> *to maintain, enhance and update skills at all levels.*

Investment in knowledge and learning

Infosys' corporate message is 'powered by intellect, driven by values' and the
company makes a considerable investment in knowledge and learning. The
human resource concerns mirror those of any large knowledge intensive company. They have moved from 15 to 6 tiers of staff and they have introduced
an Employee Stock Option Plan (the first in India). There is a competency
system in place and every individual must have a competency development
plan, based on these competencies, which takes account of individual performance, organizational priorities and, where appropriate, client feedback.

Training interventions are organized in four key areas:

- Technology and project management
- Leadership and managerial including soft skills training
- Domain training (knowledge of specific industry)
- Quality processes.

The education department also provides intervention through just-in-time
training courses, mainly delivered off-the-job and mainly project specific.

There is an ambitious knowledge management programme in place with
rewards and recognition for those staff who submit knowledge assets which
are highly rated by their peers. One of the many knowledge products is Kspeak,
which was developed some time ago. This tool provides a facility whereby
any Infoscion (their preferred term for their employees) can telephone in with
an enquiry, probably on a technical subject. The answer or solution will be generated through voice recognition and intelligent systems and mailed back to
the person concerned.

Despite this technical sophistication, there is probably more reliance on the
classroom than in a US or European firm. Dr Ravindra expresses his perspective

in the following terms: 'Learning should be supported not automated'. It is also a cultural issue and a change management programme is in preparation and they plan to roll it out soon.

The scope of the challenge

Infosys currently employs over 52 000 staff throughout the world. Three-quarters of them work in India with the headquarters at Bengaluru, in India's Silicon Valley, organized as an impressive and attractive campus. To reach the campus you have to travel on grossly overcrowded and under maintained roads – India's poor infrastructure is recognized as a major constraint for its growth.

The major impression that Infosys leaves on the outsider is the scale of its ambitions and problems. Infosys receives nearly a million and half annual applications for employment and in the last year recruited 21 000 new candidates. In India, students who proceed through the University career system are only allowed to accept one job offer. They cannot choose at the last moment or try to play one employer against the other.

The offer to acceptance ratio is therefore critical and Infosys claims that theirs is running at 85%. Across the company, all new-entrant foundation students receive 14 weeks training. To cope with an entry cohort of this size, a new induction course starts each month. Delivery is 50% classroom and 50% hands-on activity with the support of a mentor. The training facility, at Mysore, can train 4500 trainees at any one time and this figure can be increased to 6000 if electronic enablers are used.

The Clipper project (Case study 3.3) was designed to support the transformation of leadership in the South African Department of Defence. Its inclusion reminds us that alignment is not simply about achieving commercial aims – it can be about supporting broader societal change.

Case study 3.3 A leadership and management development programme to support transformation in South Africa

Background

The 'Clipper' programme, described below, forms part of a wider programme of capacity building, to offer management development and encourage diversity in public services in South Africa. It is set in the overall context of an era of transition following the transformation led by Nelson Mandela at the end of apartheid. Specifically, the programme is to develop the leadership and management skills of key managers in the South African Departments of Defence and Foreign Affairs.

In co-funding this initiative, the UK Government aims to assist the progressive transfer of knowledge and skills with the intention that the programme becomes self-sustaining, delivered in South Africa, by South Africans for South Africans.

In 1998, the new Government in South Africa issued a White Paper on Public Service Training and Education (WPPSTE). This was intended to:

establish a clear vision and policy framework to guide the introduction and implementation of new policies, procedures and legislation aimed at transforming public service training and education into a dynamic, needs-based and pro-active instrument, capable of playing an integral and strategic part in the processes of building a new public service for a new and democratic society in South Africa.

The White Paper also signalled a need for the creation of:

a coordinated framework for ensuring the provision of appropriate and adequate public service training and education that will meet the current and future needs of public servants and contribute positively to the realisation of the vision.

As part of the underlying transformation project, the UK-based Ashridge Business School developed and delivered a major programme for senior and middle managers in the South African Department of Defence (DOD).

The demands of transformation were particularly acute for the South African Department of Defence. As was the case elsewhere in the country, new government structures were put in place and new organizations and relationships were created. However, before the constitution of the country was changed, there was no civilian management structure in place. The defence forces were managed and controlled by the military. In the words of Daan de la Rey, the Head of Management Development in DOD, who was responsible for the project:

The military talked and everybody listened.

The Clipper Programme

In 1996, a team from the UK Civil Service visited the Republic of South Africa to assist in the transformation process. One particular suggestion was that the

South African Department of Defence should receive high level management and leadership development. In 1998, the UK Government agreed to fund six to eight members of the Department of Defence to attend the Higher Management Training Programme held at Ashridge for the UK Ministry of Defence.

Following favourable feedback from the South African participants, Ashridge was invited to deliver the programme in South Africa. This initiative, which became known as the Clipper Programme, forms an important part of the capacity building in South Africa. From 2005, a train the trainer programme has been facilitated by Ashridge to build a South African faculty team.

The programme is based on an agreed set of competencies. Indeed, the 1998 White Paper provided an illustration of the kinds of competence, performance criteria and outcomes that might be expected from administrative assistants and administrative officers under the headings of 'management of work, working with people, and personal effectiveness'. The examples presented were based on the actual competence, criteria and outcomes used for such grades by the UK Ministry of Defence.

The current Ashridge Programme is delivered as an eight-day residential programme held near Pretoria, but drawing from staff in the armed services as well as their civilian colleagues located throughout South Africa. The style is fast paced and draws on the experience of the participants with action learning in interactive sessions. There is work in small groups and one-to-one coaching. Psychometrics and 360° feedback instruments are used. Personal development plans are prepared and supported by access to Ashridge's virtual learning resource centre – an e-learning product built and maintained by the business school. Some 230 South African staff in the Republic's Department of Defence have attended the programme over the period 1998–2006.

Ashridge Director, Dr Mark Pegg, who has led the Ashridge team over the last five years, commented:

This programme is one of the highlights of our careers as tutors – working in Africa, we see tremendous added value as participants arrive with a real thirst for learning and leave with a huge amount of extra confidence and practical tools and techniques to take on some really tough challenges back in the workplace.

According to Daan de la Rey, many of those attending the programme had received no prior management training. Hence the strength of the programme is its style.

The type of exercises and the approach developed by the faculty encourage a high degree of involvement from the learner. This develops a willingness from participants to manage their own learning.

51

Given the challenging structure in the Republic of South Africa, the mix of the students has changed as the programme has developed. Initially, there was an urgent need to train black and coloured managers. The lists of participants have been countersigned throughout by the Secretary of State for Defence. As the first cohorts have completed the programme, so other considerations have come into play. There is now, for example, an intention to achieve a better gender balance among participants.

As the programme has gained strength and a reputation for successful learning, senior level commitment has grown too, with important interactive contributions from senior staff in the Department of Defence and active support from the UK High Commission.

Mark Pegg points to the importance of the programme as a means of benchmarking leadership and change skills against best practice in the public and private sectors globally.

> *We never compromise our learning process – it remains as highly interactive, practical and results focused as for any other Ashridge programme – and we based our programme design on models that have worked well with our flagship programmes for the UK's MOD and FCO and also our global business programmes. At the same time, we introduced many uniquely African features – such as sessions on Leadership in Africa and new team working exercises and have progressively moved to joint delivery of the programme with South African faculty who use their own models and their own tools and techniques.*

Daan de la Rey also emphasizes the importance of networking as a programme outcome.

> *For many it's the first time they've been brought together as colleagues, where they share as colleagues and they begin to network.*

For the future, Daan de la Rey points to the growing strength of the alumni event that is held each year:

> *Past participants come back for a day to share their experience, to prove the return on our investment – that they can use the learning to achieve change successfully. Many have been promoted to more senior posts and are firmly committed to send their own high potentials to the programme. Several have also become successfully involved with programme delivery and there has been a really positive dialogue between these key managers and the top military and civilian management, on the development goals we should set for the future.*

Frameworks for alignment

What is evident from the Wegmans, Infosys and South African Department of Defence cases is that alignment occurs when the interventions to support training and learning are consistent with the aims, ethics and culture of the business. We can recognize it when we see it. However, alignment is one of the more elusive concepts in people development. It is easy to understand but very difficult to achieve in practice.

One of the reasons why alignment is a difficult area for people development professions is that it takes us out of our comfort zone. We are drawn into the area of business strategy and must consider the full range of human resource activities and practices. This is inevitable and unavoidable if we are to make a significant contribution to the organization.

This next part of this chapter will consider three frameworks which take us into this broader arena. They will assist in identifying the considerations which determine the place that learning, training and development should play in the organization. They are:

■ the work of Nohria, Joyce and Robertson on the way that strategy can deliver business results
■ the people and performance model developed for the Chartered Institute of Personnel and Development
■ the ASTD's (formerly the American Society for Training and Development) introduction and advocacy of the term 'workplace learning and performance' to describe the role of the profession.

The first framework is about broader business strategy; the second and third stress the need for a widely based approach to people management and development.

What really works

In 2003, Nitin Nohria, William Joyce and Bruce Robertson wrote an influential article for Harvard Business Review and an important book [2, 3].

In an extended piece of research, they made a rigorous study of connection between management practices and corporate performance. They looked at 160 companies and divided them into 40 groups, each consisting of four companies in a defined industry. Although the four companies in each group began the period in approximately the same fiscal conditions, their progress and fortunes varied considerably over the decade under consideration (1986–96).

The authors describe the progress in terms of winners, losers, climbers (which started poorly but then performance dramatically improved) and tumblers (which began in good shape but then declined).

The decade under consideration was one in which, to quote the authors, 'entrepreneurs and venture capitalists were dismissing traditional business models as antiquated and conventional business wisdom as old school' [2, p. 43]. The researchers examined over 200 management practices which were employed by the companies with the objective of determining which would be shown to make the difference. Thomas A. Stewart, the editor of the Harvard Business Review, described the results in the following terms: 'The practices described in "What Really Works" ought to be on a plaque in every boardroom, a talisman against cognitive bias and a caution against core-group clubiness' [4, p. 8].

To quote from the authors:

> *Our findings took us quite by surprise. Most of the management tools and techniques we studied had no direct causal relationship to superior business performance. What does matter, it turns out, is having a strong grasp of business basics. Without exception, companies that outperformed their industry peers excelled at what we call the four primary business practices – strategy, execution, culture and structure. And they supplemented their great skill in those areas with a mastery of any two of four secondary practices – talent, innovation, leadership, and mergers and partnerships* [2, p. 43].

This winning combination was described as the 4 + 2 formula for business success. The authors argue that companies that consistently follow this formula have a better than 90% chance of sustaining superior performance.

What is encouraging for the human resource professional is that these practices are straightforward and easy to comprehend – if not implement. They are not magic formulas for success which only the cognoscenti can understand. We do not need to be initiated into secret or arcane processes to play a full part in the business.

Brief descriptions of the primary and secondary practices are set out below.

Primary

- Strategy: devise and maintain a clearly stated, focused strategy
- Execution: develop and maintain flawless operational execution
- Culture: develop and maintain a performance oriented culture
- Structure: build and maintain a fast, flat organization

Secondary (two of these four should be embraced)

- Talent: hold on to talented employees and find more
- Innovation: make industry transforming innovation

- Leadership: find leaders who are committed to the business and its people
- Mergers and partnership: seek growth through mergers and partnership

Before going any further, those involved in people development should ask which of these practices are evident in their organization. They should ask who is responsible for designing and maintaining these practices. Above all, they should ask how the learning, training and development function is involved and how is its contribution recognized and valued. If these are the practices that drive success the function must be intimately involved. '4 + 2' is refreshingly uncomplicated and all the more powerful for that.

The CIPD people and performance model

Research undertaken by the Chartered Institute of Personnel Development (CIPD) over an extended period has sought to identify how effective human resource activities make their impact. This is described more fully in a CIPD research report [5] and a book both published in 2003 [6] and is summarized below. Essentially, it involved an investigation into the relationship between people management practice and bottom line business performance. A research team at Bath University in the UK, led by Professor John Purcell, carried out most of this work and one of the most significant outcomes of the work was the people and performance model.

The model asserts that human resource practice alone does not result in business performance. Such practices have their effect through the intervening variables of AMO. AMO describes:

- The Ability to perform above the requirements of the job because they possess the necessary knowledge and skills including how to work with other people.
- The Motivation to do the work and do it well.
- The Opportunity to deploy skills both in the job and more broadly contributing to work group and organizational success.

The full model is set out diagrammatically in Figure 3.1.

The model also emphasizes the role of front line managers in delivering, enacting and enabling HR practices and the importance of developing a supportive culture which fosters job satisfaction, motivation and commitment which, in turn, reinforces the positive behaviours which are associated with discretionary behaviour (see Chapter 5, p. 101). This behaviour is the ultimate goal of the people and performance model and describes the willingness of individuals to perform above the minimum requirement of the job or to willingly exhibit behaviour associated with high performance.

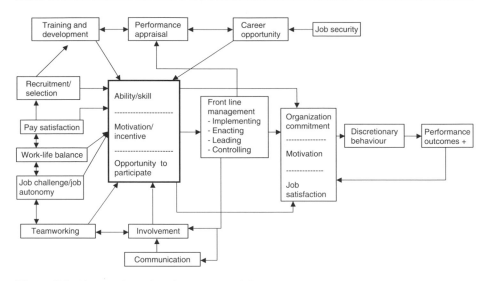

Figure 3.1 The people and performance model

One of the key messages of the research was that the combination of HR practices that would make a difference would vary from situation to situation and HR professionals would need to design a strategy that would work for them. In other words, anyone looking for a simple tick list was going to be disappointed!

Some questions based on the people and performance model are included as an Appendix to this chapter.

Training, learning and performance: the ASTD perspective

This chapter, and the previous one, have demonstrated that the world of the learning, training and development professional has changed dramatically. A new mind-set and new approaches are required. Role definitions and titles will and are changing. Titles are open to debate: what is beyond dispute is that a broader range of human resource practices must be brought into play if employees are to learn effectively at work. The chapter will end with a consideration of the way which the US professional association has responded to this broader role.

In 1999, the ASTD introduced the phrase 'workplace learning and performance' (WLP). This term has replaced 'training and learning development professional' in their work. Over the subsequent period, the ASTD has considered the implications of the change of name which is justified in the following terms:

The beauty of the WLP as a descriptor for the field and profession represented
by ASTD is that it explicitly connects learning – and all of the activities that

support learning – to the improvement of individual, group and organizational performance [7, p. 51].

To quote further from this article:

Workplace *specifies the context in which we address learning and performance. The W in WLP also acknowledges the role of workplace variables – such as goals, systems, resources and incentives – in the selection and success of learning solutions. Variations in workplace contexts influence our decisions and actions as WLP professionals.*

  Learning is, in part, a surrogate for the old term, training and development. Learning shifts the focus from external activities to what is happening in the individuals who are trained and developed. Using the term learning *broadens the scope of the professions responsibilities to include all opportunities, formal and informal, planned and unplanned, that lead individuals to learn and develop new knowledge and skills.*

  Like learning, performance *has multiple meanings in WLP. First, performance is the outcome of learning and can be viewed at three levels: individual, group and organizational. Second, performance is a perspective or mind-set that leads one to see learning as only one of many interacting variables that influence individual, group and organizational performance* [7, p. 31].

The debate on titles is less important than the substance of what is set out above. These statements on WLP seem to capture eloquently and succinctly the essence of what is at stake. As was argued at the end of Chapter 1, our preferred term is people development professional.

  Whatever job title is preferred, it is important to consider the practical implications of the changing context in which the profession is operating. One inevitable conclusion from this chapter is set out in the fourth proposition.

Proposition 4   Many different human resource roles are involved in the people development effort and the boundaries between organizational development, management development and training are becoming increasingly blurred.

Certainly, the relationship with other human resource professionals is recognized as critical by many developers. Titles vary and one of those who provided a case study made a strong case for the use of the term 'organizational development'. This forms the final case illustration in this chapter which comes from the Australian building and construction company, Boral, included as Case study 3.4.

Case study 3.4 Implementing organizational development at Boral, Australia

Background

Boral Limited is Australia's largest building and construction materials supplier; it also has a significant operation in the USA and Asia. It produces and distributes a broad range of materials including quarry and building products for the building and construction industries.

The company has over 15 000 employees working across 650 operating sites in Australia, the USA and Asia. The majority of these employees are unskilled and semi-skilled – mainly quarry workers, operatives, transport workers and production staff. Boral has a set of stated values: 'to provide a grounding for a common culture in the organization and provide the basis for consistent decision-making throughout the company'. Boral's values place considerable emphasis on leadership – seeking an environment where people: 'can excel through a management style which is participative, encouraging, demanding and supportive'. Recently, particular attention has been placed on identifying and developing those managers who are capable of offering this style of leadership – about 1000 individuals fall into this group. This is the target population for an extensive range of organizational development interventions.

Organizational development

Almost 40 years ago, the leading US academic and writer on leadership, Warren Bennis, defined organizational development as: 'a response to change, a complex educational strategy intended to change the beliefs, attitudes, values and structure of organisations so that they can better adapt to new technology, markets, challenges and the dizzying rate of change itself' [8, p. 2]. Organization or organizational development (both words seem to be used interchangeably with OD as a favoured abbreviation) has been, with varying degrees of fashionability, a key concept in human resource development ever since. As can be seen from Warren Bennis' definition, the emphasis is on the organizational change process rather than the narrower conception of individual training.

OD is the term preferred by Mary Dahdah, Boral's Learning and Organizational Development Manager, to describe her initiatives and activities. There are a number of reasons for her preference. The first concerns the perceptions of managers. In her view, learning and training can be seen by senior and line managers as 'fuzzy', soft terms, whereas OD, with its change implications, is more likely to be recognized as offering a hard contribution to business goals. To an extent the issue is one of appropriate branding of the human resource development function.

Certainly, OD is a more holistic discipline and Mary Dahdah has responsibility for broader interventions, including those that could be considered constituents of talent management, such as management development, career management and succession planning. Again perception is important, as Mary Dahdah comments:

> *Surveys within Boral have indicated that staff are happy with the development opportunities that are available, but they do not think that satisfactory career management systems are in place.*

One further advantage of a holistic view of human resource development is, in Mary Dahdah's opinion, the scope that is offered for more effective measurement. For example, retention figures are a clear indication of success as are improvements indicated in 360° feedback scores and the percentage of internally filled roles as opposed to externally sourced employees – whereas training evaluation data are a less satisfactory indicator of the impact on company priorities. Effective measurement can also permit benchmarking against outside companies.

A key issue in implementing a holistic approach based on OD is the need to ensure that all parties play their part. Progress cannot be achieved by learning and training specialists acting alone. Indeed, Mary Dahdah sees her main challenge as educating and influencing stakeholders who have not come across OD and do not appreciate its potential value to the organization. Ironically, one of the most demanding groups are fellow human resource professionals outside learning and training. Often they can be drawn to focus on short-term transactional aspects of human resources, rather than those that build a longer-term strategic capability. This can create problems. In Mary Dahdah's view, it is essential to manage people's development proactively; if not, staff who are critical to succession plans become frustrated and seek opportunities elsewhere.

In the longer term Mary Dahdah has aspirations that:

> *All the potential development processes, systems and strategy are in place and are aligned to the business goals; people at all levels are fully on board and play their part.*

Progress to that end will be achieved through the introduction of a set of consistent initiatives – currently one focus is the Executive Development Programme (EDP).

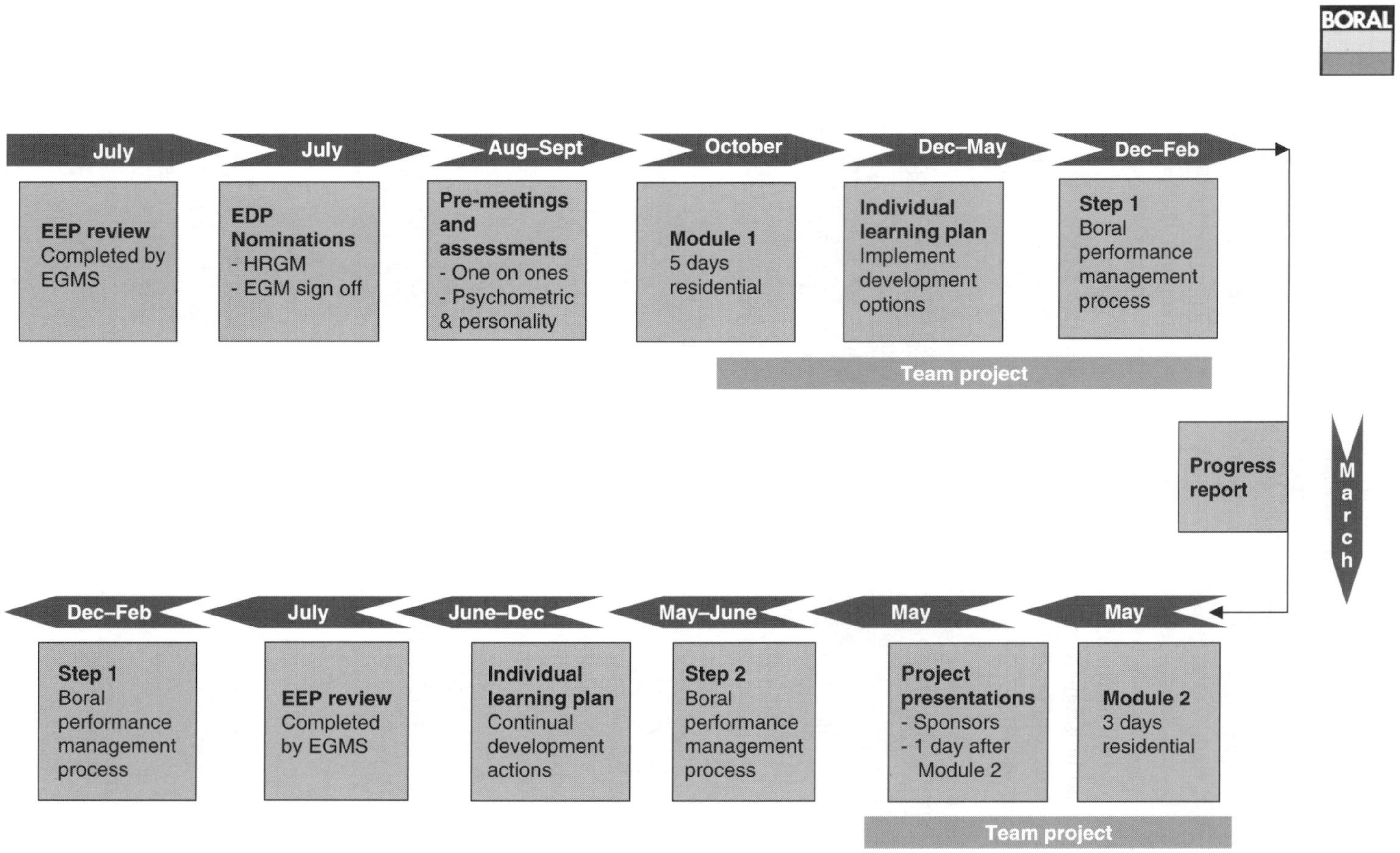

Figure 3.2 The Boral Executive Development Programme

The Executive Development Programme

The EDP has been a feature of Boral's management development initiatives for many years. However, it has recently been restructured and the focus has shifted from top-down instruction to embedded individual learning. The current programme design is set out in Figure 3.2. The programme lasts 18 months and some 24 individuals are chosen to participate against declared selection criteria – for example, they must have been in a senior management role for a year and have demonstrated high potential.

It can be seen from the diagram that there are two residential elements. The first, which follows shortly after participants have completed and received feedback, is a series of psychometric assessments focused on self-awareness and the softer interpersonal skills – for example, coaching. Participants then prepare an individual development plan which is skills orientated. Recent examples have included extending leadership and promoting the capability of subordinates. It will be seen from Figure 3.2 that there is a two-stage team or group project. This is firmly business orientated and implementation is expected to pass a financial threshold – examples here have included the more effective management of equipment. The results of the group project are presented back to senior managers. In Figure 3.2, Employee Estimated Potential (EEP) is the talent identification and succession planning tool used in Boral, which is integrated into the EDP participant selection criteria. The second residential session concentrates much more on harder technical subjects – for example finance.

It can be seen that the emphasis on the EDP is on encouraging learning over an extended period. A similar emphasis applies to development programmes in place at lower levels in the organization.

The important thing, according to Mary Dahdah, is that learning is seen as a continuous activity, not as something that is associated with attendance at discrete events.

Appendix

Some practical questions

1. Does the organization operate a formal process for reviewing the performance of employees?

   If yes, which categories of staff does the process cover?

- Senior management
- Middle management
- Operational/front-line management
- Administrative/office-based staff
- Production/blue-collar staff
- Other

2. How often are formal performance reviews/appraisals conducted?

3. Which of the following are formally included in your performance appraisal/ review arrangements?

- Discussion of organizational priorities or objectives
- Discussion of workgroup or team objectives
- Discussion of appraisee's role and accountabilities
- Agreement of appraisee's objectives
- Review of appraisee's performance against objectives
- Review of appraisee's skills or competencies
- Agreement of development plan for appraisee
- Identification of career potential
- Identification of career opportunities
- Other elements

4. What processes does the organization apply to evaluate the performance review/ appraisal arrangements?

- Feedback from organizational attitude survey
- Statistical audit of completed documentation
- Quality audit of completed documentation
- Statistical audit of performance ratings
- Formal feedback from appraisers
- Formal feedback from appraisees
- Review of completed documentation
- Review against organizational requirements

5. How does the information collected influence the provision of training, learning and development plans?

- The organization does not have a central training plan
- All review/appraisal documentation is formally collated centrally to inform organizational training plans

- All review/appraisal documentation is informally reviewed centrally to inform organizational training plans
- Review/appraisal documentation is not analysed centrally but major requirements may be built into plans

These questions were prepared by Jennifer Taylor based on extracts from the People and Performance tool – designing HR processes for maximum performance delivery which is available to CIPD members on www.cipd.co.uk/subjects/corpstrtgy/busiperfm

References

[1]. Johnston, R. and Hawke, G. (2002) Case Studies of Organisations with Established Learning Cultures. Australia: National Centre for Vocational Education Research (NCVER)/Australian National Training Authority (ANTA).
[2]. Nohria, N., Joyce, W. and Robertson, B. (2003) What Really Works. Harvard Business Review, 81(7), 43–52.
[3]. Joyce, W., Nohria, N. and Robertson, B. (2003) What Really Works: The 4 + 2 Formula for Sustained Business Success. New York: Harper Collins.
[4]. Stewart, T.A. (2003) From the Editor: Thinking Rationally about Irrational Thinking. Harvard Business Review, 81(7) p. 8.
[5]. Purcell, J., Kinnie, N., Hutchinson, S., Rayton, B. and Swart, J. (2003) Understanding the People and Performance Link: Unlocking the Black Box. CIPD Research Report, London: CIPD. See also Purcell, J., Kinnie, N. and Hutchinson, S. (2003) Open Minded. People Management 9(10), 15 May, 30–37.
[6]. Sloman, M. (2003) Training in the Age of the Learner. London: CIPD, pp. 10–12.
[7]. Sugrue, B., O'Driscoll, T. and Blair, D. (2005) What in the World is WLP? T + D, January, pp. 51–52.
[8]. Bennis, W. (1969) Organization Development: Its Nature, Origins and Prospects. Reading, MA: Addison Wesley.

4

Extending our leverage

What's in a name?

One indication of the impact of the shift from training to learning is the way that job titles have changed and are changing. The ASTD's introduction of the phrase workplace, learning and performance outlined in the previous chapter is a good illustration.

In 2003, to support an investigation into the future competency model for the profession, the ASTD surveyed practitioners about their preferred name. The survey results are set out in Table 4.1 and were reported in an article entitled 'The future of the profession formerly known as training' [1]. The author, Pat Galagan, the Managing Director of Content for the ASTD, wrote that:

There is no topic that inflames more passion at the moment than what to call the profession formerly known as training. Medieval theologians debating the number of angels that could dance on the head of the pin could not marshal more arguments than the defenders of competing nomenclatures. Is it performance? Is it intellectual capital development? Is it knowledge management? Is it learning facilitation? Is it human process engineering? Is it workforce development? Is it organizational stewardship and transformation? [1, p. 26].

Pat Galagan's article brought together the views of a number of experts on the future direction of the profession. It concluded on an optimistic note from the ASTD's Chief Operating Officer, Tony Bingham. He cited an ASTD competency study and described it as:

an important step towards mobilizing all parts of this dynamic profession behind a common goal of maximizing the talent in organizations [1, p. 38].

The phrase 'common goal of maximizing the talent' is a useful statement of modern objectives. This chapter considers how this objective can be achieved and will begin with a consideration of the term 'talent management' itself.

Table 4.1 Which name or label would you prefer our profession to be called? ASTD survey results

	Response percent	Response total
Training	1.4	19
Training and development	31.0	416
Human resource development	14.3	191
Workplace learning and performance	31.9	427
Workforce development	10.7	144
Other (please specify)	10.7	143
Total respondents		1340

Before doing so, we will briefly return to the question and ask 'what's in a name?' The answer is potentially quite a lot. Job titles do matter if they reflect a mind-set or attitude on the part of the job holder and suggest that they see their role in the organization in a limited way.

The argument advanced at the beginning of this book was that the shift from training to learning, a consequence of new business models, means that the creation of knowledge and skills has become a much broader activity. It is no longer solely about activities that take place in the training room. To an extent this argument seems to have been won – but only to an extent. The idea that 'trainer skills' need to be displayed in a different context has gained wide acceptance; the idea that we must work with and through others less so.

For instance, one phrase that is in common usage, certainly in the UK, is: 'From the sage on the stage to guide on the side'. This aphorism was originally articulated by Alison King, a Professor of Education at California State University [2]. The sentiment behind its use is clear: we have moved away from a top-down classroom-based instructional model to one which is based on support and challenge, inviting the individual to form their own solutions to their problems (this concept is considered more fully in Chapter 8). Without question, a broader role and better organizational relationships lie at the heart of all these discussions on the future of the profession.

Talent management

The term 'talent management' was explored in the CIPD Learning and Development 2006 survey and in a companion 'Reflections' discussion document [3, 4]. The survey showed that 51% of the 630 respondents claimed to undertake talent management activities – although only 20% reported that they had a formal definition for it. Developing high potential individuals and growing future senior managers were identified as the two main objectives for talent management activities and in-house development programmes, coaching and succession planning the most common mechanisms. The 'Reflections' essay suggested that:

In its broadest sense, talent management can be used to describe the:

- Identification
- Development
- Engagement/retention
- Deployment of 'talent within a specific organizational context' [4, p. 1].

The essay went on to consider whether 'talent management' is something different or a new label for well-established activities.

But what makes talent management different? For many, talent management represents a shift from static succession planning processes towards 'action-oriented' activity. It is also seen as a far wider-reaching, holistic approach that moves towards better 'joining up' of HR practices and processes behind a clear business and personal set of goals. Others describe talent management as a 'mind-set' that needs to permeate and be owned by an organization [4, p. 1].

On this basis, the emergence of the term 'talent management' can be seen as a reflection of the changing role of learning, training and development. It is an inevitable consequence of the move to a service-led and knowledge-driven economy where people development becomes a critical activity.

However, there is a danger in taking an overly narrow view of talent management in two respects. As the 'Reflections' essay puts it:

Should 'talent management' be focused on 'high potentials', in the sense of an elite sub-group of 'future leaders of the organization', or at least those capable of progressing through a number of promotions? An alternative more inclusive definition might consider 'organization capability'. This definition recognizes that there are various key positions that it is important to fill in any organization and a future pipeline of the 'appropriate' skills to fill all these positions needs to be in place [4, p. 1].

There is also a related danger in seeing talent management as an activity which only takes place in knowledge-intensive organizations and is less relevant to routine production or blue collar work.

In fact, the challenge of developing talent is one facing all organizations. Whether the term 'talent management' is here to stay or is a passing fad is not the important issue. What matters is how thoughtful practitioners are proceeding with their work. Three case studies illustrate this point. The first, Sukut Construction, is set out in Case study 4.1. It describes the work of the Talent Director at an earth-moving company in California. The need to engage all parties and to build personal credibility will be evident.

The second (Case study 4.2) describes the Motorola University initiative in the People's Republic of China. It shows how talent management can be particularly important for multinational organizations who are endeavouring to build management capability overseas.

The third (Case study 4.3) concerns the international development programme undertaken at the design company Diesel. It highlights two challenges that have already been introduced: aligning any learning and training intervention with business activity; and the need to move beyond course-based activity if learning is to be transferred effectively to the organization.

Case study 4.1 Developing talent at Sukut Construction, California

Background

Sukut Construction was founded in 1968 and began as a small Southern California earth-moving company. It has achieved rapid and sustained growth and, with annual revenue of $142 million, is now ranked among the largest 300 contractors in the USA. Since its establishment, Sukut has moved over one billion cubic-yards of Californian soil. It has expanded into new activities and new regions within the State and has expertise across a whole range of areas in the heavy construction sector. These include all facets of mass excavation and grading: residential; commercial; public works; golf courses and resorts; land fills and clean-ups; highways and roads; storm drain systems and emergency landslide repairs.

Currently, Sukut employs some 600 people – the number varies depending on the number of contracts in place. Approximately 70 employees are involved in management and administrative roles, but the workforce is mainly based at the construction sites undertaking the tasks involved in earth-moving. Field jobs range from foremen, employees driving heavy equipment, through to ground based staff. These tasks are physically demanding and can take place in hot and dirty conditions. As will be seen, safety is an important consideration. The operatives are hired from a pool of workers who belong to the International Union of Operating Engineers and are typically transferred to Sukut's books for the duration of a project, though some remain on assignments with Sukut for the long term.

In 1988, Myron Sukut offered a select group of his most valued team members the opportunity to purchase shares in the company. In 1990, Myron transitioned from active management of the company and a new Chief

Executive, Mike Crawford, was appointed. The practice of offering select employees of the company the opportunity to buy shares in Sukut has been extended and there are now some 60+ shareholders, including a mix of office and field personnel.

The company operates in an industry where 'soft' people management skills and employee development are not always given the highest priority. However, the founder, Myron Sukut, believed that, even in this most capital intensive sector, people are the key to business success. The company has declared and practises a set of people values which stress the importance of enjoyable work, work–life balance and honesty and ethics. These values contributed to the company's selection by Orange County Metro magazine as one of The Best Companies to Work For in 2000.

One key to the company's successful growth has been the encouraging of employees to pursue their areas of expertise and interest. A recent example of this philosophy occurred when a Project Manager developed Global Positioning Satellite (GPS) technology from an embryonic state at Sukut into a major area of emphasis. Mike Crawford believes strongly that people development is an essential key to continued success for both individuals and the company:

> *The talented individuals working in our organization need to be engaged in meaningful work and provided with opportunities to grow. Otherwise, the best and brightest might stop enjoying themselves and look for opportunity elsewhere. Historically, we have mentored our workers and cleared the way when they had a desire to help define the future direction of the company, but now I want to take it further by establishing systems focused on fostering even more sustained, consistent growth of the talent within the company.*

The role of the Talent Director

In 2004, Sukut hired a Talent Director, Mary Ellen Copek, to lead its people development activities. She is the only female member of the company's executive leadership team. Copek is a human resource professional with extensive expertise developed through strategic work in various industries including pharmaceuticals, computer software and cable television; she reports to the Chief Executive Officer and, with a colleague focused on operational human resource activities, Mary Ellen is able to maintain a long-term and strategic focus on the company's human capital needs.

One of Mary Ellen's major goals is the establishment and implementation of a 'Sukut University'. The correlation between training, motivating and empowering employees and significantly improving productivity and employee satisfaction is well documented. Mary Ellen is confident that the company's financial performance will be positively impacted by these improvements as well.

> *My long-term goal is to create a culture where an employee and his/her manager sit down together, using Sukut University as a central resource, and craft a customized development plan that stimulates excitement, growth and engagement.*

There are some areas where there is an immediate talent deficiency and one in particular concerns the development of capable project managers. The Project Manager at Sukut oversees contracts from inception to completion: bidding for work, negotiation of tender, monitoring progress and billing. Finding individuals externally who are experienced and talented enough to take on this breadth of work immediately is not easy. For this reason, Sukut has traditionally brought in junior employees and mentored them informally to develop their talent internally.

In her first year at Sukut, Mary Ellen has been instrumental in creating a more formal Project Management Competency Development Plan with the help of 'resident experts'. The programme has been launched as the initial product of Sukut University with the goal of significantly reducing the time it takes for new employees to develop the competency required to function as Project Managers and oversee multimillion dollar projects independently.

The safety initiative

As well as the more strategic objectives, there are immediate tasks that require, or would benefit from, a training and learning intervention. The important area of safety training offers a good example and has become the second major initiative to be launched under the Sukut University umbrella.

As would be expected in the construction industry, safety is a high priority with on-going concern. Approximately one year ago, Sukut joined a consortium organization, American Contractors' Insurance Group (ACIG), which was established to negotiate premiums and make financial savings on these costs by bench-marking, sharing and promoting best practice on safety. The stated desire is to keep employees safe by creating a zero-accident culture.

Recognizing that employees know the safety risk factors best, a new initiative was put in place at Sukut. This seeks to secure the input of front-line operatives whose views would be collated and articulated by the foreman. Each division held meetings at which they identified 10 ways in which practices could be improved. Typical outputs included:

- Mechanics noted a growing practice of operating grinders without a guard in place. The discussion led to the purchase of larger, more expensive grinders so mechanics would not need to remove the guard to perform their task.
- Improving signage at job sites; it is important that directional signs are updated regularly as both Sukut and non-Sukut employees can get hurt if they drive on the wrong roads when they deliver materials.
- Reminders to wait for non-verbal acknowledgement when communication is required between ground personnel and those driving moving vehicles.

Mary Ellen Copek has facilitated and documented these initial safety meetings, ensuring consistency of approach and managing the collation of documentation. The improved safety practices are communicated by foremen at so-called 'tail-gate' meetings (the on-site meetings that take place round a convenient truck). Data are provided to support these meetings. In addition, the new employee induction material is being updated to include the newest safety initiatives.

Immediate challenges and aspirations

Given the ambitions surrounding Sukut University, it may appear that the support of a safety initiative might not be the best use of Mary Ellen Copek's time and resources. She would argue otherwise. Essentially, she feels that her involvement has given her a chance to gain a deeper understanding of the core business while delivering results on safety, which is universally accepted as an important business issue.

Other programmes that foster continued human capital development at Sukut have been initiated by Mary Ellen. These include formal policies on tuition assistance, the development of partnerships with local universities and organized methods for new talent acquisition. In the near future, Mary Ellen plans to implement an automated learning management system that employees will access through the company intranet. At that time she will add additional on-site curriculum tracks aimed at various segments of the office staff group. E-learning will be an exciting addition that will help meet the challenge of making information and support available to employees in the office and the field. As Mary Ellen says:

> There is nothing as rewarding at the end of the day as to have a positive impact on the life of employees while also growing the company's bottom-line.

Case study 4.2 Developing talent at Motorola University

Background

Motorola is a Fortune 100 company known for innovation in wireless and broadband communications. It has a global presence and achieved almost $37 billion of sales worldwide in 2005.

Motorola University (MU) was established in the 1980s as a consequence of a strong commitment to learning and development held by successive Chief Executive Officers. Its mission is:

> To provide best-in-class practice to Motorola employees, customers, suppliers, partners, and other potential customers as a change agent through breakthrough performance improvement with sustainable financial results.

Motorola has had a presence in China since the early 1990s. Some 10 000 staff are currently employed in the People's Republic and are involved in manufacturing and assembly of a range of Motorola products including hand-phones, semi-conductors, two-way radios and automotive and infrastructure equipment.

Motorola University Asia

In 1993, MU was established in China and began to deliver a range of courses and training interventions which reflected Motorola's global learning programmes. These covered leadership, quality management, sales and marketing and soft-skills training. Increasingly, however, MU has been seen as a way of developing a local management capability in the People's Republic.

Almost half of the original management staff in China were expatriates so Motorola developed an integrated strategy to identify and train local managers chosen from their workforce. Some 500 high potential managers have been selected and received training to date. Currently, almost 90% of middle managers and above are Chinese nationals and all of them will have received some training from MU.

The China Accelerated Management Programme (CAMP)

One key building block in the process has been the CAMP programme. Participants are nominated by their business area following consultation between local leadership and the human resource function. They then undertake a compulsory assessment of their capability to complete a training programme in the English language. Those selected join a group of between 20 and 25 participants who attend a one-week classroom course. Instruction is given by external consultants and internal faculty staff from the MU team. Most importantly, the curriculum reflects Motorola's competency domains which are agreed globally. These include business acumen skills, interpersonal and leadership skills and people and project capabilities, as well as more specific customer-related competencies which must remain confidential.

Learners spend a total of eight months participating in CAMP and the programme involves a combination of instructor-led content, e-learning and observation and feedback in the workplace. When it was first introduced, the programme was amended to meet the needs of the Chinese learner. One important consideration, for example, was the way that decision-making takes place in the Chinese culture. Local potential leaders also learn strategic thinking and systematic problem-solving skills from the CAMP programme which Chinese employees can hardly learn from other career opportunities.

A central element of the programme is the identification and completion of an individual project. The topic must be agreed with local management or be of value to the business. However, the emphasis is on creating an opportunity for the learner to develop and deploy the competencies in the workplace. Coaching support is provided by MU staff and other internal specialists over this extended period. Specific e-learning modules are identified to assist the participant and he or she will spend another four days in the classroom on compulsory modules and have the opportunity to attend optional classroom electives. At the end of the CAMP programme the learners make a formal presentation on their project.

The training challenge

There is a strong demand for CAMP and, at the time that this case study was written in June 2006, 190 further potential candidates had been identified – 87 had been enrolled with the remainder on the waiting list. Jenny Yan is the Director of Motorola University Asia Operation and she sees meeting rising demands as her biggest challenge. Resources are stretched to meet increasing requirements. There are a range of more senior programmes beyond CAMP on offer, including a Leadership Accredited Development Programme and a Talent Rotation Programme (TRP) available across the Asia Region.

MU provides services to clients and suppliers and a particularly attractive initiative is six sigma training. This is a methodology developed to improve business processes and has been used internally and externally to offer accreditation at a range of capabilities – from green to black belt. A newly launched internal programme is 'Mentor Motor' – designed to identify and train internal managers to act as mentors.

Jenny Yan sees part of her role, and that of her team, as ensuring that global MU programmes are fully grounded in the reality of working life in China. There has, in the past, been a tradition of rote learning – where the word of the instructor is taken as received unchallenged wisdom. However, this mind-set has changed a lot and will continue to change; this will allow more workshops and teaching through case study discussion to feature in programme design.

Jenny Yan feels positive about Chinese learners – they are eager to learn and see joining Motorola as a major opportunity to enhance their skills. They are highly motivated when they arrive at training events. Her major challenge, therefore, beyond managing scarce resources, is the continuous need to develop programmes which meet the changing needs of a fast moving sector. As she puts it:

> *How can we design really good programmes which reflect the changing business?*

Case study 4.3 An international development programme at Diesel

Background

Diesel is an innovative, international design company, producing a wide-ranging collection of denim, clothing and accessories. With headquarters in Molvena, in the Veneto region of North-East Italy, Diesel employs more than 4000 people worldwide and is present in over 50 countries with over 190 company-owned stores.

When Renzo Rosso founded Diesel in 1978, he wanted to create a company which took chances and carved out a niche for itself in its field. He surrounded himself with creative, talented people – innovators who, like him, rejected the 'slavish trend-following' typical of the fashion industry. From the start, Diesel was committed to a more dynamic and imaginative line of clothing. Renzo Rosso gave his open-minded new designers broad stylistic freedom to create a line of clothing perfect for people who follow their own independent path in life and who decide to express their individuality by the way they dress.

Through this vision, Diesel has remained, for nearly 30 years, at the edge of fashion. Seen by many as having achieved iconic status, it has now set itself the further challenge of being leading premium brand.

At Diesel, the desire for formal processes for assessing and developing people comes from the business. HR's role is to provide the tools to make it happen.

Three of Renzo Rosso's values that provide particular direction for the HR team are:

- . . .creatives must create, change, challenge, experiment . . . . . managers must create a system able to translate ideas into reality.
- Diesel does not impose anything to anybody, we are to be chosen.
- . . .strategies, processes . . . . OK, but how do you feel about it?

Six years ago, Tiziana Rosato, HR Director for the Diesel Group, recognized that, to keep up with rapid expansion, it was no longer possible to 'shop' for external talent. To maintain consistency and quality, while at the same time keeping true to Diesel's core values, a structure was needed to develop talent internally and on a global basis.

International development programme

The first step was to identify the qualities needed to manage the brand. Working with an external consultancy, Tiziana Rosato and her team carried out an exercise that identified the key capabilities for being a successful manager at Diesel. Some of these, such as relationship skills, communication, negotiation, teamwork and managing people, were the strengths displayed by the top team who had developed the brand. In addition, they identified other capabilities as critical to future success and drew up the framework on which the international development programme is based.

Managers start the programme by attending a one or two-day intensive assessment programme, from which participants draw up an individual development plan. They then move onto the formal training consisting of three modules, working with business school professors and training consultants, learning in cross-functional and cross-cultural groups. The third part, back at the workplace, is encouraging a culture of continuous learning.

Assessment programme

The overall aim of the assessment programme is to develop people to their full potential. In a successful organization such as Diesel, it is easy to identify the high performers. However, to manage talent effectively, it is also important to identify potential and this is a key purpose of the assessment programme.

The project began in November 2001 with the whole top team and was then cascaded to middle managers. Participants use simulation, role plays, case studies, self-analysis and reflection to look at how they deal with situations, solve problems, plan and control events, develop and maintain relationships, cope with stress, adapt to changes and organize themselves. The programme is intensive but also stimulating. Most participants come away from it saying that they have gained new insights about themselves and that they have already identified how they can start their self-development.

The way the assessment programme is positioned, run and communicated in Diesel is of prime importance. The programme is not about identifying high-flyers, but it is about helping management and the company to grow as a team. The first top management group who went through the programme are still among its most enthusiastic exponents and they have been key in emphasizing that at Diesel everyone is important. Formal and anecdotal evidence shows that the participants value the programme as a process for development and see it as Diesel paying attention to each of them individually.

Each person receives their feedback report in a one-to-one session with one of the external consultants. This is highly valued by participants who appreciate the confidential nature of the session, as well as the chance to ensure they understand the feedback and can formulate development plans. This is also part of the Diesel HR way of providing the tools to make things happen without interfering or imposing.

The international dimension

In 2003, the project was extended overseas. A key challenge in doing this was to give managers a sense of Diesel's corporate identity and values without losing their own local cultural identity and their individuality. They rejected the idea of using an international company who would manage everything centrally as being inconsistent with this challenge. The external consultant was charged with guaranteeing the methodology but rolling the programme out through local partners who specialized in assessment and development and who were also compatible with Diesel and its culture.

To set up the programme, Tiziana Rosato held meetings, discussions and presentations in each country and there was complete transparency over the process. Although the methodology was consistent, material and delivery were adapted to each national culture and translated into the local language. Assessing people in their own language means that you are assessing their capabilities without the intrusion of linguistic ability. It is consistent with the Diesel way of not imposing but of valuing the individual and what they have to offer.

Participants share their assessment feedback with their line managers who, together with local and central HR, support their self-development. An added benefit of the assessment programme is that it gives line managers a language and a framework for holding meaningful conversations with people about their development and for then supporting them appropriately. Self-development is run locally but coordinated through Diesel HQ. It consists of a series of questionnaires, checklists, a bibliography and self-development exercises. Line manager support is critical to its success.

Once the roll-out of the assessment programme was completed, the results were analysed and the following key messages were developed and used to underpin the training and development programmes that are being run through the International Development Programme:

- Everyone must invest in the critical competency of being a good manager.
- All managers must be strong in people management. This is the DNA of the organization.
- Everyone is important to the organization. There is no question of excluding those who are weaker.

The analysis of results also revealed weaknesses that were common throughout the organization and the first training programmes of the International Development Programme were based around these. In running these programmes, people came together from across the Diesel Group. This mixing together of countries and functions has proven popular and has also been a part of Diesel's focus on cross-cultural management to reinforce the international identity of the Group.

Other development initiatives include coaching. A successful international coaching programme has been run for senior managers, first at group level but is now being extended. Technical training is provided, generally through local initiatives and special projects are being set up for country managers.

Managing the growth of an organization like Diesel means creating a mindset where instability, change and speed are a daily requirement. There is no typical management style. This is a particular challenge that the international development programme has to be designed to meet.

A partnership model

If we are to 'maximize the talent in organizations' (to return to Tony Bingham's phrase), we must be seen as key organizational players working in collaboration with others. This is the justification for the creation and promotion of the CIPD's partnership model set out diagrammatically in Figure 4.1.

The notion of partnership has attracted considerable attention in the HR community in recent years. In 1997, academic and consultant Dave Ulrich of the University of Michigan wrote a book which had a major influence. In 'Human Resource

Champions' [5] he identified four roles for HR professionals: employee champions, administrative expert, change agent and strategic partner. Subsequently, in 'The HR Value Proposition', written jointly with Wayne Brockbank [6], his thinking evolved and he argued that value creation must lie at the heart of the HR agenda.

In this second book, he revisited his suggested roles for human resource professionals. Five roles were now outlined: HR leader, functional expert, employee advocate, strategic partner and human capital developer. Both 'change agent' and 'strategic partner' had evolved into a single role which, in an article that appeared in 2005, he and Wayne Brockbank described in the following terms:

> *In their role as strategic partner, HR professionals bring know-how about business, change, consulting and learning to their relationships with line managers. They partner with line managers to help them reach their goals through strategic formulation and execution* [7, p. 27].

In the same article the human capital developer was described thus:

> *Increasingly people are recognised as critical assets and HR professionals as managing human capital: developing the workforce, emphasising individual employees more than organisation process. As human capital developers HR professionals focus on the future, often one employee at a time, developing plans that offer each employee opportunities to develop future abilities, matching desires with opportunities. The role also includes helping employees forget old skills and master new ones* [7, p. 27].

'Implementing Ulrich' absorbed much energy for the HR community in the period after the appearance of the 1997 book. A key part of the organizational re-design that took place was the desire that generalist or operational HR professionals became 'business partners'. This has proved difficult in practice: organizations frequently complained that their HR professionals were unable to adapt to the new role and/or they were unable to recruit suitable staff from the outside. Generally, a demanding range of skills is required.

Figure 4.1 illustrates some important elements of the development professional's role in promoting learning in organizations, in particular:

- The continuous nature of the move from an isolated role for training to a culture where learning is seen as relevant to the needs of the business and of the learners and integrated in the day-to-day activities. This element is shown in the two arrows at the top and bottom of the diagram.
- The shift to a learning culture is an aspiration; in practice it will take a long time and success in any organization may be patchy, or even go into reverse on occasion.
- The heart of the diagram shows the roles and relationships of the stakeholder in a continuous, integrated learning culture.

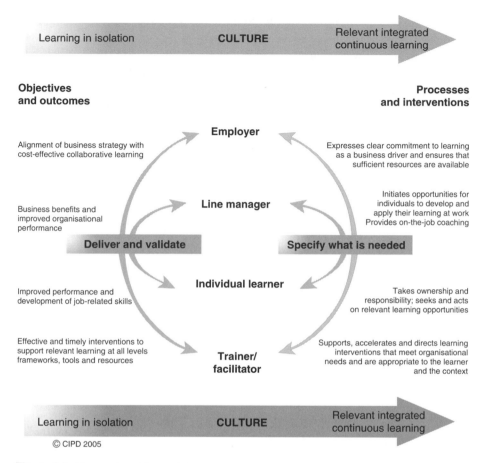

Learning in isolation   CULTURE   Relevant integrated continuous learning

Objectives and outcomes

Processes and interventions

Employer

Alignment of business strategy with cost-effective collaborative learning

Expresses clear commitment to learning as a business driver and ensures that sufficient resources are available

Line manager

Business benefits and improved organisational performance

Initiates opportunities for individuals to develop and apply their learning at work Provides on-the-job coaching

Deliver and validate

Specify what is needed

Individual learner

Improved performance and development of job-related skills

Takes ownership and responsibility; seeks and acts on relevant learning opportunities

Effective and timely interventions to support relevant learning at all levels frameworks, tools and resources

Trainer/facilitator

Supports, accelerates and directs learning interventions that meet organisational needs and are appropriate to the learner and the context

Learning in isolation   CULTURE   Relevant integrated continuous learning

© CIPD 2005

Figure 4.1 The partnership model

To emphasize, the partnership model is put forward to express how learning should be embedded in the organization. It is about the approach required from all parties and is not intended simply to re-define the role of the people development professional. Some questions for practitioners, based on the partnership model, form the Appendix to this chapter.

Cultural transitions cannot be achieved overnight, so organizations must move forwards through a series of interventions. For these to occur, all the relevant parties must recognize the importance of this transition and be prepared to play their part; all these parties – the employer as represented by senior management, line managers and individual learners – must understand what is required.

In particular, if senior management do not understand the importance of promoting learning as a business weapon, it is hard to see how the development professional can achieve his or her objectives – this is emphasized in the next proposition.

> **Proposition 5**   Those in Senior Management need to be aware of the implications of the shift from training to learning and give their full support to the new processes and practices that must be implemented in the organization.

Case study 4.4 illustrates the point. At Dublin City Council Finance Department, the need for fundamental changes in leadership attitudes and practice was identified by senior managers. This was seen both as a means of maintaining the service the department offered and keeping pace with the changing demands of users. A steering group of managers, including the Head of Training and Development, planned and executed the change programme.

Case study 4.4 A change framework for the Finance Department at Dublin City Council

Background and context

Dublin City Council is the largest local authority in the Irish Republic and one of the biggest employers in the City. As well as planning and economic development, it manages housing, environmental services, refuse collection, water, roads and streets and the fire brigade. In 2005, its large programme of revenue spending amounted to €780 m while capital spending was €1.1 billion. The Council as a whole employs 6500 staff, of whom 500 work in finance, the subject of this case study.

The Finance Department embraces a range of different activities – with half of the 500 staff working in the Motor Tax Office. Activities extend beyond financial and management accounting and include internal audit, procurement, payroll, claims management, coroner's court and treasury. Only some 25 of the department staff are qualified accountants pursuing a role based on their professional discipline. The other jobs require numeracy rather than accountancy skills and many can be described as routine administrative processing. Although technology has had a considerable impact, much of the activity is paper-based and the introduction of technology to eliminate routine work presents its own challenge. In the words of Kathy Quinn, the Head of Finance:

> *Very efficient systems can steal the opportunity away from people to learn and understand the underlying processes.*

As a result, the job can be less demanding and interesting. Enjoyment and motivation can suffer; gaps can appear between professional workers doing interesting work and others who perceive their job in a less favourable light.

The approach adopted

In 2004, the senior team within the Finance Department recognized that change was imperative to ensure that service did not begin to deteriorate and, in addition, acknowledged the need to be positioned to meet the changing demands of users; such change would necessarily involve a new approach to leadership. A series of workshops was held with the senior team to cultivate a sense of ownership and engagement. Consequent changes would need to cascade downwards throughout the Department, but the starting point would need to be the senior team of 12 and the next tier of 28 managers. Together these 40 formed a strategic group who would need to offer leadership which would inspire, motivate and develop people. It can be seen that this initiative is much broader than learning, training and development; a change in the climate towards learning was, however, recognized to be an essential outcome and, in the longer term, a driver of continuing change.

The immediate focus on senior leadership was given additional impetus by changes that were demanded in the broader context of local government in Ireland. In the mid-1990s there was a national commitment to strengthening Local Government through a central government initiative 'Better Local Government'. Arising from this, local authorities were encouraged to develop a new approach to management development; three of the four authorities in the Dublin area implemented an initiative for senior staff developed by the Irish Management Institute. This initiative had run its course by 2004 and an internal evaluation undertaken by the Dublin City Council Training Department identified a need to strengthen senior managerial capacity and focus on developing leadership qualities. A pilot Department was sought and, given the need for change outlined earlier, the Finance Department agreed to fulfil that role.

Given this background, it was recognized as essential that the senior team in Finance owned the initiative. Accordingly, a vision statement was developed as an integral part of the ongoing business planning process. Progress against that vision continues to be monitored as part of the ongoing business review process. Additionally, a steering group consisting of four of the senior finance team and the Council's Head of Training and Development was established; at a later stage external consultancy support was sought and the lead consultants became members of the steering group.

The initial vision statement developed by the senior team clearly indicated the need to build on the softer skills as well as maintaining the process or technical skills. These key additional areas were identified as follows:

- to be highly regarded by choice rather than obligation
- to be the preferred internal employer with high staff retention rates
- to be seen as an internal partner and resource
- to take initiative, rather than to be reactive
- to focus on outcomes rather than process
- to develop a strategic overview capability.

The same document emphasized that additional leadership strategy and people management competencies would be required along with their existing professional competencies.

The process adopted

What was at issue therefore was the need to develop a new leadership style. As Kathy Quinn emphasized, this is all about 'building networks, creating good relationships, taking initiatives and establishing time to reflect and develop'. Such changes are not about procedures, they must be embedded in day-to-day activities within the Department. Senior managers and, as the initiative cascades down, other managers and team leaders must not only accept such changes of style they must become champions of this change.

Processes to encourage this acceptance have begun with the development of a competency framework and set of related behavioural indicators. An external consultancy, John O'Hehir Associates (John O'Hehir and Dr Corinna Grace), was commissioned to undertake a series of interviews with the Department's internal and external stakeholders and to develop a set of competencies and behavioural indicators. These competencies will be used in a redesigned performance management development system (PMDS); performance review is based on a nationally agreed process – it is the locally designed PMDS that is seen as the development tool. The development of competencies was followed by a sustained series of away day workshop events for the strategic management group.

As soon as the behavioural indicators were in place, the 12 senior staff received coaching support by the external consultants. Initially this consisted of two hour sessions with a gap of three months in between. Differences and gaps against these competencies and indicators were identified and discussed and up to five key action steps agreed. For most of the recipients this was their first experience of external coaching and underlined the importance of the initiative. One of the issues facing the Department is how on-going support can be delivered: the external coaching support may be extended; internal provision may be put in place; another alternative could involve the creation of action learning sets.

The most important tangible indication of the commitment to on-going change has, however, been the creation of a development pack for all staff. This consists of a set of exercises and support material embracing a wide range of areas. These include: career and lifestyle assessment; how to seek feedback; issues on personal development and action planning. Importantly, this pack is intended to encourage individuals to take responsibility for their own development by equipping them with the tools and providing a framework in which this is encouraged.

The consequences for learning

What has been described can be seen to be a wide-ranging change initiative. It embraces all aspects of leadership and extends far beyond learning and development. Kathy Quinn emphasizes the importance of new styles of communication inside and outside the Department. This was identified as a requirement in the stakeholder interviews and are reflected in the competencies.

However, the desire for engagement and initiative should lead and be stimulated by recognition of the need to extend individual knowledge and skills and for greater individual ownership of that objective. This is implicit throughout, but made explicit at key points in all the documentation. '*Demonstrates determination to build on knowledge of the organization continuously seeking opportunities to develop and learn new skills and encouraging the development of others*' is one of the key competences in the 'proactive leadership' cluster.

The acceptance of responsibility for learner self-development is clearly set out in the Development Pack. The Pack, using self-assessment exercises, enables staff to assess their own strengths and weaknesses in each competency and also suggests possible activities to strengthen their individual performance against each competency. It both assists and places responsibility on the individual to develop the competencies needed in their current role and those that would contribute to their future career development.

According to Maire Twomey, the Council's Head of Training and Development, who has been involved in the initiative from the start and sits on the steering group:

> We want people who work in finance to develop their own personal motivation for learning. We are striving to create an environment where this motivation is developed but it must be facilitated, encouraged and actively supported by the organization.

A change in the leadership style of the senior team in the Department is seen as an essential first step.

Moving forward

One feature of the partnership model, as set out in Figure 4.1, is the emphasis on gradual progress. The arrows at the top and the bottom emphasize the need to move from an isolated role for the trainer to a culture where learning is continuous. There is nothing new in the idea that the learning culture can and should be advanced gradually in this way. Almost 20 years ago, researchers at the Ashridge Management Centre (part of a leading UK business school) suggested that training and development could be characterized by three different levels of sophistication.

These were:

- a fragmented approach (where training is not linked to organizational goals and is delivered in a non-systematic way)
- a formalized approach (where training and development becomes more structured and is linked to organizational processes such as appraised systems)
- a focused approach (where the emphasis moves from formal training to personal development) [8].

The idea of moving the organization through a clear ladder of progression in stages, ending up at an ideal state is attractive. It is certainly possible to identify what good (or even best) practice looks like in the modern service-led and knowledge-driven economy. Achieving it is a different matter. We will return to this idea of a ladder of progression in Chapter 11, when we consider its relevance in the international context.

Some US research, undertaken by the Consultancy Accenture Learning, illustrates this point. In 2004, Accenture Learning surveyed 285 organizations over a nine-week period. They had an average 23 000 employees. As a result of their study, seven characteristics of the High Performance Learning Organization (HPLO) were identified and 23 of the 285 surveyed organizations were stated to have achieved the level of an HPLO. The seven characteristics are set out in Table 4.2.

Jeanne Meister, the organization's Vice-President, summarized the report's findings as follows:

It is a marked change. Organizations are not looking to the learning departments to just manage their own operations efficiently and effectively. . .CEOs are looking to the learning departments for innovations. Specifically, they

Table 4.2 The seven traits of high-performance learning organizations

- Alignment of learning initiatives to the business goals of the organization
- Measurement of the overall business impact of the learning function
- Movement of learning outside the four walls of the organization to include other members of the overall value chain, such as customers and channel partners
- A focus on competency development of the organization's most critical job families
- Integration of learning with other human performance systems and functions, such as knowledge management, performance support and talent management
- Blended delivery approaches that include classroom as well as both synchronous and asynchronous e-learning
- Mature design and delivery of leadership development courses

want to know how learning can help drive revenue growth and an innovation agenda for the organization [9, p. 35].

The list set out in Table 4.2 is a useful summary of the aspirations that many organizations have embraced whether implicitly or explicitly. These are demanding: each of the seven characteristics presents its own challenges. To an extent, such aspirations can only be achieved in larger organizations where there is the scope, the research and professional expertise available.

Accenture Learning's term 'high performance, learning organization' deserves some consideration. Its strength is that it combines the high performance model (thus taking us outside the training box) and emphasizes learning not training. As has been noted the challenge is to achieve progress through involving others.

Those who have been involved in people development for some time will of course recall a period when the term 'learning organization' achieved tremendous popularity. This followed the publication, in 1990, of a book by the US commentator Peter Senge [10].

In a complex and challenging book, Senge differentiated learning organizations from traditional controlling organizations. In the years following publication, the concept of the learning organization excited many practitioners, but interest in the term (though not the ideas behind it) has subsequently declined. In retrospect, there was a lack of debate and agreement on the steps that should be taken to ground the concept and the climate that would be needed for a 'learning organization' (however defined) to flourish.

What is beyond doubt is that more and more organizations see the need to create the conditions for effective individual and organizational learning. For many this is central to their strategy and articulated as such. This is especially true of 'new economy' organizations and the chapter concludes with Case study 4.5 from India, i-flex.

Case study 4.5 Developing competitive advantage at a niche Indian IT firm

Background

The creation of a virtual university and the use of on-line learning has been central to the success and expansion of Indian IT services provider PrimeSourcing, a division of parent company, i-flex Solutions Ltd, which is an Indian IT solutions provider with a niche (domain) focus in the financial services industry. i-flex was established in 1992 as Citicorp Information Technology Industries Limited, when its two co-founders Rajesh Hukku and R. Ravisankar, along with a handful of other colleagues, spun it off from Citicorp Overseas Software Limited, an Indian subsidiary of Citigroup.

i-flex has grown rapidly from employing 250 employees when it first started operating to its current size of just over 7100 members of staff. It serves some 660 customers located in more than 120 countries and employs staff from 17 different nationalities. Nearly half of i-flex employees work for PrimeSourcing, which offers a comprehensive portfolio of services, mainly in the form of customized IT solutions to meet clients' needs for specific solutions.

PrimeSourcing's key selling proposition to its customers is its in-depth (domain) expertise in the financial services industry, covering corporate banking, investment banking, private banking, retail banking and insurance. PrimeSourcing recognizes that the effective delivery of training and learning are essential to achieving the company's source of competitive advantage, which is built on its employees' specialist knowledge of the banking industry. It also emphasizes that the case for effective people development is even stronger in knowledge-intensive industries like software and when an organization is expanding fast, with a corresponding need for employees to pick up new skills and knowledge rapidly.

Knowledge development: Prime University

This emphasis on training and knowledge development led to the creation of Prime University – a collaborative initiative between PrimeSourcing and i-flex's Training Department. Prime University is a forum for inquiry, discussion, experiential learning and knowledge sharing. The University offers three kinds of training programmes: Technical (covering IT certifications); Functional (including Finance/Banking programmes; and Behavioural or People Skills (covering soft skill advancement). Every employee, irrespective of their specific rank or role, undertakes foundation-level training (Finance Foundation Programme) on the banking industry. This programme equips all employees with a basic understanding of the financial services industry and includes modules covering Money and Risk, Financial Statements, Raising and Investing Money, Retail Banking and Corporate & Investment Banking and Financial Markets. Successful completion of this programme leads to certification. Since employees are based in different locations across the world, this programme is delivered as a blended learning programme through the use of LearnLinc, an on-line tool for e-based learning. There are several self-paced modules, which put the onus of learning on the learner. In March 2005, 100% of the approximately 2500 employees in PrimeSourcing had successfully completed this programme.

Some of the other training programmes include: a fresher induction programme for new graduate recruits; a lateral induction programme for those who are recruited from the industry, with some previous exposure to the finance industry; behavioural training programmes for managers who required soft skill training; technical workshops; and process awareness workshops.

To embed the importance of continuous learning, development and knowledge sharing within the culture of the company, senior managers are encouraged to deliver the training programmes. To reinforce this process, they are required to incorporate training and coaching objectives in their annual performance goals. Participants are encouraged to put themselves forward for training programmes, not just as a result of annual identification of development needs through the appraisal process, but also by a system which awards them credit points for learning. Similarly, the trainers are also awarded credit points for teaching.

Formalized knowledge sharing

Prime University is one of several initiatives designed to integrate the concept of knowledge development and sharing into the culture of the organization. *Thursday Thoughts* is a forum through which people increase their knowledge through real life experience sharing by senior managers. This is delivered live over PrimeSourcing's intranet through video-conferencing. Employees across the world can log in to view this and, to take into account the time variations of the offices in different countries, talks are scheduled round a time when the maximum number of employees across all countries can participate. Another learning initiative is 'One-on-One', a project led by HR that encourages the view that senior managers have a responsibility for coaching. Through this scheme, any employee can request a talk with any senior manager to discuss projects, ideas and learning.

Learning and training and knowledge sharing is seen as essential for the future of i-flex. According to a member of i-flex's Training Department,

'Our business growth demands have made knowledge enhancement a necessity'. Multiple modes of learning are being exploited to cater to a widespread audience and there is growing emphasis on learners accepting responsibility for their own learning. As V. Shankar, Executive Vice-President, PrimeSourcing, puts it:

> *Going back to University was never this easy or exciting! Neither was it so rewarding. With its promise of enhancing domain and technical knowledge, behavioural and managerial skills, our University at i-flex is all set to increase the competency of its students in the financial services industry.*

This case study was contributed by Deepali Prashantham.

Appendix

Some practical questions

1. What actions do senior managers take to demonstrate their commitment to a learning culture? Highlight one box in each row – pick the statement that most closely represents the current position in your organization.

Low commitment			High commitment
Score 1	*2*	*3*	*4*
Doesn't talk about learning	Offers only rhetoric or lip service to the learning strategy	Talks convincingly about the importance of people skills	Models good people management behaviour
Sees training as a stand alone activity	Listens to training professionals	Understands training professionals' explanations of what a learning strategy can do to support business performance	Gives learning and development resources such as budgets, time and people
Doesn't engage in on-going learning	Engages in on-going learning by introducing programmes	Engages in on-going learning by taking part in delivering interventions	Engages in on-going learning by participation as a delegate
Equates learning to the provision	Understands that learning may occur	Ensures there is consistency in learning	Follows up after learning interventions

Low commitment		→	High commitment
Score 1	2	3	4
of traditional courses	in a variety of settings	and the delivery of training across the organization	to check that things are happening
Expects task performance only from line managers	Communicates the importance of line managers having people skills	Ensures that line managers have the people management skills required	Enforces high standards of people management through the performance management, promotion policy and reward system

2. What other signs are there in your own organization that senior management practice and attitudes are moving to appreciate the value of a learning culture? How far along the commitment arrow (see Figure 4.1, p. 78) would you assess these to be?

3. How involved are your line managers in learning interventions? Some ways that different levels of commitment might be demonstrated are shown below. Highlight one box in each row – pick the statement that most closely represents the current position in your organization or one for which you are a consultant.

Low commitment		→	High commitment
Score 1	2	3	4
Line managers call in training professionals to organize courses	Line managers carry out on the job instruction and collaborate with trainers on general needs	Line managers have the skills and capability to coach their teams	Learners look to line management for skilled coaching assistance
Line managers driven only by task accomplishment	More driven by tasks, but relationships are important	Relationships seen as the way to get the task done	Line management gives equal weight to relationships as the task
HR professionals interfere with manager's need to get the job done	Line managers are involved in HR initiatives	Line managers are part of working parties on HR initiatives	Line managers are driving people initiatives themselves

Low commitment			→ High commitment
Score 1	*2*	*3*	*4*
Line managers 'park' people issues with the specialist functions	Line managers ask for consultancy advice from training professionals	Line managers analyse the training needs of their staff	Line managers come to training with issues, looking for their help with solutions
HR jumps in and takes people issues away from line managers	HR gives guidance to line managers to resolve issues	HR coaches line management	Line and training professionals work together to build the best solution

4. What other measures of the involvement of line managers in learning interventions exist in your organization?

These questions were prepared by Jennifer Taylor based on extracts from the People and Performance tool – designing HR processes for maximum performance delivery, which is available to CIPD members on www.cipd.co.ut/subjects/corpstrtgy/busiper.fm.

References

[1]. Galagan, P. (2003) The Future of the Profession formerly known as Training. T+D, 37(12), 26–38.
[2]. King, A. (1993) From the Sage on the Stage to Guide on the Side. College Training, 41(1), 30–35.
[3]. Chartered Institute of Personnel and Development (2006) Learning and Development Annual Survey Report 2006. London: CIPD. Available at: http://www.cipd.co.uk/NR/rdonlyres/97BE272C-8859-4DB1-BD99-17F38E4B4484/0/lrnandevsurv0406.pdf
[4]. Chartered Institute of Personnel and Development (2006) Reflections on Talent Management. London: CIPD. Available at: http://www.cipd.co.uk/NR/rdonlyres/F473B522-DD49-49E2-9021-59E0B2BDA288/0/reftal-manca0306.pdf
[5]. Ulrich, D. (1997) Human Resource Champions. Boston, MA: Harvard Business School Press.
[6]. Ulrich, D. and Brockbank, W. (2005) The HR Value Proposition. Boston, MA: Harvard Business School Press.

[7]. Ulrich, D. and Brockbank, W. (2005) Role Call. People Management, 59(8), 25–28.

[8]. Barham, K., Fraser, J. and Heath, L. (1988) Management for the Future. Berkhamstead: Ashridge Management Research Group.

[9]. Sussman, D. (2005) What HPLOs Know. T+D, 59(8), 35–39.

[10]. Senge, P.M. (1990) The Fifth Discipline: the Art and Practice of the Learning Organization. New York: Doubleday.

PART 3

Current practice

5

Becoming Learner-Centred

In the previous three chapters, which together made up Part two of this book, we set out the new context in which the development professional must operate. Hopefully, this will help to determine the desired position for the function in the organization. In this third part of the book we will ask what should we do: what are the problems we encounter and how should we seek to overcome them? We will consider in turn some implications of the move to a learner-centred approach, some key processes, the place of the training course, non-course interventions and issues on technology and value. First, we will offer some general comments on how the profession can shape its future.

One of the underlying themes of this book is that we can learn a great deal from sharing good practice. Indeed, it is the author's view that the future of people development practice will be shaped by the energies and initiatives of individuals in organizations. In an earlier section, the importance of adopting a contingent approach was emphasized. Throughout this book a whole series of case studies has been presented. These describe good practice interventions that are intended to help professionals elsewhere in their thinking. However, everybody must determine and map their own way forward using interventions that are appropriate in their circumstances. There is no alchemy out there waiting to be discovered. Progress will be achieved through discrete improvements. John Kay, the economist and former head of the Said Business School at Oxford University, offered the following observation:

> *Because the world is complicated and the future uncertain, decision-making in organizations and economic systems is best made through a series of small-scale experiments, frequently reviewed, and in a structure in which success is followed up and failure recognized but not blamed* [1, p. 108].

Although he was writing mainly about economic systems, his words have a resonance for people development professionals. In this sense, the future will be determined by those who have recognized the importance of the propositions, can act on them within their organization and will share their results with their fellow professionals.

Barriers to progress

In the course of the research for this book a series of workshops was held with participants who held a particular interest in the changing role of the trainer. Participants were self-selecting; these audiences are not claimed to be representative of the profession as a whole. They were all asked to identify 'one key issue, challenge or consequence that you believe is important for effective learning, training and development in the modern world; one that will occupy the professional's time and needs to be addressed'. The form they were asked to complete is set out at Figure 5.1; the exercise outlined at the bottom of the Figure was used to structure the subsequent discussion.

In all, 17 separate workshop sessions were held between October 2005 and June 2006; eight of the sessions were held in the UK and three in the USA and Canada. A special session was held at the European Commission's Training Day in Brussels – where the participants came from a wide-range of countries. Sessions were held in the Republic of Ireland, Bahrain and Bulgaria. In all, 314 valid usable responses were collected and analysed [2]. Using a slightly different format two sessions were held in the People's Republic of China.

The themes that emerged are set out in Tables 5.1 and 5.2 and are illustrated with representative comments taken directly from the returned exercise forms.

Inevitably, there is considerable overlap among the categories; however, Table 5.1 lists the four themes that were mentioned most frequently and Table 5.2 lists another eight themes that emerged.

An analysis of the data showed how people developers see themselves as facing common problems. The same issues arose irrespective of business circumstances and, seemingly, location. Certainly, it would be hard, through analysis of the data, to detect any major national differences, beyond some indications of different stages in the ladder of progress (to return to the point made following the discussion of the Ashridge model in the previous chapter (p. 83). Such transatlantic nuances (and they are no more than that) as did emerge are summarized in Table 5.3.

One special but very interesting case concerns some data collected from the People's Republic of China. In June 2006, the author was invited to speak to the Central Training Committee of the Chinese Communist Party. The results of their completed submissions to the same questions are set out in Table 5.4. It can be seen, without overstretching the point, that these 17 statements are consistent with those received from elsewhere in the world. One can extend a fellow professional's sympathy to the respondent who reported: 'participants are not interested in political theory training'. Given the nature of the job, this does indeed present him or her with a problem!

The Changing Role of the Trainer

Exercise I: General

Please write below one key issue, challenge or consequence that you believe is important for effective learning, training and development in the modern world; one that will occupy the professional's time and needs to be addressed.

Key issue:

Your Name: **Role**

(Please print)

Organization:

Under guidance from the facilitator, five different people will be asked to award up to 10 points for each issue. 10 is the highest rating (I agree: this illustrates an important issue facing the profession) and 0 is the lowest rating.

1	2	3	4	5

Figure 5.1 Workshop Form

Table 5.1 Major themes from workshop sessions

Developing a learning culture
- Creating an organizational culture (behaviours, systems and processes) in which training and learning can flourish
- How to create a learning environment with people who are reluctant toward traditional learning solutions
- How to motivate people to learn; how to get people committed
- Going beyond rhetoric of self-learning and creating or enabling space/culture for people to do it effectively

Gaining management buy-in
- How to achieve complete 'buy-in' by the Board/MD for all levels of learning/training and development
- Convincing managers that training/L&D is good for business and not a drain on overstretched resources
- Director's perception of the benefit of learning when the company hits hard times
- Lack of buy-in from management – requires massive culture change in people who don't understand learning; management send staff on training courses to 'tick the box'

Overcoming barriers to learning
- How to enable people to have time to learn and develop in busy work environments
- Not to be distracted from learning by job pressures
- Time needed for training versus a very results driven business; where time is money!
- Give staff time out to learn (organization paid to deliver service, not train)
- Time for training courses

Analysing learning and development needs
- Understanding the requirements and needs of the business, the job role and the individual
- Ensuring that training and development actually meet organizational needs; how core competencies meet organizational requirements
- Relevance: trying to make sure that the training is relevant for all groups
- Knowledge of the learner, their learning requirements and aspirations

Table 5.2 Other themes that emerged in workshops

Involving line management
- Responsibility of line managers to facilitate appropriate learning
- Transfer of learning requires support from line management
- Taking responsibility for the success of the outcome (the role of the manager and individual)

Encouraging learners to take ownership
- Individuals to take responsibility for their learning
- Encouraging learners to see the value in learning as a self-managed process
- To convince management and staff to take on responsibilities/ownership of self-development/learning

Addressing specific learning interventions
- Delivering training and learning that supports and enables staff to be assessed as competent against occupational standards
- Matching learning to recognizable transferable qualifications

Knowledge sharing
- Getting people to share ideas, skills and knowledge across the organization: fear of loss of power, culture change or due to geographic spread which does not facilitate people getting together to learn from each other

Evaluating training
- Evaluation of training – pre and post: evaluation being key into discerning the 'next round' themes for training. Did it work – why/why not; what's the next step?
- How to evaluate training where the individual/manager takes responsibility for the success of the outcome

Ensuring the transfer of learning
- How to transfer learning and subsequent organizational and individual benefits
- Getting the organization to encourage the learner to use new skills when they return to work after a course

Assessing learning
- Measurement of performance, how it should be conducted and what values can actually be attributed to successful delivery of training and development of learning environments
- Training – learning: measuring what has been learned

Establishing the benefits of learning
- Show how learning will create value in the role
- Selling the value of the learning *before* it happens, as well as being able to demonstrate return on investment

Table 5.3 A transatlantic comparison

UK and Ireland
The key issue is the need to make a cultural shift from managing training to managing a learning environment within an organization, which requires ownership and commitment from stakeholders in the learning process

USA
The key issue is the need to make time for learning in busy/fast-paced working environments. Also understanding the needs of learners and ensuring training keeps pace with technology

Both the UK and USA had issues regarding time for learning in organizations. Whereas the UK focused on developing a 'learning culture and gaining management buy-in', the USA focused more on correct analysis of needs and use of technology in the learning process

Table 5.4 Exercise returns collected from the Central Training Committee Chinese Communist Party

- Trainers' lack of ability to design proactive content
- Participants have high education level but low skills level
- How to handle big volume with different education level
- Learners lack pressure of motivation to learn
- Not all training content can meet the learners' requirement
- Don't have enough motivation to learn because the participants don't know whether or not they can get new skills by training
- Old and bad learning habits affect getting better results
- From 'be asked to learn' to 'want to learn'
- Participants are not interested in political theory training
- The way of business training is boring and results can't match the expectation
- Lack of learning skills in the creation of atmosphere to solve real problem through organization training (learning)
- The expected results of managers and trainees to training are different and the managers do not always like to pay so much
- The biggest problem in transferring from training to learning is lacking of motivation or drive
- Lack of motivation, they always think 'ask me to learn' but not 'I want to learn'. The reason is that training and learning are not aligned with the promotion and utilization
- Not enough time
- Training content lack of practicability
- Change the learning attitude of participants, from passive to initiative

The reader is asked to excuse the imperfections in English which arose from the need to compromise between the requirements of agreed translation and elegance of expression

How do people learn?

Many of the themes that were uncovered in these workshops will be explored further in the remainder of the book. In this chapter, we will consider one important issue that underlies them all: how can we become learner-centred? It seems reasonable to start by outlining what we know about individual learning and to ask the question 'how do people learn?'

In 2002, the Chartered Institute for Personnel and Development (CIPD) commissioned Cambridge Programme for Industry (CPI) to review and synthesize the theories that govern our understanding of learning in organizations [3]. The CPI research report suggested that the learning theories that have exerted most influence over the past 50 years could helpfully be placed into the following four clusters:

- learning as behaviour
- learning as understanding
- learning as knowledge construction
- learning as social practice.

Fuller details of their analysis are set out in the reports, but the broad definitions and summaries are set out in Table 5.5.

No one learning theory is 'correct'. There is a continuing on-going debate on their value. All of them can assist our thinking. All can help to clarify the steps that can be taken to assist learning and the learner. All have their place. For example, there is considerable interest in knowledge-intensive organizations in what is known as social-constructivism (or sometimes socio-constructivism) – a combination of the third and fourth categories. Learning is then a process of knowledge construction undertaken by the individual in a specific environment.

Why do people learn?

However committed managers are to learning, ultimately it will be the learner himself or herself who will determine progress. We will now consider the above question, which is about individual motivation and engagement. Here we will draw on the work of both US and UK commentators.

Writing in the ASTD's (formerly the American Society for Training and Development) magazine in 2003, Neal Chalofsky of George Washington University presented a useful overview of relevant motivation theory. He asked:

How do we help people change in order to reach the goal of meaningful work?
[4, p. 55]

Table 5.5 Summary of learning theories

Learning as behaviour
The first cluster is concentrated around the theory of behaviourism and the work of
B.F. Skinner. These theories originate from the natural sciences. Behaviourism
asserts that any change in an individual's behaviour is the result of events, known as
stimuli, and the consequences of these events. Reinforcing responses through reward
is the behaviourist's way of encouraging the desired behaviours. By rewarding the
desired behaviour the behaviourist conditions the individual to perform the action
again and again.

Learning as understanding
Unlike behaviourism, which focuses on the conditioning of behaviour, cognitive
learning theories view learning as a process of understanding and internalizing the
principles, connections and facts about the world around us. Seen this way, the
learner is like a powerful machine that processes information and internalizes it as
knowledge.

Strategies for cognitive development frequently deploy facilitation to assist
understanding. By exposure to learning materials and guidance, the learner can pass
through developmental stages more quickly than if left to their own devices. Clearly,
the facilitator needs to have a good understanding of where the learner is starting
from in order to guide them effectively.

Learning as knowledge construction
Constructivist theories view the individual as an active agent in their own learning.
Constructivists believe that all knowledge is personal knowledge – in other words
knowledge is not something 'out there' ready to be grasped. This means that
knowledge is subjective, tacit and highly dependent on context. Constructivists
would argue that knowledge management systems in fact manage information rather
than knowledge, since the latter only exists inside people's heads.

Individuals assign meaning to knowledge that they have obtained through their
own experience and only then does it become useable. This focus on the learner
contrasts with behaviourism where the 'expert' is the source of learning, or the
cognitive approach where 'content' is emphasized. In constructivist theories, the
learner is at the centre of the learning experience. Interaction and dialogue (with
other learners or with a facilitator) are used by the learner to enhance their own
personal experiences and understanding.

Learning as social practice
Social theories of learning do not contradict the behavioural, cognitive or
constructivist theories. Instead, they simply argue that learning is more effective
when it arises and is applied in a social setting. This idea goes back to the work of
L.S. Vygotsky who observed children interacting with older individuals. He discovered
that they could perform well above their age if given the chance to interact with
someone older. This led him to conclude that social interaction was crucial to some
forms of learning.

Table 5.5 (continued)

Anthropologists, sociologists, social psychologists and cognitive theorists have all contributed to this cluster of theories. There are several different forms of social learning theories. Cognitive-social theories, as exemplified by Albert Bandura, regard learning as the outcome of social interactions which foster shared standards of behaviour. Activity theories regard established patterns of social interaction as the source of learning, for example, problem resolution within established work processes and patterns. Lastly, theories of social practice, made famous by Jean Lave and Etienne Wenger, point to the importance of participation in communities of practice as the source of learning. Here individuals don't so much learn facts and principles about the world; they learn, instead, how to 'be'.

and answered:

By sticking to the roots of individual change. There are two aspects of organizational behaviour that three legendary content motivation theorists – Maslow, Herzberg and Alderfer – advocated that are even more critical now than when they were first proposed: intrinsic motivation and growth (learning) [4, p. 55].

and went on to argue that:

Since the mid-1970s, new theories have emerged that focus on intrinsic motivational processes and on self-systems that determine an individual's behaviour. Intrinsic motivation is an internal emotional preference for a task that gives it satisfaction and meaning [4, p. 56].

Certain things seem evident to those who are wrestling with the practical problems of motivation in organizations. One is that such problems are complex – it is not easy to 'read' people and to know what will activate that intrinsic motivation. This must strike a chord with every parent of every child who is not achieving their full potential at school. Secondly, encouraging individual motivation will involve the full range of human resource interventions.

The CIPD People and Performance model (see Chapter 3, p. 55) offers a very useful insight here. This research suggests that the crucial factor linking HR practices to performance is the way that these practices lead to discretionary behaviour. This was defined in the following terms:

Discretionary behaviour means making the sort of choices that often define a job, *such as the way the job is done – the speed, care, innovation and style of job delivery. This behaviour is at the heart of the employment relationship, because it is hard for the employer to define and then monitor and control the amount of effort, innovation and productive behaviour required. The most obvious example here is front-line service work dealing with customers either face to face or over the phone. It concerns the sort of everyday behaviour that the employer wants but has to rely on the employee to deliver. It may involve emotional labour (smiling down the phone), using knowledge to solve a problem or suggest an alternative to the customer, or it may be internal to the work of the organization, such as cooperating with team members, helping probationers learn shortcuts or sharing new ideas on work processes. One way or the other, the employee chooses how conscientiously to undertake the job.*

Most jobs are built up of many tasks, so the level of complexity can be surprisingly high, even for seemingly routine ones. This choice of how, and how well, to do things is not necessarily made deliberately: it can be unconscious – just part of the way people behave in their organization. But discretionary behaviour can certainly be withdrawn, often in the sense of adopting an uncaring attitude. This may be a reciprocal response to a belief that 'the firm no longer cares about me, my future or my opinions.'

Ultimately, whatever the incentives or sanctions the firm tries to use, it lies with the employee to 'give' discretionary behaviour and to withdraw it. Although this is described in terms of the action of an individual (we all have bad days), it is the collective withdrawal of discretionary behaviour that is so damaging. Our own experience tells us that there are times when morale is low, or the 'buzz' has gone, or everyone just wants to go home as soon as possible [5, p. 5].

A shift from training to learning is entirely consistent with the emphasis on discretionary behaviour. If employees are encouraged to exercise appropriate initiative, seeking to acquire and develop the knowledge and skills to do their current and future jobs must be seen as a particularly welcome way in which they exercise that discretion.

Employees can be made to attend training courses; they cannot be made to learn skills. Certainly, in no sense can they be made actively to seek learning opportunities. It is up to them. What organizations can do is put appropriate structures and processes in place to encourage and support the learners. It is perhaps easier to see how this applies in the case of knowledge workers. Here, there is an expectation that an individual's professional ethos includes a commitment to update his or her expertise. The case of the Interpreter Service at the European Commission, set out in Case study 5.1, offers a good illustration.

Case study 5.1 Developing the Interpreter Service at the European Commission – the role of learning

Background and training objectives

With 500 professional conference interpreters and 160 support staff, the European Commission Interpreter Service at Brussels is the biggest employer of interpreters in the world. Taken together its staff have the capability to interpret in and out of all 20 languages used among member countries

Most staff are, of course, fluent in at least one of the two widely used working languages (French or English). In addition, a number of 'pivotal' languages have been identified (German, Spanish, Italian, Dutch and Portuguese) where an in-depth capacity is required. For the smooth running of multilingual meetings, knowledge of all other official languages – including the new ones of the 2004 enlargement – is also vital. The Interpretation Service is a full Directorate General (DG) within the European Commission.

Claude Durand is Head of the Unit in the Directorate which provides professional support for interpreters. The main activity is the provision of appropriate training but, in addition, his unit is responsible for facilitating meeting preparation and improving awareness among meeting organizers and participants to the needs for efficient multilingual communication. Claude Durand emphasizes that, to be a successful interpreter, 'languages are not the only thing'. It is important to be versatile and flexible, to learn new things and subjects and, at all times, to understand client needs and the context in which the interpretation facility is required.

The training challenge

As is the case in all organizations, there is a need for on-going training in management, interpersonal skills and IT. The DG staff can take advantage of the training provision offered centrally in the Commission and the training delivered in the Directorate General. The very specific nature of the function, however, leads to an additional set of objectives for learning and training. Some obviously relate to extending the interpretation capabilities through immediate training in languages. However, there is a general requirement to build the capability and capacity of the service. This extends beyond training and, as will be seen, solutions involve developing relationships beyond the boundaries of the Commission. In Claude Durand's view, this approach is necessary for both the maintenance of the service and its growth.

One positive feature is that the approach to training and learning can start from the assumption that the professional staff are committed to develop their own skills and knowledge. Such a commitment is a characteristic of choosing to work as an interpreter. Equally, line managers within the Directorate General recognize the need to improve and extend the skill base.

However, one of the major challenges facing Angela Gossez, Claude Durand's assistant who is responsible for course and event provision for interpreters within the Directorate General, is planning and logistics. Interpreters have assignments at various places inside and outside Brussels.

Those with a capability in languages where there is a high demand for conference interpretation can be difficult to release from their jobs. In many cases where interpreters are released to participate in training or learning, they must be replaced in the short-term for assignments by freelance or contract provision drawn from an approved network. In that case, the replacement cost can be a very high burden on an already tight budget.

Language training and the pedagogical assistance scheme

All professional staff recruited are mostly qualified linguists (but not exclusively) and trained interpreters. As well as the usual induction procedures, one of the immediate tasks is to assess their training needs and to prepare a training path.

An early interview is undertaken by the line managers to discuss training needs and opportunities. For many new entrants, one of the first learning objectives is to develop proficiency in a new pivot language. Once the new entrant has spent some time in the Directorate General, the acquisition of extended language proficiency is discussed together with other training needs, at the annual performance review.

As a result, there is an on-going provision for language training. About 100 participants will be undertaking some sort of language course at any given time. Courses are generally delivered by approved external contractors in training rooms in the Directorate General, generally in groups with a minimum of three participants. Where there is a particular need, but the number of volunteers does not reach the three participants limit, an individual learner will be sponsored on an external course – for example, in 2006, an interpreter whose first language is Spanish will be given full financial support to learn Maltese, but outside working hours.

It is important for the future of the Directorate General that a wider view is taken and is not limited to language training. To make sure that universities' training interpreters provide the European Institutions with the high-quality graduates that they need, the policy of the Directorate General has been to develop a cooperation programme with more than 50 European universities. This means that it is essential for the implementation of this programme that a significant number of staff within the Directorate understand and are able to convey the way in which people are trained as conference interpreters meeting the highest standards. These trainers need to be capable of assisting university teachers working in specialized departments training interpreters and to represent the Directorate General effectively in universities and to assess and support outside institutions.

This significant new initiative, introduced in the late 1990s, is called the 'pedagogical assistance scheme'. This was designed to achieve the above aims and also improve recruitment by encouraging applications from aware and capable entrants. Pedagogical assistance was based on the experience gained within the European Commission from over 30 years of training interpreters in-house. This training course for graduates was run by experienced interpreters to fill a pressing need for young interpreters which could not be met by universities at the time. This course was so successful that some interpreting units were made up almost exclusively of former in-house trainees.

Some 50 universities and schools have been identified and the Directorate has established an on-going relationship with them. Every year, some 120 members of staff are chosen to participate in the scheme. They will spend anything from a day to 10 days at the institution and develop an understanding of the teaching approach and contribute to its development. Much of the emphasis has been on institutions in countries which gained access to the European Union in 2004 – recently, an interpreter spent 10 days at a Lithuanian university, for example. The overall resource commitment is considerable; some 600 interpreter days can be devoted to this programme in a given year.

The use of workshops

Much of the emphasis within the Department is on shared learning through workshops. A good example is the two-day events held two or three times a year to prepare participants for the pedagogical assistance programme. The aim is to get all eligible and competent staff through this programme so they were held more frequently in the earlier years when the scheme was developed. The format was designed by Claude Durand and the workshop delivered by two senior interpreters. The intention is to learn through sharing of experience rather than formal instruction. This two-day event has been recently supplemented by four half-day workshops where various topics are given more detailed treatment by participants.

A similar format (two-day event) is used to prepare those staff who will be involved in recruitment and selection. Here, the challenges facing the Directorate are almost unique. They have, over time, designed and developed their own tests and exercises which must be appropriate and effective in the assessment of candidates. Those people who will deliver the speech that will be interpreted by candidates at selection tests must be trained so that consistent standards are achieved in assessments. All those involved in selection – whatever their role – attend a two-day workshop where, again, the emphasis is on sharing experiences and knowledge.

One other feature of the training and learning provision is the regular thematic workshops. Experts from outside the Directorate General will present sessions to 15 or so interpreters on current topics. Examples would be bird flu (which became an important topic in 2005), criminal law, food safety, securities trading etc. Sessions which are particularly relevant or successful are repeated and participant interpreters will suggest improvements and new topics.

Flexing round the learner

What is evident from these brief discussions on 'how do people learn?' and 'why do people learn?' is that research output from the pedagogy (defined in the science of teaching instruction or training) or psychology in general will not offer us easily transferable blueprints. There is only so much that can be drawn from such material; people development professionals will need to show confidence in their judgement and supply what we can call their 'craft skills' in the situations they are facing.

We can illustrate this point further by a consideration of learning styles. This short section will be drawn from a research paper prepared by Andrew Fleming of the British Educational Communication and Technology Agency [6]. It will come as no surprise, given the previous discussion to discover that learning styles is a complex area; to quote from the research paper:

The term 'learning styles' has no one definition. It is used loosely and often interchangeably with terms such as 'thinking styles', 'cognitive styles', 'learning modalities' and 'multiple intelligences'. Learning style theorists draw on the fields of pedagogy, psychology and neuroscience but generally fail to engage fully with any of them. This has led to a confusing array of models and terminology, and a body of research that is characterised by conflicting findings and methodological weaknesses.

And:

A number of researchers have attempted to break down the concepts and processes which underlie the term 'learning styles'. At risk of over-simplifying a complex subject, learning styles might be said to consist of three inter-related elements:

- *information processing – habitual modes of perceiving, storing and organising information (e.g. pictorially or verbally)*
- *instructional preferences – predispositions towards learning in a certain way (e.g. collaboratively or independently) or in a certain setting (e.g. time of day, environment)*

■ *learning strategies – adaptive responses to learning specific subject matter in a particular context.*

To quote again from the research paper:

Any theory or model of learning styles is necessarily a simplification of the complexity of how we learn.

There is no secure evidential base to support any one theory of learning styles – it is important to be aware of the limitations of any learning styles model and indeed the field as a whole.

Learning styles are at best one of a range of factors determining how learners react to learning opportunities – environment, culture (both the learners and the institution's) teaching methods and learning aims are all part of a complex pattern of interactions.

So, as far as practical action is concerned:

It may therefore be both more practical and more effective to think in terms of accommodating, rather than matching, modalities and styles. There is evidence that presenting information in a variety of formats has benefits in terms of both achievement and motivation. For example, presentations which include both visual and auditory elements can be more effective than those which cater for only one modality. Learners certainly seem to perform better when a range of instructional approaches are used, though it is open to debate whether this is an issue of cognitive style or simply avoiding boredom.

The ability to flex or adjust interventions to suit a learner's needs is self-evidently attractive, but the conclusion must be that we are not likely to find a process map on how to do this through a consideration of learning style theory. Andrew Fleming's research paper shows how far we have to go on learning styles. In mitigation, it must be said that many people development professionals, current author included, have found that the introduction of a learning styles exercise in a classroom of considerable value in increasing learner self-awareness. Honey and Mumford's Learning Styles Questionnaire has proved of particular value for many of us in the UK.

Moving forward, in practical terms there seem to be two different sorts of strategies that people developers are adopting to flex or adjust round the learner.

The first involves an explicit recognition of the limitations of what might be called 'remote' learning and proceeds through one-to-one focus on the needs of the individual learner delivered by a sympathetic intermediary. Such interventions will be considered more generally in Chapter 8 where they will be described as 'support and challenge'. The second consists of putting a variety of processes in place generally to make it easier for the learner to understand what is required of him or her and what support that they can receive. Some of these processes will be considered later in the next chapter.

Two case illustrations will be presented to bring this chapter to a conclusion. Both describe the use of 'sympathetic intermediaries'.

In the first case, the processes involved putting a system of peer group assessment in place. Case study 5.2 describes the way in which skills are developed and performance reinforced through feedback at the ethnic minority services at Swedish Radio. Here, the nature of the job itself presents the challenge in terms of determining a strategy for individual learning.

The second case, set out in Case study 5.3, describes the support for learning with disabilities in Ontario, Canada. The challenge here arises from the starting point of the learner himself or herself. In both cases, the way forward involves a highly customized or individualized approach.

Case study 5.2 Learning through feedback at Swedish Radio

Background

Sveriges Radio (Swedish Radio, SR) is the country's national public service broadcaster. Since 1994, SR has been operating as a limited liability company owned by a foundation. It has a nine member board who determine policy and board objectives. Some 1800 staff are employed by SR, 60% of whom are journalists, some 15% are engineers with the remainder involved in a range of management and support functions.

As part of its public service obligation, SR provides national broadcasts for minorities resident in Sweden. Output is delivered in Finnish, Sami (the language spoken by some Swedish nationals in the north) and other official minority languages. This case study, however, concerns the radio broadcasting that is delivered to immigrant communities. Eight groups of languages are covered: Albanian, Arabic, Aramaic, Kurdish, Persian (Farsi), Bosnian/ Croatian/Serbian, Somali and English (which is a common second language understood by people who have come to Sweden from a wide range of countries, for example, Africa). Sarah Roxström, who is Head of Programming for Ethnic Minorities, has a total of some 35 journalists reporting to her. She is supported by two editors who form her management team. The nature of the work means that a flat organizational structure is appropriate, therefore, the support from peers is critical.

As an illustration of output, the service broadcasts in Arabic for 20 minutes a day Monday through Friday and 30 minutes on Saturday. These broadcasts are repeated on a local frequency in Stockholm.

Resourcing the service

The Ethnic Minority service requires a very particular set of skills and capabilities from its journalists. They are easy to state but hard to secure in practice. Successful journalists must be fluent speakers of both their broadcasting language and Swedish; they must be capable journalists and they must understand the purpose, ethics and values of public service broadcasting. The need to recruit journalists across eight languages means that recruitment is demanding and new entrants can have different starting points in terms of their capabilities.

Some may have had all their formal education in Sweden with another language (for example Farsi) as a second home language. Others could have no problems on linguistic fluency but have no background in journalism. These could include former lecturers in political science or language teachers.

A third set of issues arise when people have trained, or acquired journalistic experience in another country with different traditions. As Sarah Roxström observes:

> *If someone has left Iraq to train in Moscow as a journalist, their ideas of public service broadcasting may not accord with what we regard as good practice.*

In her view, this can be so in lots of little ways. One example is what would be regarded as an acceptable criticism or challenge to the government. Another would be what constitutes impartiality or balance in items and quite simply: 'how much you can allow politicians to use the service as a platform for their option?'

When a new starter joins the service, they are likely to undertake some basic training courses – for example a centrally run course on 'An Introduction to Swedish Radio' or courses on how to speak on radio. However, the requirement to identify, develop and maintain skills can only be resourced within the Department.

The feedback meeting

At the heart of the development process is a feedback meeting where a journalist submits a programme and participates in a review discussion with Sarah Roxström, the two editors and colleagues in that language service. The review meeting will last some two hours and each journalist will participate in two review meetings a year. The output from this meeting will be fed into the annual performance review process.

What is important is that these reviews take place against a clear set of criteria which were developed and agreed in the workshops held in 2005. These include, among others:

■ Were the concepts or issues addressed likely to lead to a good item or programme?

- Were they relevant?
- Was the information given of value to the audience?
- Was the subject treated with appropriate balance or impartiality?
- Was sufficient variety of approach used (for example, did the presenter/ reporters go to different locations for input or was it a studio piece)?
- Was it delivered with presence (did it sound as though the presenter was talking to you?) and a good 'sound picture' painted?

A set of critical questions is associated with each of these concepts. The journalist responsible for the piece is to undertake a self-assessment, be receptive to comments and to identify any deficiencies.

It is evident that this process lies on the boundary between performance review and learning and development. However, Sarah Roxström and her colleagues place the feedback process as critical to any realistic development through learning.

She argues that only if the journalists themselves recognize the areas where they are deficient are they likely to learn: you cannot learn concepts like impartiality through instruction. The next stage is learner motivation: are they willing to seek to improve? Once these two preconditions have been established – recognition and motivation – the journalist can learn through support and feedback from experienced colleagues within the department.

Some issues

Support and challenge through feedback requires a deal of commitment – especially from the more senior and experienced members of the service.

The emphasis on supported self-development must mean that a degree of failure must be accepted – people will try different approaches and may not get it right. Feedback takes time and requires skills and Sarah Roxström is concerned that not all her staff can deploy the necessary coaching techniques:

As a Department we need better coaching skills.

Moreover, Sarah Roxström recognizes that not everybody takes easily to feedback and cultural background and prior experience can be an issue. As she puts it:

It has taken us some time to learn what is considered respectful.

Some of the staff will be more circumspect than others. Some middle-aged men can find it difficult to accept critical feedback from a younger person or from a woman. However, the feedback review approach is seen as the only way forward. As Sarah Roxström puts it:

> *In many ways it was much easier just to send people on a course, but the results would simply not be effective.*

Case study 5.3 Supporting the Disabled Learner in Ontario

Background

L. Tara Hooper and Associates is a small company operating in Branford – a town 50 miles from Toronto in Ontario, Canada. The company aim is to assist people with disabilities to secure long-term employment or self-employment. Lisa Tara Hooper, the founder, is supported by a team of three staff – all of whom are disabled. The founder herself was born with cerebral palsy and in adult life developed a back condition and now requires the use of a wheelchair. It is Lisa Tara Hooper's personal experience of coping with disability that has inspired her to create the company. She trained and worked in the hotel industry but experienced harassment in the workplace when employers and co-workers would not recognize her desire to achieve her potential contribution. Her view is that false perceptions underpin a lot of the problems that arise and that disabled people: 'do not demand or need special treatment – it is simply a matter of allowing them to do their work effectively'.

Some 30 clients a year take advantage of the company's services. All are referred from the National or Federal welfare services; L. Tara Hooper and Associates is a recognized service provider by both tiers of Government in Canada. Clients include people with a wide range of physical and mental disabilities. Success rates are impressive: 86% of clients enter full-time employment or self-employment at the end of their period of support; 83% are still working some six months later.

The approach

The first contact takes the form of an interview with Lisa Tara Hooper to explore the client's issues, ambitions and aspirations and to determine whether the company can assist. If a decision is made to proceed, the client can expect a series of sessions lasting two hours which are held twice a week over a six-month period. As well as these timetabled sessions clients receive assistance with resumé (curriculum vitae) preparation and the services of a job placement specialist and support in the workplace during the early period of transition to employment.

The skills imparted during the timetabled session are ones which would be recognized in any organization which supports people returning to employment: communication skills (written and spoken); issues in presentation in the workplace; and basic IT skills. However, in this case, the approach used needs to differ in two respects: first, because considerable efforts must be made to build learner confidence; secondly, because delivery must be flexible to take account of the learner's disability without creating a 'special case' mind-set which would run counter to the ethics of the organization.

One-to-one intervention

According to Lisa Tara Hooper, one of the main challenges is to help a disabled person discover his or her own potential and then persuade them to see the workplace as an environment 'to uncover their dreams'. Almost all clients have spent a period at work but have failed to maintain continuing employment. They are likely to have experienced unsupportive responses based on false perceptions from colleagues and may have developed negative self-perceptions, undermining their capability and potential.

The training and learning agenda will be based around skills, but much of the process is designed to build self-belief. Lisa Tara Hooper argues that her own experiences in overcoming the problem of disability allows her to understand and empathize – indeed, it would be difficult to offer support without this personal understanding.

The delivery of training support requires the customization of material so that the learner's disability is not a barrier. Given the wide range of disabilities, it is inappropriate to develop formulas or templates. Illustrations of the customized or bespoke approaches that have been adopted are set out below.

Physical conditions could include cerebral palsy, spina bifida, multiple sclerosis, stroke victims and accommodations include:

- change in physical office setting
- wheelchair access facilities
- all training undertaken by oral communication with the trainer becoming the note taker in cases where the learner is not able to write
- frequent breaks, with the training schedule reviewed regularly with the client and altered according to their needs
- modified keyboards.

For blind and visually impaired learners, training materials need to be presented in a format that can easily be scanned (this requires more emphasis on text than graphics). For deaf learners, if the client lip-reads, trainers need to speak normally and directly and furniture must be arranged so that it is easier for the learner to see the trainer. For those individuals who suffer from Tourette syndrome (uncontrollable motor and vocal tics), the key to successful learning is the understanding of the situation: 'tics' are prevalent when the client is ill or nervous with anxiety. What is required is to allow the client to discuss the situation, achieve a comfort level and relax when learning.

Mental health issues could include schizophrenia, obsessive–compulsive disorder, anxiety/panic or depression and accommodations could include:

- a quiet environment
- a slower pace
- lots of repetitions
- giving the client lots of reassurance – they are doing a good job and progressing
- establishing and reviewing individual boundaries at the beginning of learning and throughout
- altering the scheduled programme and the length of the training module.

For learners who have mental health problems, there may be a particular need for mentoring and coaching and other supportive relationships with co-workers. Indeed, one of the major challenges that Lisa Tara Hooper and her colleagues face in achieving their objectives occurs not when the learner is undergoing training but when they return to the workplace. A different set of pressures can arise, support may not be immediately available and something can go wrong.

Given the wide range of disabilities experienced by clients, it can be seen that individualized and bespoke training is essential. Although this approach is resource-intensive, Lisa Tara Hooper argues that it is impossible to proceed in any other way than one-to-one support and coaching. The specific needs of the individual are taken into account; the atmosphere is calmer and the learner can relax; the client is the only focus of attention from the trainer and there is no pressure on the learner to answer in front of others.

One obvious challenge for the company is the need to cope with such a wide range of disabilities. Here, Tara Hooper comments:

Having a disability myself I have learned to adapt. I have needed to look at different ways of doing things, of getting tasks accomplished. The key is to display sensitivity – treat clients with respect and ask them what they need and want. The first step is to get the client to overcome their fear. I can understand how that fear arose.

References

[1]. Kay, J. (2003) The Truth About Markets. London: Allen Lane.

[2]. I am grateful to Toni Borsattino, a Masters Student at Kingston University, for her analysis of the data from this exercise and to members of the Alphasta Consultancy, Beijing, for their translation of the returns submitted in Chinese.

[3]. Reynolds, J., Caley, L. and Mason, R. (2002) How Do People Learn? London: Chartered Institute of Personnel and Development. Available at: http://www.cipd.co.uk/NR/rdonlyres/EE171F3B-A2D1-4A6F-A4A3-2AFBBE164688/0/2438howpeoplrn.pdf9

[4]. Chalofsky, N. (2003) Meaningful Work. T+D, 57(12), 52–58.

[5]. Purcell, J., Kinnie, N., Hutchinson, S. et al. (2003) Understanding the People Performance Link: Unlocking the Black Box. London: Chartered Institute of Personnel and Development.

[6]. Fleming, A. (2006) Learning Styles. London: Chartered Institute of Personnel and Development. Available at: www.cipd.co.uk/onlineinfodocuments

6

Some Key Processes

In the previous chapter, we considered some ways in which the learner could be supported on an individual basis. In this chapter, we shall consider the processes that can be put in place to build a more effective learning culture.

The underlying argument is straightforward. There are certain key building blocks that must be put in place if the motivated learner is to advance and the unmotivated learner is to comply (however grudgingly). Some of these building blocks concern information on what is desirable or, in some cases, what is required. Others concern the provision of immediate support and encouragement. This chapter, like the previous one, will rely heavily on case studies. There will be a brief discussion on the place of competencies and, later, on the role of line managers, but the main emphasis will be on some practical illustrations.

The effectiveness of any process must be based on an understanding of the learner and what will motivate them to acquire the knowledge and skills that help the organization achieve its business objectives. This will depend on the prior experience of the learner, their ambitions and the context in which they can achieve them. One interesting example is provided by Linklaters – the subject of a fuller case study in Chapter 2 (p. 27). Linklaters is considering the framework in which the fee-earners can manage their own development and their conceptual thinking in this area is set out in Table 6.1.

Competencies and competency frameworks

In 1982, the US academic Richard Boyatzis wrote a book entitled 'The Competent Manager: a Model for Effective Performance' [1]. This proved to have a considerable influence on the profession and, over the following two and a half decades, competency frameworks became an increasingly accepted part of modern HR practice.

Table 6.1 Learner motivation at Linklaters

Entry into partnership is a compellingly attractive goal for lawyers. If they cannot achieve progress towards partnership they are likely to leave to pursue opportunities elsewhere; it is essential for continuing relationships that any parting is amicable.

Such a statement emphasizes the self-reliant learner and the clear link to career development as well as the business objectives. The challenge is to create an appropriate climate and an organizational context and the related opportunities. As an indication of a possible approach, Des Woods, the Global Head of Learning and Organizational Development, has suggested that there may be four different sorts of employees, each with different motivations to learn.

	Career-aggressive achievers	*Transitioning achievers*	*Aspiring backpackers*	*Life stylers*
Characterized by	Focused on going as far as I can (achieving partnership)	Early career focus changed by significant life event, e.g. marriage or children	I want to broaden my horizons – take a break – do something different for a while	I want a job that I like and I am good at – and a life I can enjoy as well
Purpose of learning	Learning which grows my reputation and skills	Help and clarify around what I want do	Portable knowledge and skills and/or a deal that may keep me in touch with you	Learning that keeps me up to date, confident and secure in my role

When thoughtfully applied, competencies are a valuable tool. They can act as a signal from the organization to the individual of the expected areas and levels of performance. They can provide the individual with a map or indication of the behaviours that will be recognized and, in some organizations, rewarded.

Competencies can also provide an essential link with other human resource systems. This is demonstrated in two case illustrations drawn from the Jardine Matheson Group, an Asian-based conglomerate. Competencies provide an important underpinning for the group's overall talent management system (see Case study 6.1) and efforts to develop a learning strategy and appraisal system in a subsidiary (see Case study 6.2). Some headings of the Group Competency Model are reproduced as Figure 6.1, with appreciation, as are the full set and development plan from the subsidiary as Figure 6.1 and Table 6.3.

Case study 6.1 Developing talent at Jardines

Background: the competencies

The Jardine Matheson Group is an Asian-based conglomerate with companies involved in engineering and construction, transport services, motor trading, property, retailing, restaurants, hotels, transport services, financial services and insurance broking. Many of the companies in the group have their headquarters in Hong Kong. Just over 230 000 people are employed across the group.

There is a strong commitment to organizational and individual development. Even in adverse business circumstances, there has been no concerted effort to cut training. Jill Dodwell-Groves, the Hong Kong-based Head of Executive Development, has responsibility for creating and managing learning opportunities for the most Senior Executives (some 400 in total). A key driver in the process is the staff planning system. Once a year every company in the group must submit a succession plan based on their organization chart. This plan is colour-coded and identifies potential successors for each position and the potential of the individual in the existing job. The classifications include: capable of advancing a number of levels; capable of advancing to the next level; need to develop within the level – through to 'at risk'. Those Executives who are capable of moving readily across different businesses are also identified. This central reporting only embraces the most senior levels. In addition, however, central staff planning applies to the finance and HR functions and to a number of high fliers across the group.

A key element of the group-wide development process is an agreed set of competencies. Some of these competency headings are set out at Table 6.2. These permit a common development approach and vocabulary to be put in place at senior levels across the group, via the appraisal and development centre processes. According to Jill Dodwell-Groves, the competency list inevitably reflects an international/ British originated organizational culture, but there has been no difficulty in gaining acceptance for them across a wide range of nationalities and different business situations. Many companies within the group have their own industry specific competencies.

These competencies underpin the Group Development Centres which are held for Executives across the region and held at Hong Kong, Malaysia, Indonesia and mainland China. Centres are organized as intensive workshops in which participants undertake a series of simulated management tasks and receive feedback from observers. These are followed by two-day

Table 6.2 Extracts from Group Managerial competencies

Business focus
- Maintains a broad overview of his/her area of business: sees beyond the detail
- Identifies and develops strategies for the core business
- Demonstrates an enthusiastic interest in the business (its competitors, customers, brand and market)
- Thinks in terms of cost, profit and added value
- Uses financial data to assess the balance of cost, risk and opportunity
- Seeks new business that accords with business goals and the vision
- Demonstrates awareness of the need to develop the corporate brand and give it value
- Takes pride in the business and the quality of products or services. Will not compromise on quality. Encourages a culture of continual improvement

Customer orientation
- Accepts that customers are in the best position to know their own needs; takes steps to stay aware of these
- Uses customer data scientifically and proactively; probes in greater depth when required
- Formalizes systems for receiving customer feedback and the process for reviewing and taking action
- Takes customer complaints seriously; shows empathy. Takes both corrective and preventive measures to deal with complaints
- Looks for ways to improve standards of service and quality for customers. Seeks innovative ways to add value and exceed expectations
- Convinces others of the overriding value of the customer as a business driver and partner. Rewards customer-focused behaviour
- Engages with customers directly and personally; values these contacts and develops relationships
- Sees customer satisfaction as a key performance indicator for the business. Regularly monitors this

Analysis and judgement
- Gathers and analyses pertinent facts, data and information, including the advice of others, to establish the cause of a problem
- Produces new ideas and insights, readily making connections between previously unrelated events or systems
- Thinks laterally and innovatively when generating options to solve problems
- Creates practical solutions
- Considers the implications, risks and outcomes of proposed solutions on all aspects of the business
- Makes sound decisions where conflicting data or uncertainty exists. Can rationalize seemingly ambiguous data
- Uses available data and intuition to take calculated risks in situations of uncertainty
- Can make quick and sound decisions on incomplete data, balancing the need for further analysis with the need for a timely decision when under commercial pressure

June 2005 Copyright © 2005 Jardine Matheson Limited – All rights reserved.

training workshops designed to improve skills and enhance individual development needs in the areas identified.

Shared learning

At the most senior level, there is an emphasis on bringing managers away from their jobs into shared learning experiences. However, there has been a move away from the more traditional taught course. Many of the most senior managers have received extensive business school education and there is little point in repeating these activities. Indeed, there is a danger of engendering a negative reaction. Instead, Groups of Directors have been taken on corporate visits – known as the Directors Development Initiative – to gain an appreciation of the business challenges outside the Jardine Group and the Asian region. There is also a Business Enhancement Initiative, for those with potential to become Directors, which addresses a recognized need in the group to develop their wider business awareness. The participants will, as part of a group of 10–12, spend 12 days over a four-month period visiting other companies within the group and see how they operate in different countries across the region. They also meet connected companies and competitors to understand the whole market and supply chain.

Increasingly, Jardines has sought to build up their own capability in management and skills training and transfer programme design from external consultants. In this way, it is possible to build a stronger link with business objectives. As Jill Dodwell-Groves puts it:

> *We are fortunate in the level of support we get from the top. For example, our Chief Executive recognizes that leadership development is not something that can easily be measured in financial terms and therefore he sees the 'proof' of the value of learning in terms of improved performance and the increased self-confidence and motivation of the executives, rather than in specific dollar terms. However, we will only maintain this position if we focus on the business requirements and not on learning for its own sake.*

Case study 6.2 Implementing a competency framework at the Jardine Engineering Corporation

Background

Jardine Engineering Corporation (JEC) is a wholly-owned subsidiary of the Jardine Group. Originally established in Shanghai in 1923 to support the

Group's engineering operations in China, it now employs 3370 staff; a third of these staff are working in Hong Kong, where JEC has its Headquarters and the remainder work from other offices in Asia.

JEC provides high value engineering and project services. These include bespoke solutions for clients and the distribution of building products and materials. Over half the JEC staff have a technical background, many of whom are qualified engineers. Overall, the staff are divided into two broad groups: project engineers who coordinate the work undertaken for clients and manage sub-contractors; and a sales force who secure the contracts and liaise with current and prospective clients. In addition, there are the staff involved in the normal management, administrative and support functions.

The JEC workforce is mostly between 35 and 40 years of age. Many have been working for JEC since they left school. Some have become set in their ways and need to develop new skills to meet the challenges of an increasingly competitive market. One particular problem that has been identified is that project engineers and sales staff can operate in independent silos and miss opportunities for cross-selling. One senior JEC manager reported a customer as saying: 'on occasions we have had three JEC salesmen arriving in the same day and we have had to introduce them to each other'.

A new Chief Executive Officer was appointed to JEC at the end of 2004. He identified people development as one of the top priorities for the company. Accordingly, he has given his fullest support to Alice Wong, JEC's Director of Human Capital, in her efforts to devise and implement processes to support the acquisition of appropriate skills and behaviours.

The competency model and the development plan

Alice Wong's initial approach has been to design and implement two basic cornerstones of development: a competency framework and a development plan. Competency models are now in place for the engineering function, for the sales function and for technical services. The model for technical services is reproduced in Figure 6.1. As can be seen, the model embraces the requirements at craft apprentice level, technical and functional skills and management and soft skills. Five basic approaches to skills acquisition are identified: classroom training; on-the-job training; external programmes sponsored by the company; knowledge gained through experience sharing; and knowledge gained through experiential learning. The competency models were devised through detailed interviews with relevant senior

Competency Model - M&R Technical Services

Category		CA1	CA2		CA3		CA4	
Training Subjects		Introduction of Air-conditioning System	Updates of Air-conditioning System	Motor & Pump	Trouble Shooting	Reciprocating & Screw Compressor Overhaul & Service	System Control	Centrifugal Overhaul & Services
Training Approach		TA1	TA1	TA1	TA1	TA1	TA1	TA1
Job Position								
Apprentice		R	R	R	R	R	R	R
SM	A/C	--		--	--	--	--	--
M1	FS	--		--	--	--	--	--
M2	EL	--		--	--	--	--	--
Sr Supvr	A/C	--		--	--	--	--	--
Supervisor	FS	--		--	--	--	--	--
Sr Foreman	EL	--		--	--	--	--	--

Category		Technical/Functional													
Training Subjects		Air-conditioning related Knowledge	Electricity-related Knowledge	Pumping-related Knowledge	Fire Service-related Knowledge	Job-related Advance Courses	Job Rotation	Occupational Safety & Related Legislation	Briefing on Labor Law & Industrial Accident Cases	Quotation & Material Sourcing	Site Supervision & Quality Control	Understanding of Technical Drawing	Trouble Shooting	Computer Skills	Business/ Report Writing
Training Approach		TA2	TA2	TA2	TA2	TA1 TA3	TA2	TA1	TA4	TA2	TA1 TA2	TA4	TA1 TA4	TA1	TA1
Job Position															
Apprentice		R	R	R	R	E	R	R	--	--	--	--	--	--	--
SM	A/C	R	R	R	R	E	R	R	--	--	--	S2	S1	--	S3
M1	FS	--	--	--	R	E	R	R	--	--	--	--	S1	--	S3
M2	EL	--	R	--	R	E	R	R	--	--	--	--	S1	--	S3
Sr Supvr	A/C	R	R	R	R	E	--	R	R	S1	S2	S1	S1	S2	S3
Supervisor	FS	--	--	--	R	E	--	R	R	S1	S2	S1	S1	S2	S3
Sr Foreman	EL	--	R	--	R	E	--	R	R	S1	S2	S1	S1	S3	S3

Category		Management/Soft Skills								Lic
Training Subjects		Supervisory Skills	Motivation & Staff Management	Negotiation Skills	Customer Services	Handling Complaint	Teambuilding	Communication & Interpersonal Skills	Time Management	Job-related Licenses
Training Approach		TA1	TA1	TA1	TA1	TA4	TA5	TA1	TA1	TA3
Job Position										
Apprentice		--	--	--	S1	--	S2	S3	--	R
SM	A/C	S3	S2	--	S1	S3	S2	S1	--	R
M1	FS	S3	S2	--	S1	S3	S2	S1	--	R
M2	EL	S3	S2	--	S1	S3	S2	S1	--	R
Sr Supvr	A/C	S1	S2	S2	S1	S2	S3	S1	S3	R
Supervisor	FS	S1	S2	S2	S1	S2	S3	S1	S3	R
Sr Foreman	EL	S1	S2	S2	S1	S2	S3	S1	S3	R

TA1 = Classroom Training
TA2 = On-the-job Training
TA3 = Company-sponsored Program
TA4 = Experience Sharing
TA5 = Experiential Learning

R = Required
E = Elective
S1 = Stage 1
S2 = Stage 2
S3 = Stage 3

A/C = Air Conditioning
FS = Fire Services
EL = Electrical

CA = Craft Apprentice
SM = Senior Mechanics
M1 = Mechanics 1
M2 = Mechanics 2

Figure 6.1 Competency model – M&R Technical Services

Table 6.3 Staff Individual Development Plan

(A) STAFF INFORMATION

Name & No:	Job Title:
Department:	Immediate Manager:

(B) DEVELOPMENT ACTIVITIES/PLAN

What new or additional experiences, responsibilities and development activities would help you achieve your immediate and long-term career goals? What are your plans to accomplish this? Include skills and competency development.

Your plan might include participating in a cross-functional team, taking on a special project, job assignment, rotation, identifying and working with a mentor, taking educational courses or training, etc.

Skills/Competences to Develop	Development Activities	Target Date
1		
2		
3		
4		

(C) DEVELOPMENT RESULTS

Expected Results/Measurables:	Result Date
1	
2	
3	
4	

(D) REVIEW AND ENDORSEMENT

Prepared By (Staff's Signature): ———————————	Date: ———————
Review By (Manager's Signature): ———————————	Date: ———————
Comments: —————————————————————	
—————————————————————	

managers in the business. They will be used for devising the company's learning strategy, for the appraisal system and, at a later stage, to underpin recruitment.

The second document in place is the staff development plan – this is set out in Table 6.3. This plan is completed annually, after an interview between the employee and his or her boss. Alice Wong will be collating the returns and they will be fed into the design of the training plan.

Implementing the system

Once they had been agreed, the competency models were placed on JEC's corporate intranet and promoted through Departmental meetings. In Alice Wong's view, all staff in Hong Kong now have a good awareness of the initiative and its consequences, but there is still a selling job to be done elsewhere in the region. It is essential that there is a high degree of awareness since, in Alice Wong's words:

The company can provide the environment and tools, but it is the responsibility of the individuals themselves, together with their supervisors, to manage their development.

As Alice Wong would readily agree, the design of systems is easier than getting them to work. There was some initial resistance from some managers to what was seen as a paper-intensive and potentially bureaucratic process. As a result, she has offered to make any necessary revisions after a trial period. However, she remains optimistic, not least because results from the company's annual engagement survey indicate a clear and growing demand for development opportunities.

Literature on competencies abounds and point to some challenges as well as advantages. They are a compelling, perhaps too compelling, way of indicating what is required. They can be used, for example, to underpin national qualification structures and some governments (and this has certainly been true in the UK) have displayed an obsessive and certainly counter-productive desire to map the entire workforce in this way.

Within the organization, competencies can be very beneficial in signalling required standards – particularly if technology is used to facilitate transmission and access. At Ford, the case illustration set out Case study 6.3, a career development framework is applied across a large professional workshop in a number of different countries.

Case study 6.3 A career development framework for IT professionals: Ford Motor Company

Background

Ford is one of the best-known global companies and over 300 000 people are employed across the world in automotive, financial and adjacent activities. Effective IT is a critical component of business effectiveness. Currently, approximately 11 000 staff are involved in IT services: 4500 are Ford employees and the remainder work on contract or through agencies.

In 2001–02, a major reorganization took place within IT designed to achieve greater efficiency through standardized processes, competent professionalism and effective governance within the function.

One consequence was a move away from agency staff towards greater development of internal resources. A second consequence was restructuring around four key departments: Information Technology Infrastructure; Application Development Services; Process & Technology Group; Information Technology Strategy & Organizational Development. This last group (ITS& OD) has been responsible, together with the human resource function, for developing and implementing a major competency-based framework. This is designed to give Ford IT staff throughout the world clearer development opportunities consistent with the requirements of a competent professional in a leading organization.

The framework

The approach adopted by Ford has been to develop a Career Development Framework (CDF). The vision statement for this initiative is reproduced below.

We will provide the right IT resources at the right time and place to support current and future business needs, as we grow:

- *An IT culture in which learning is a core value, integrated into every project and operation.*
- *IT people who think of themselves and are regarded by their customers as proud competent professionals.*
- *IT professionals who take ownership of their career development.*
- *IT leaders who take responsibility for the continuing development of employees as a core element to their role.*
- *The best infrastructure among all large companies for encouraging, supporting, tracking and rewarding IT professional development.*

Underpinning the CDF are 22 competencies defined for IT staff. Seventeen distinct job families have been identified within the function across the four key departments. For each job family a subset of the 22 competencies have been identified as 'core' (the most relevant and, in some cases, critical), others are identified as qualifying (here the individual should have demonstrated that competency in the past, though they may not need it to perform their current role, particularly at senior levels). These competencies and the related tools and paperwork are available on the web and the CDF process proceeds as follows. Individuals should become aware of the relevant competencies for their role; they should conduct a self-assessment against those competencies; they should conduct a gap analysis designed to highlight deficiencies which should then, in agreement with their manager, be addressed through participation in relevant developmental activities. A set of learning opportunities are set out on the web. These include courses, websites, references, e-learning and suggested individual action (for example, presentations at professional groups).

Implementation of the CDF processes should produce clear benefits for both company and individual. According to Ford's Global IT Competency and Learning Manager, the framework was introduced for the following reasons:

> *We needed a framework in which we could direct people's learning in the company's interest. Within IT there are four areas of specific skills and knowledge – the company needed a model that ensured consistency of standards. Most importantly, we needed people to have pride in their role, to be motivated and energized for development. Further, we wished Ford IT to be at the forefront of the profession.*

Considerable resources have gone into building a robust framework; efforts have been made to secure appropriate buy-in at all levels. The Competency and Learning Manager emphasizes that CDF is not a process defined by a tool; it is its effective use by IT professionals within the global business that will produce the benefits. Here the company is refreshingly candid about previous difficulties and the issues that were encountered.

Practical issues on implementation

Ford was able to benefit from the lessons of earlier efforts with competency frameworks. A previous system, based on self-assessment against competencies introduced in the late 1990s, exposed many of the practical problems.

For example, there was a large volume of paperwork downloaded for self-reporting and the extent of the skills gaps revealed could be demoralizing for the individual. Moreover, inevitably, given the company's structure, the initiative was driven from the USA. According to the UK IT Learning and Development Strategy Manager, there were occasions when the recommended 'solution' to a deficiency was only available in the USA.

Effective implementation of CDF is therefore seen as a long-term task. Importantly, it must be delivered and supported in the IT functions across the globe. Culture and practices differ: 'coaching' is interpreted differently in the USA from in South-East Asia and Europe. Moreover, the resources available for local support and development vary considerably.

Competency centres

One approach, which has been developed in the USA, UK and Germany to support the initiative, has been to establish a centre with staff whose role is to assist implementation. In the UK, some seven staff are employed as coaches. Their role is to conduct one-to-one discussions with all IT staff up to the level of first line management and to provide guidance and support on career development. This means that the individual takes responsibility for self-assessment and gap analysis but is helped and advised by an experienced coach. The development plan must then be agreed with the line manager, who has a responsibility to ensure the individual is able to implement their plan.

The USA operates a similar arrangement but, given the greater scale, the staff at the Competency Centre are able to specialize and focus on the needs within particular job families.

The future

Ford's emphasis on individual learner responsibility supported by a published competency framework is by no means unique. However, their commitment is considerable and they have reflected and learned from previous experience. They are conscious of the challenges posed by a global initiative. Both individual and company benefit from successful implementation. Given the time scale, it is important to demonstrate the business benefits to ensure continuing long-term commitment to skills development against the framework.

At the Hilton Group, which manages a number of hotels across the world, there is a process to take a new joiner from induction to full effectiveness. This is described in Case study 6.4. It also introduces an important concept – that of time to competence.

Case study 6.4 Time to competence: the TBS at Hilton Hotels

Background

Hilton International is well known for its operation and management of hotels throughout the world. With headquarters in North London, it has over 400 hotels in more than 80 countries, employing more than 70 000 team members who are serving more than 10 million guests a year. Hilton International is organized into five geographic areas and operates all the Hilton hotels outside of the USA.

New entrants to their hotels in UK and Ireland can come from a variety of different backgrounds (and nationalities) and with very different prior experience and skills. In the UK and Ireland, following initial induction training, familiarization and assessment are dealt with through a structured process known as Technical and Behavioural Skills (TBS). Similar processes are in place at other hotels in different countries throughout the group.

The TBS

TBS was introduced to the company in the late 1990s and is aimed at getting new team members up to the level required to work competently in their particular department/role. The system was designed to link closely to the Government-promoted vocational qualification standards (this enables learners to progress their initial skills development into a recognized qualification). TBS was introduced to raise the level of skills and knowledge in team members and to provide new team members with a structured programme of training on joining the company. The comprehensive records enable learners and trainers (and managers) to see at a glance how each team member is performing and where the gaps are and ensures there is evidence available to support progress to a vocational qualification. The TBS training also supports new processes, procedures or initiatives which are rolled out in the company.

TBS training starts on day two of employment when the team member meets with the departmental TBS trainer. At this initial stage the aim is to identify what the team member currently knows and can do and thus where the training needs lie. Subsequent on-the-job skills training and knowledge building is supported by training records. An extract from an example from the Reception area is shown in Table 6.4. The training records reflect the key brand and service standards as well as legal standards for each role. The TBS typically takes 12 weeks to complete; at this stage the new team member should have completed their probation period. Subsequently, the team member

Table 6.4 Hilton Technical and Behavioural Skills training and assessment record

	TECHNICAL & BEHAVIOURAL SKILLS TRAINING & ASSESSMENT RECORD
[tab]**Hilton**	

RECEPTION

Technical & Behavioural Skills	I have been trained		My progress has been reviewed		I feel competent	Competence achieved
	Trainee	Trainer	Trainee	Trainer	Trainee	Assessor
Specific Product Knowledge						
I know our competitors' current availability.						
I know the hotels selling strategy.						
I positively describe the range and key features of all the hotels bedrooms.						
I know the name of the top ten companies that use the hotel and the bookers' names.						
I know the scope within which I can negotiate rates.						
I know the location and distance of the nearest Hilton.						
I know and can find out the names and location of all Hilton hotels in the UK and Ireland.						
I positively describe the benefits of Hilton HHonors/Meeting Planner Bonus.						
I know the current Loyalty/Frequent Flyer programmes.						
I understand the market segment definitions.						
I know how to read the hotel's availability board or use F5 key and I use this information when making decisions on reservations.						
I use guest history whenever possible to ensure best possible customer service.						
I know the benefits of HHonors and Shareholder Privilege Cards.						

has a discussion with his or her line manager to determine their level of performance/competence. The team member receives a certificate in recognition of their completion of the TBS training.

Within each hotel a group of designated TBS trainers deliver on-the-job skills training; they receive training themselves in the form of a one/two-day programme. They then embark on a path of development called 'Going for Gold', which enables them to earn recognition and status depending on their achievement of set criteria. TBS trainers are monitored and audited monthly which determines their progression through the level (bronze, silver and gold) and to their monthly departmental score. There is a TBS trainer of the year and TBS department of the year award in each hotel and for Hilton UK & Ireland as a whole.

All of the TBS information was initially made available at the hotels in a hard copy format. It is now available through the corporate intranet portal (HiWay). The support comprises: TBS records, handbook for trainers, guidelines on Going for Gold and trainer of the month criteria. The regional Learning and Development team support the HR managers in ensuring that training is implemented and they also train the HR manager to enable them to train the TBS trainers.

Some issues

The Hilton HR team believes that the TBS approach is very effective, but they also recognize that there is a continuing need for improvement. At present, the system is paper intensive and lots of signing off is required. The focus can appear to be more on the completion of the forms rather than the quality of the training. TBS can also be a long process for more experienced team members and some less experienced TBS trainers would welcome more training support materials to help them in delivery. In February 2006, it was announced that Hilton Group plc had sold its Hotel Division, Hilton International, to the Hilton Hotels Corporation, headquartered in the USA. Garcia Williamson, the Director of Talent Development, offered the following comment:

> *TBS has been an essential tool for providing consistently high quality training for team members. However, we are about to revisit all of the TBS records and supporting training materials to ensure that they map to the new People First standards and our new international brand standards. With the recent merger announcement we are in for an exciting time as we realign our brand and operational training.*

The role of front-line/first-line managers

Given the discussion in this chapter to date, it came as no surprise that one of the least contentious propositions proved to be the one set out below.

Proposition 6 The delivery of effective people development practices requires a considerable increase in commitment and enhanced skills from all managers, particularly first-line managers.

In a 2004, CIPD publication, which built on the People and Performance research outlined in Chapter 3, front-line managers (the term preferred by the researchers) or FLMs were defined as managers who had first-line responsibility for a work group of approximately 10 to 25 people [2]. They were accountable to a higher level of management and are placed in the lower layers of the management hierarchy, normally at the first level.

The research discovered that front-line leaders were often crucial in making the difference between low-performing and high-performing firms. Occupying a key position in the organization, they were the deliverers of success by implementing strategies that focus the efforts of individuals on business goals and translating them into positive outcomes.

Team leadership was an important aspect of motivating and managing people in all the organizations studied and required the use of what are sometimes called 'soft' skills – for example, communication, involving, listening, asking and problem-solving. FLMs often had to implement policies such as appraisal or team briefing and had a major role to play in bringing these policies to life.

Leadership is important in influencing employees' attitudes towards the organization and their job and FLM behaviour is the most important factor in explaining the variation in both job satisfaction and job discretion – the choice people have over how they do their jobs. It is also one of the more critical factors in developing organizational commitment.

The policies that are most supportive of line managers were identified as:

- ensuring good working relationships with their managers
- providing career opportunities
- working to support their work–life balance
- allowing them to participate and feel involved in decisions
- having an open organizational culture that allows them to raise grievances or discuss matters of personal concern
- giving them a sense of job security.

Communicating what is required is essential and many organizations are considering how this can best be done in the context that they operate. Within the TNT Express delivery service there is a large dispersed workforce. Its operations in China are the subject of a full case study in Chapter 14. The UK and Ireland business unit employs over 10 700 staff. The majority of these employees work at one of over 60 major depots as drivers or operational loaders, servicing both domestic and international markets. The company firmly believes that individual learning, rather than directive training, is critical to business success. This view is articulated and promoted through the implementation of TNT's 'Commitment to People Development'. This one-page document is displayed prominently throughout all

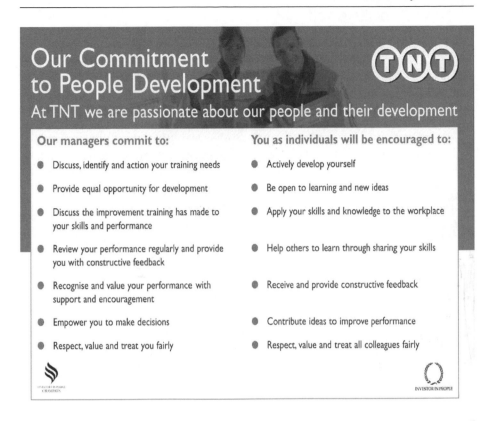

Figure 6.2 TNT's Commitment to People Development

offices and depots and is highlighted as part of the induction process. The 'Commitment' outlines what is expected from managers and staff and is reproduced in Figure 6.2.

Basing interventions on the assumption that front-line managers will play a critical role will only be effective if these managers have the necessary skills; in many organizations this has become associated with building a coaching capability at operational level. A final case study illustration for this chapter is set out in Case study 6.5. It is drawn from Piccadilly Supermarkets, Bulgaria, an organization facing the challenge of rapid expansion using a less-experienced and sophisticated workforce. The immediate solution adopted was to build an in-store coaching capacity. Coaching will be discussed more fully in Chapter 8, but here we need to recognize that it is increasingly seen as a key element of a manager's role at all levels.

Case study 6.5 Developing a coaching network at Piccadilly Supermarkets: Bulgaria

The business challenge

In 1994, Boliari Limited, the holding company for Piccadilly Supermarkets was incorporated. The first supermarket was established the following year in Varna, a resort town on the Black Sea coast. Subsequent growth has been rapid. By mid-2006 Piccadilly operated six supermarkets in Varna and two in the Bulgarian capital Sofia, together with six separate smaller format 'Mambo' convenience stores. Plans are in hand for expansion across Bulgaria with another two stores due to open shortly in different towns in the country.

Currently, some 1500 staff are employed by Piccadilly, all but 100 work in the supermarkets. A very flat management structure is in place, with three levels: store managers, supervisors and operatives (cashiers, warehouse workers/common workers/storage workers and sales assistants). The largest supermarket employs some 180 people and most employ on average 120.

The company has ambitious growth plans and intends to be the leading supermarket in Bulgaria. Its size and growth makes it a significant force in the local economy. Its emphasis is on quality and Piccadilly seeks to offer a wide range of goods in an attractive shopping environment (to provide shopping experience). The company motto is 'load high spirits' and the aim is to sustain the high level of service achieved throughout the chain.

The average age of the staff is under 30 and the company targets the recruitment of young people and students – over 50% of the current workforce are engaged in some form of university or college studies. Bulgarian higher education allows students to study for a limited number of hours in the day and to live at home. Inevitably, this approach to recruitment produces some challenges – for some of the staff it is their first real job and some of them face difficulties adapting to a pattern of regular work. For some, they have the option of seeking parental support for their studies, so attrition rates can be high, especially in the early stages. Moreover, the company has a policy of growing its management from within, so the management staff have not always gained the breadth of experience that comes with a mature workforce. Set against this, the staff are intelligent and many are willing to commit if the organization treats them fairly and offers them promotion opportunities.

Creating human resource policies

Marionela Bojkova was appointed Head of Human Resources in August 2005. Her biggest challenge to date has been coping with the operational demands of recruitment and initial training, while putting routine procedures in place for the long term. Initially, for example, selection proceeded in a haphazard fashion and candidates were sourced by word of mouth or personal contact. Similarly, promotion was based on immediate availability or personal observations rather than considered choice and internal competition. She has now introduced a system of written requests to fill vacancies and systematic selection of candidates through a series of interviews and tests giving the process transparency and guaranteeing a better choice of candidates.

Importantly, she has introduced a process for the regular assessment of operative staff by their line managers. Supervisors, who would typically manage up to 15 staff, are required to submit an assessment using a spreadsheet on a weekly basis. Cashiers, for example, are assessed using four criteria: speed and dexterity; quality of service; reliability and discipline; and appearance and hygiene. The ratings are now used to monitor staff performance and are used as a basis of bonus formation and incentive programme involvement.

At first the introduction of such systems was resented by some supervisors and managers as an imposition from human resources. However, there is now a general acceptance that effective personnel procedures are necessary if the company is to continue to recruit and retain the staff it needs to fuel its growth.

In-store coaching

One key element of Marionela Bojkova's policies has been the development of a cohort of in-store coaches – experienced, excellent work performers, ready to pass their knowledge to the large number of newly selected company employees.

Coaches were nominated by the store manager in agreement with the managers responsible for purchasing goods. They were then trained by the central human resource team in two critical aspects of induction. First, they received training in how to pass to the new people the hard skills and product knowledge: the company standards and the basic procedures – for example, how to cut cheese or operate a till. Secondly, they were trained in the softer skills of selling and the psychology of customer relationships. This training took the form of one-day courses spread over intervals.

The trained coaches were then responsible for managing the induction and on-the-job training of new joiners at store level. Using material designed by the Human Resource department and by the Company Standards department, procedures for on-the-job training were put in place. For one week the new joiners worked alongside the coach, at this stage merely shadowing the job. In the next week, the new joiner worked by himself or herself but was observed by the coach. At the end of this second week, there would be an evaluation or assessment meeting with a representative of the Human Resources department present, together with the coach and the trainee. At this meeting any problems were discussed and the coach would offer recommendations for improvement. The trainee then worked closely with the coach for a further week and this would be followed by a final week of almost independent work and assessment. This whole process, known as the coaching project, was seen as the only effective way of ensuring that the large number of new staff could meet organizational requirements. In Marionela Bojkova's view:

> *This coaching project was necessary because our goal was not only to train quickly and efficiently this large number of new people, but also make them part of Piccadilly culture. We wanted to transfer the specific atmosphere Piccadilly has in our new supermarkets. This project worked because it gave a chance to many employees at all levels to be personally involved in the company growth and success. The joined utmost efforts of our best people, both management and staff made it work.*

Moving forward

In a supermarket employing 150 people there can be as many as 25 trained coaches. Following internal discussions, in recognition of their importance to the company, it was decided that the coaches should receive extra bonus to their salary on a regular basis.

However, as the company moves into its next stage of growth, Marionela Bojkova would like to see the network of coaches play an even more important role. The company has just opened its own training centre in Varna where her human resource team, together with the best coaches, will undertake more of the initial training before the joiner starts at the store. Every new trainee will be issued a certificate of capability (for example as a cashier on successful completion of training). This would enhance the individual's employment prospects in the longer term and signal the company's support of individual development.

The HR department is also planning the coaches network to support and deliver other development initiatives at store level, aiming at motivation and involvement of employees and improved work performance. In the longer term, Marionela Bojkova would like to see a more professional approach to management – she would like to introduce management by objectives and see a greater flexibility and wider deployment of management styles (away from command and control). In the short term, 'there is so much to be done'. She places value on the coaching network as an instrument of effective development because, in her words:

> *When you inspire the best people of a company to work for the best of the company the success is inevitable.*

The message from this chapter is straightforward. Expecting learners to take more responsibility for their own learning is only possible if certain preconditions are met. One of these is that what is required is clearly communicated; a second is that adequate support is in place. How this is achieved must depend on both the nature of the organization and the circumstances of the learner.

References

[1]. Boyatzis, R.E. (1982) The Competent Manager: A Model for Effective Performance. London: Wiley.
[2]. Hutchinson, S. and Purcell, J. (2004) Bringing Policies to Life: The Vital Role of Front Line Managers in People Management. London: Chartered Institute of Personnel and Development.

7

The Training Course in Context

It has been argued throughout that the progress of people development will be determined by capable practitioners. It will be those professionals who grasp the initiative in their organizations, achieve their objectives and share the results, who will shape the future. People development is a practical activity and theory can only offer us so much.

This book is a product of a series of exchanges with what the Chartered Institute for Personnel and Development (CIPD) would define as 'thinking performers' [1] in the world of learning, training and development. As has previously been emphasized, such people are not representative of the profession as a whole. They are the more interested and aware. Later in this chapter, Iain Thomson, will use the term 'thoughtful practitioner' to describe this same population.

Given that it is these more thoughtful members of the profession who have been the ones contributing to this research, it is significant that the proposition that received the least support was the seventh.

> **Proposition 7**   While off-the-job classroom-based training still has a place, it no longer occupies the central role in training provision as other terms of intervention are becoming more important.

It is important to consider why this is the case. Is it a desire to operate in the comfort zone and a fear of the future? This is neatly captured in the following, anonymous comment on an evaluation form following a session delivered at the 2005 ASTD Conference:

If classroom training went away I wouldn't have a job.

Or is it, to repeat the earlier introductory discussion on the propositions in Chapter 1 (p. 6), that many respondents see a move to a more varied approach to delivery and a shift to a more interventionist 'organizational development' type role as being desirable if they are to do their jobs effectively. However, such a transition takes time. In their organizations, they may be progressing slowly and may, indeed, be meeting some resistance.

The place and value of the training course will be explored in this chapter. What however, is not in dispute is that other forms of learning and training interventions are growing at the expense of the course. To quote from an article summarizing the results of the 2006 CIPD Learning and Development Survey:

> *The slide of the formal training course from its once pre-eminent role in workplace learning continues. Fifty-six per cent of learning and development professionals tell us that on-the-job training is the most effective way for people to learn, with only 17% saying this is true of training courses. Progress towards an individual-centred style of learning does appear to be taking place. The vast majority of respondents report that they are currently using a much wider variety of activities, that their jobs involve a greater element of consultancy and that learners are being encouraged to take more responsibility for their own learning. However, other signs are less positive. Only a third report that managers are trained in the appropriate skills to support the development of their teams, and only a fifth report that efforts are made to find out what motivates employees to learn. The good news, however, is that two-thirds believe that learning and training is now taken more seriously by senior and line managers, and almost 60% believe that the department has far more credibility than before [2].*

The discussion will begin by considering the positive benefits of the training course in terms of learning. At the conference and workshop sessions held in the course of research for this book, participants were presented with the definitions of training and learning. They were then asked: 'what are the positive features of an off-job training course as a vehicle for learning?'. The answers offered invariably cluster round the five categories set out in Table 7.1.

Table 7.1 Attractions of the off-the-job training course as a vehicle for learning

- A course offers protected time for learning.
- A course offers the chance for participants to share ideas with each other and learn from shared experience.
- A course may offer participants the opportunity to practise skills in a risk-free environment.
- A course instructor can give feedback immediately and in a non-threatening way.
- A training course can signal what matters to the organization. Compulsory courses are a strong signal that this knowledge is still important.

All of the statements set out in Table 7.1 have substance.

The argument that a course offers protected time for learning has gained new currency with the emergence of e-learning. Learners who are at their desk undertaking e-learning at their PC are visible to all – they run the risk of frequent short inter-ruptions from colleagues. Sending someone to an off-the-job training event is, at least, a signal to others that they are there to learn and should be left in peace for that purpose.

The second statement in the table reflects the socio-constructionist model of learning considered in Chapter 5. The sharing of ideas is often best undertaken away from the workplace and, as all experienced developers know, participants often say that the main benefits arise in the bar or over dinner.

The opportunity to practise skills in a risk-free environment arises mainly in soft skills or interpersonal training. Certainly, the greatest intensity and commit-ment on the part of participants can occur when they are involved in role playing, giving performance feedback to an under-performing subordinate. A skilled instruc-tor, to move to the fourth statement in the Table, can in effect give one-to-one coaching in an environment where the learner is at his or her most receptive.

The fifth and last statement is different from the rest. Here, we are not talking about the benefits to the individual learner, but about some perceived advantages to the organization. The argument that compulsory courses are a signal that some-thing matters is legitimate. A compulsory course can also mean that the organiza-tion knows that something required has happened, for example health and safety or regulatory requirements can be 'satisfied' if an employee has attended an event. However, the evident danger is that a course can be the easy option. Line managers can send people on courses as a visible indication that they are doing something – and often something that requires little commitment on their part.

All this is well-known and well-trodden ground. It leads to a well-known con-clusion. The off-the-job training course has its place. What we must determine is what its place in our strategy is and how it can be made more effective.

Moreover, an off-the-job training course is not one and the same as trainer-led-instruction. As Jake Reynolds, of Cambridge Programme for Industry, writing in 'Helping People to Learn' puts it:

> It is important to appreciate that a course is simply a period of dedicated learning time that may be used in whatever way necessary to promote the development of its participants. There is nothing in the name to suggest that it must be instructor-led, be wholly content based, or indeed, follow any other design philosophy. Many courses place greater emphasis on process than content, and some even place the design of the process in the hands of the participants [3, p. 45].

Such sentiments explain the continuing popularity of outdoor training. Providing there is a well facilitated debriefing session afterwards, participants can learn a lot about team-working from climbing Creag Dhubh in Scotland or white water raft-ing on the Tully River in Australia.

So, the off-the-job course will remain a feature of training provision so long as there are learners. In some cases, it is the essential delivery mechanism – or indeed the only option. Case study 7.1 offers an interesting, if contentious, illustration. The NATO mission in Iraq faced probably the most demanding challenge considered in this book. It operated in a situation where the infrastructure, however defined, had collapsed. There was a need not only to 'teach the learners the basics' (the training needs), but to rebuild their confidence and change their perception of what is required to learn the job.

Case study 7.1 Building a training infrastructure for the Iraqi armed forces

Background

One of the most significant events in global politics in recent years has been the Iraq war and its aftermath. In March 2003, armed forces from a group of coalition partners defeated Saddam Hussein and replaced the regime in that country. This case study describes the subsequent initiatives put in place by a NATO Training Mission to aid the rehabilitation and recovery of Iraq. This took the form of officer training and it also included an equipment programme and doctrine development and may, in time, expand to include the training of non-commissioned officers. These elements are recognized as an essential contribution to the establishment of modern and robust Iraqi armed forces of a size and capability consistent with a Middle Eastern country facing border security issues and involved in counter-insurgency operations. It required a huge cultural change and took place in the most difficult and demanding of circumstances.

Readers may have different views on the politics of the Iraq war and its consequences. However, what is beyond dispute is that a highly professional task is being undertaken by NATO. A training infrastructure was built under the most demanding security conditions and against tight time pressures. Moreover, this involved cooperative working from professionals in different countries and with different languages. A consideration of the approach adopted by NATO highlights a number of the challenges involved in modern training and learning.

The time-line

After the military conflict ended in May 2003, the Iraqi armed forces were disbanded. Officers and men left their posts and went back to the community;

equipment disappeared or was destroyed and the infrastructure collapsed. The problems of counter-insurgency that later began to develop and the need to underpin withdrawal in the long term meant that a new armed force structure needed to be put in place once the cessation of hostilities made this possible. The coalition forces led by the USA, and in which the UK participates, immediately began the long and difficult business of rebuilding the Iraqi armed forces and the infrastructure to support them. This meant reconstituting units and manning, equipping and training them. A NATO summit held in the Summer of 2004 agreed that it could contribute to this gargantuan effort in a modest way through a focus on officer training and education and also assistance with equipment.

Accordingly, NATO formally agreed to commit resources to officer training in Iraq and establish the NATO Training Mission in Iraq (NTM-I) for that purpose and work began during August and September 2004. A mission of 250 staff from 18 different countries was created and, from August 2004 to February 2005, it planned operations, set up NTM-I at its HQ in Baghdad and initiated training activities. This meant that the design of the training had to be undertaken by NTM-I as soon as it could feasibly be done. This training would take the form of on-the-job training aimed at senior Iraqi officers, as well as the establishment of a military Staff College catering for both middle ranking and senior officers. Instructional delivery in the Staff College would be undertaken by Iraqi nationals. The strategy was designed to build capacity: increasingly, ownership would pass to the Iraqi armed forces and development of the infrastructure would take place on the basis of joint consultation.

Implementation took until March 2005 and from then until August 2005, NTM-I was involved in on-the-job training for senior officers in the new Iraqi armed forces (described in more detail below) and, the main focus during this period, the planning of the Staff College. This included writing and delivering a four-month Train the Trainer course, writing the Junior and Senior staff courses and developing the infrastructure to house and support the whole effort. NTM-I also needed to obtain training equipment and to produce training material appropriate for the situation.

From September 2005 to August 2006, the Staff College was established in Al-Rustamiyah some 9 or 10 miles South East of central Baghdad, site of the original Iraqi Military Academy. Additionally in this phase, a Defence Strategic Studies Institute and a Defence Language Institute were created and the National Defence College (NDC) was planned.

In September 2006, the National Defence College located alongside the NTM-I HQ in Baghdad, was opened. The NDC provides courses for officers of Colonel and Brigadier rank dealing with strategic and operational planning.

The use of the term 'college' is deliberate because it emphasizes the benefits of bringing students together and encouraging learning that is mutually supportive. In this way, the wealth of talent and experience prevalent in a group of senior people like this can be fully tapped.

Some issues

Colonel Steve O'Connell, a British Army education and training officer, was Chief of Staff at the NTM-I between February and August 2005. He describes the challenges in the following terms:

- securing resources: both money and physical resources
- creating a modern training and education regime at a time when all the previous doctrine, knowledge and training materials had dissolved
- operating in a hostile security situation.

Although the NTM-I would recognize that training is not normally about letting building contracts and putting physical security measures in place, a safe physical environment was needed at the earliest opportunity. In Steve O'Connell's own words:

You must realize that, in that difficult situation, the Iraqi officers working with NATO were taking a huge personal risk simply by turning up to work!

It was necessary to rebuild the former Staff College facilities, provide physical security barriers including fencing, obtain desks and furniture, modern PCs and training materials.

Given the situation, the initial training went hand in hand with recruitment. A new ethos of fair selection was implemented, allowing some of the most capable officers in the armed forces to be selected as Staff College instructors, while others who had previous experience in the former Iraqi regime, but had retired, returned to service as well. This 'open' approach to selection ensured that the very best talent available was recruited to run this important institution. Additionally, there were important issues on military doctrine to sort out. Broadly defined, doctrine is the strategic military principles from which all else follows. If the training NTM-I put in place was to remain valid, doctrine had to be written and this work was embarked upon.

Essentially, there is an enormous difference between what is required from armed forces that are supporting a repressive regime and the modern forces needed for border security and counter-insurgency operations. It requires a completely different approach with a different mix of forces, different skills and different equipment. Even if a training legacy had been in place in Iraq, it would have needed to be scrapped and rebuilt. Moreover, the previous regime had created a particular mind-set so far as learning was concerned.

Steve O'Connell offers the following illustration:

When running educational courses for military officers, a typical method is to present a topic or scenario and open it out for discussion – the instructor asks: 'What do you think?' Initially, doing this in Iraq resulted in a stony and embarrassed silence. They simply could not understand that they were being asked to express an opinion.

However, once the Iraqis realized that this was an appropriate approach to learning, they grasped what was required and learned the techniques rapidly. Indeed, the realization that they were positively being encouraged to speak their mind after so many repressive years brought tears to more than one pair of eyes. As Steve O'Connell emphasizes, motivation was high and learners were keen to embrace the model of conduct in modern armed forces. Another dimension of adjustment was the need to demonstrate commitment by working longer hours than had been prevalent in the previous regime.

This legacy could have easily led to a model based on top-down, instructor-led training. However, the need to build capacity and develop local ownership meant that, throughout the design stage, an attempt was made to produce materials which emphasized the learner's responsibility for their own learning. This also involved more use of technology: materials and learning aids were made accessible through PCs.

One-to-one instruction

One other aspect of the training and learning strategy developed by the NATO mission deserves consideration. This was the on-the-job training which began in 2004 and was further developed throughout 2005. The officers newly employed in key command and control centres needed to get up to speed very rapidly.

Despite the time pressures, some training needs analysis was undertaken and this highlighted an urgent need for what may be described as military processes; how to conduct operational planning, undertake briefing, write orders and task military units. As well as that, there was a need to develop basic IT skills and to teach the use of written and spoken English.

Given all the considerations, the best method of delivering this requirement was seen to be one-to-one instruction. NTM-I delivered this on-the-job training in three separate operations centres employing Iraqi officers. The NATO instructors were present for most of the working day from the outset but, as their numbers in Iraq increased, they supported training twenty-four hours a day, seven days a week. They would sit and work on a one-to-one basis with the Iraqi officers and so develop the skills the Iraqis needed to undertake their daily tasks effectively. During this period, the one-to-one instruction was supported with a regular series of lectures. Although this approach was recognized to be resource intensive in terms of NATO mission time, the circumstances demanded this highly tailored and supportive approach. In short, it was not possible to release Iraqi officers in key roles for full-time training while they were fighting a major counter-insurgency campaign.

Reflection

Looking back on this whole period, Steve O'Connell offers the following comment:

> *I had never known a situation where so much had to be done in so short a time, let alone under the threat of constant attack by insurgents. It brought home to me the value of the investment in good military training. Your actions have to be second nature; there is no time to make mistakes. The Iraqis, for their part, willingly took risks and made personal sacrifices to get their country back on its feet; they were extremely grateful for the risks taken by others too.*

The issue, then, is not how to eliminate the course, but how to make the course provision more effective. This involves both a consideration of delivery – what happens in the training room – and the context – when is the course most effectively deployed.

A thoughtful contribution was made to an internal CIPD debate by Iain Thomson, a writer and consultant. His discussion paper offers many stimulating insights and it has been placed on the CIPD website at www.cipd.co.uk/helpingpeoplelearn. Extended extracts from his paper are in Case study 7.2. At his request some helpful references have been reproduced at the end of this chapter [4, 5, 6, 7].

Case study 7.2 Trends in training delivery in the training room – some personal views from Iain Thomson

Want, need and supply

From a supply point of view, many large (often public sector) and some small (relatively under-resourced) organisations still rely heavily on standard, 'one size fits all' courses from menus put out by major training groups (i.e. those commoditising training). This reinforces unhelpful collusion on three fronts: organisations want easily identifiable training packages ('Three of your standard presentation skills courses, quickly, please'), participants want an uncomplicated attendance record ('Right, I can now tick the PDP/appraisal need box and get back to real work') and training salespeople can breath a sigh of relief ('Another £x in the bag towards my sales target this month').

'Thoughtful practitioners' are those relatively scarce trainers who have real-life experience, who can share wisdom, who are flexible, who can respond rapidly to participants' needs on a course, who have the confidence to apply 'accelerated learning' techniques and who are not afraid of challenge or emotion (particularly in soft skills training). These trainers often find themselves providing one-to-one help for participants outside the planned sessions (e.g. how to deal with a difficult boss, dealing with poor performance in the team, personal and career issues etc). 'Thoughtful practitioners' include those technical trainers who can enliven structured topics such as IT and finance and adapt their style and planned approach to meet the needs of trainees.

On the other hand, there are many 'treadmill' trainers who can steadily churn out essential, basic-skill training courses. Their events tend to be well planned, but narrow and, sometimes – under time pressure and in the absence of focused objectives – 'treadmill' trainers may try to cram in too much at the expense of some deeper learning points.

'Thoughtful practitioner' training trends

Within technical training – be it MBA-type or operating skills – the sequence of training is generally still along the lines of Input-Application-Discussion. 'Thoughtful practitioners' in management and interpersonal skills sessions, however, are generally finding that a Discovery-Reflection-Input cycle is more powerful. Thus, in technical training, facts and concepts precede practice to test understanding and skills (e.g. on a standard case study about a balance sheet, or on a lathe or other machinery process), while in management training, practice precedes consideration of possible frameworks to explain an experience (e.g. on an exercise designed to bring out planning or conflict issues – to explore meaning and how any insights can be applied to everyday work). Notably, Discovery-Reflection-Input proves popular even where there is a preponderance of Reflector-Theorist learning styles (common in the public and financial sectors).

In some cases, 'thoughtful practitioners' are able to harness opportunities to encourage Argyris' double-loop learning (i.e. personal learning that encourages change in organisational systems and processes). Thus, for example, in sessions about communication (the most commonly-cited organisational problem), participants can learn from training experience how improved horizontal communication at work can be achieved – by extending the concept of networking during a course to temporary job swaps between teams on return to work that lead to new processes or cost savings. Alternatively, to satisfy a desire for improved vertical communication, Senge's systemic thinking can be applied to the all-important 'feedback-about-results-leads-to-better-performance' sequence – so that participants are first more inclined to celebrate work achievements with their own staff, then to report more successes upwards and thus to encourage more information on overall organisational results and strategies to be divulged by their boss.

Generally, greater realism is being sought by all involved in classroom training. Case studies are more often based on careful research within the organisation before the training – in some cases trainers encourage the generation of case studies by the participants themselves, as part of the greater levels of involvement accompanying modern training. A shift to less fixed and briefer role play scenarios (e.g. 'You have a member of staff whose performance is beginning to dip. . .how do you approach them?') is popular, as is on-the-spot 'rehearsal' of what a participant is going to do/say on return to work (e.g. with a distant but demanding boss) when such issues arise in the training room. Also, oral feedback from fellow participants about behaviour and the practice of interactive skills is preferred to being videoed. Practicality, activity and innovative training techniques are clearly enjoyed by nearly all participants.

Overall, 'thoughtful practitioners' are increasingly coming out of Adult-to-Adult and andragogical rather than pedagogical, mindsets. This means less lecturing and 'talk and chalk' (less PowerPoint and theory in today's language), more participant-led discussion, less 'being the expert' by trainers, more variety in the shape of exercises and activities, and more readiness to help participants to see what something means to them and how they relate to others (including their organisation). This shift in attitude might not be observable in the outlines of a course or in a cold read of any handouts or case studies, but it is clear in the manner in which good trainers interact with participants.

What more is needed?

Firstly, the relationships between trainers and learners/participants, and how they fit best to different types of training, would benefit from serious exploration. Secondly, all involved need to stop seeing training courses and programmes as discrete 'projects' to be ticked off as soon as they have been 'completed'. Finally, more attention to business/bottom-line outcomes is essential if classroom training is to retain its credibility amongst alternative options (which often look more attractive).

It would be helpful to learn just how much more effective is facilitated adult learning (relatively close trainer-participant relationship) compared to traditional training (relatively distant trainer-participant relationship). The former is preferable for behavioural/attitudinal change, but can be time expensive; the latter may be more effective for information/knowledge transfer, but less lasting. Manual skills acquisition may be more dependent on how the manager/foreman treats learners/apprentices.

It is not helpful to see training courses and programmes as isolated in time and space, away from the requirements, management and politics of particular organisations. Benefits for all would stem from better TNA, learning strategy selection, pre-course briefing and preparation, and post-course follow up (particularly by participants' managers – one suggestion here is to invite them to attend end-of-course presentations). 'Thoughtful practitioners' also need to beware of the growth of a purchasing mentality in many companies and to be on their guard to avoid falling into the trap of merely providing commoditised courses.

It is clear that, particularly in soft skills training, greater links to the business or bottom line measures are required. Interestingly, some public sector organisations now openly recognise the need to shift from 'what the individual wants from the organisation' to 'what the business wants of the individual'. Worryingly, however, in some evaluations of management training in the financial sector the junior to middle managers being trained have been far more able to specify concrete benefits than their senior managers. Evaluation efforts are, of course, often better directed at reinforcing learning and post-course performance (action-oriented evaluation) rather than merely proving the value of the training (conclusion-oriented evaluation).

All in all, more efforts are needed to see training as an input or activity, the essential output from which is learning, motivation, self-belief and changed mindsets, and with the desired outcome from those being raised performance. Trainers who can make this happen clearly qualify as 'thoughtful practitioners'.

The course in context

Iain Thomson's paper sets out some of the issues that should be considered in improving the effectives of course-based provision. This chapter will end with three case illustrations which demonstrate the value of the course when it used appropriately.

At call centres, course-based training can be the most cost-effective way of ensuring that new joiners gained an initial appreciation of what is required to meet customer needs. To return to a phrase introduced in the previous chapter, this is about 'time to competence'. This is illustrated by the case of Convergys in India (Case study 7.3) and Ventura in the UK (Case study 7.4). Both of these cases demonstrate that a course is far more effective when embedded in a wider human resource development strategy.

The provision at Qatar Petroleum (Case study 7.5) shows how the value of the instructor is greatly enhanced if thorough consideration is given to the following: effective design, the delivery mechanisms, all the prior experience of the learner and the context in which they will be learning and applying the content.

Case study 7.3 Training at Convergys Contact Centres, India

Background

Convergys is the world's largest operator of call or contact centres. It was established in its current form in 1998 and grew out of the US Cincinnati Bell telecommunications company. Revenue in 2005 was $2.58 billion and there are four operating divisions: customer management (the contact centre business); employee care (outsourced personnel activities, including payroll, benefits, learning and recruitment); information management (IT outsourcing, with specialisms in billing platforms); and finance and accounting (the outsourcing business recently acquired from Deloitte).

Currently, Convergys operates over 65 contact, service and data centres worldwide. The largest number of service centres (54) are in North America where the company was founded. There are seven centres in India (the subject of this case study) and six in the Philippines. Total capacity in India is some 6000 'seats' which, given shift working arrangements, means that some 9000 people are employed by Convergys in the country.

Programmes (the term used to describe a discrete activity centred around a product, service or market) are delivered for overseas clients. Convergys operates 'third party' centres for clients as opposed to 'captive centres' where a contact centre is established in India solely to meet the needs of the overseas parent company. The challenge therefore is to ensure that staff have both the technical and business knowledge to assist the client's customers and the communication skills and empathy so that this is put across in a way that leaves a positive and favourable impression.

Recruitment and retention

In its centres of operation (three in Gurgaon on the outskirts of Delhi and one each in Mumbai, Bengaluru, Pune Thane and Hyderabad), Convergys is a prominent employer. The largest centre at Gurgaon, for example, has over 2000 agents (the term used for the staff who deal with client calls). As has been well observed, India has a current surfeit of capable and ambitious young people leaving its education system. Though the recruitment market is becoming more competitive, Convergys remains an 'employer of aspiration' for those who wish to work for the leader in the global contact centre business.

The majority of staff are young, mainly in their early 20s and half are female. Given that the majority of calls come from North America, much of the work takes place from evening until early morning and the company puts a lot of resources into providing meals, transport and security.

For many staff, it will be their first job since leaving full-time education, much of the initial induction is therefore focused on the transition to work – what the company offers and what is expected from the employee. Retention rates can be a problem: some people leave after a transitory period to move on to a different career or into higher education. Others simply 'don't know why they joined'. However, given the need for staff to acquire the knowledge and skills demanded by clients, Convergys puts a considerable effort into training, as Gyan Nagpal, Organizational Development Director based in Gurgaon, puts it:

> *If an organization engages with its staff, offering them a career with prospects and progression, they will stay and develop.*

Initial training

After the initial induction, which typically lasts two days, the new agent will be supervised through two training modules. Both last three or four weeks and it can therefore be up to seven weeks before the new joiner takes their first customer facing call.

The first module is designed to increase 'cultural sensitivity' to the country where the calls will originate and to understand the context in which the client operates. All staff have English as a spoken language and dealing with variations in accent is an issue in two respects. First, the agent needs to be comfortable understanding the caller's accent: five different groups of accents have been identified from North American callers alone. The second issue is the agent's accent – an element of 'accent neutralization' can be needed. Although, as Gyan Nagpur puts it:

> *A person can't change their accent in three weeks even if it was necessary. We emphasize the need for clarity and encourage our agents to speak more slowly.*

Those modules are delivered in the classroom in groups of approximately 20 people, with feedback offered from the trainer and peers. Recording devices and audio support the programme.

The second module, which is again classroom based, also introduces technology-based training screens. The module is focused on the client's products and systems and the questions that are likely to arise. Much of the detail is determined by the client's requirements and, while some clients are keen to avoid any situation where a customer sees a difference in approach between the client's home staff and the agent in India, others are less concerned. The nature of the client's product often determines the depth of understanding that the agents need to have.

All new agents must, before they can deal with the client's customers over the phone, acquire both the generic skills of client handling and the specific knowledge to answer the underlying request. Agents are brought up to speed in an efficient and timely way: driving minimum 'time to competence' measures is an important consideration.

On-going support: the role of the team leader

Convergys' contact centres operate a relatively flat management structure and the normal progression for the agents is to the role of team leader: typically a team leader will have 15 to 20 direct reports. Team leaders are invariably chosen from high performing agents, so their technical understanding of contact centre work will be good. However, for many, the management of staff will be a new challenge.

From start to finish, the training period for new team leaders can be as long as 90 days. The classroom component of this training is delivered in five day modules. Critical elements include the modules that focus on staff development – one of the five-day modules is mainly centred on coaching – and modules on tools that the team leader will use to monitor and drive performance. Feedback to agents regarding their call-handling capability is critical to the team and the business' success and the team leader must have the skills and confidence to perform this task.

As part of the preparation for the new role, during this 90-day period, team leaders are required to undertake 13 modules of on-line e-learning (from two to four hours each). The majority of the modules have been specifically developed by Convergys, as the organization increasingly deploys e-learning as a preferred means of training delivery within a blended approach. Convergys acquired Digitalthink, a US-based e-learning organization in 2004 and has used these skills to deploy a learning portal that is available for Convergys agents throughout the world.

Convergys recognizes that the quality and motivation of its agents is critical to the success of the organization. The delivery of focused training in a cost-effective, globally consistent fashion drives higher standards of service from Convergys' centres, while simultaneously reducing turnover and the associated bottom line costs.

Case study 7.4 Training for the business at Ventura

Ventura, a wholly owned subsidiary of Next plc, is one of the UK's leading outsourcing providers operating customer contact centres. Clients include well-known public, private and voluntary sector bodies. More than 7500 people are employed at four contact centres in the UK and Pune, India. Almost half the UK agents (front-line staff who receive calls and offer advice to customers) are located in two large state of the art call centres in the Dearne Valley, South Yorkshire – here Ventura is the dominant employer in what used to be a mining area.

Outsourced customer service management is a very competitive business and, two years ago, Ventura underwent a major restructure to permit a more competitive approach to pricing. A key element in securing and retaining business is the quality of the agents: they must demonstrate a good telephone manner, understanding and empathy with the customer's requirements and have the written communication and keyboard skills needed to prepare accurate and appropriate reports. Certain contracts also require selling skills and, in some cases, a specialist interest or awareness. For example, those agents serving a client who specializes in Internet and broadband services benefit from a technical appreciation and IT knowledge, while those agents working on a client's charity helpline have expert knowledge and share empathy on the subject.

The human resources function at Ventura has close links with local schools and colleges. As the largest employer in an area where the profile of employment has changed rapidly, they need to signal clearly what skills are desired and work in improving the quality and aspirations of the local labour pool. In addition, contact centre work has previously been seen as a 'stop-gap' job and not a long-term career option. However, while there can be a degree of repetition to the task, call centre work can be highly varied with many opportunities for promotion. The working environment is good, there is plenty of opportunity for interaction with colleagues and there is satisfaction in assisting people with their problems or meeting their requirements. Beverley Connor, Ventura's Recruitment and Training Delivery Manager says, 'We must strive for recognition for our training efforts and seek to remove the stigma associated with contact centre work'.

Recruitment and training

Following the restructure, the combined recruitment and training function has expanded in size. A reorganization of training delivery was designed to create a much closer link with the business areas. In the UK, there are six training managers each of whom are supported by six to fifteen training officers. Training is mainly focused on core individual skills (interpersonal and the use of the systems) and product knowledge and awareness.

The main challenges faced by the recruitment and training functions are, first, attracting quality candidates from a demographic pool where core skills might not naturally exist, in high volumes, over long periods of time. Secondly, providing expert 'niche' training from a centralized resource, where each client is just as important as another, making prioritization a continuous agenda item.

There is a close link with the recruitment process which proceeds through assessment and interviews. The interviewing process is conducted around seven key competencies – for example convincing and assertiveness, team working and communication skills.

A particular challenge, closely linked to the business offering, is the need to deliver training against very tight timetables. If a new client is secured, it is important to be able to deliver their requirements quickly. This will prevent the client's customer experiencing any uncertainty of service provision. In the space of as little as four weeks from signature it may be necessary to set up a unit, design material, organize IT infrastructure and install trained agents at their desks. Minimizing 'time to competence' is a major determination of the success of the Recruitment and Training function.

Induction and beyond

This emphasis on 'time to competence' requires that relevant business training is delivered at all times, but particularly at induction: initial classroom training, reinforced by a planned transition to the work-team is the preferred method.

Given the demands of the clients, between 15 and 60 new people can start each week. They are grouped from the outset into units of 15 or so who will be serving the needs of a designated client. After an orientation to the area where they will be working, the cohort will undertake up to five weeks' training for full-time courses, delivered by the training officer who has responsibility for this particular client. The subjects covered will include behavioural skills and IT/keyboard training as well as product knowledge.

This customer-specific training takes place in one of the on-site classrooms and a special technology system (SMART) allows the tutor to project what is happening on any individual's training-room PC. In practice, call handling, keyboard entry skills and product knowledge are inextricably linked as the new joiner progresses to competence.

Once this classroom training has been completed, the new staff members are placed in a special part of the work area known variously as a 'development centre' or 'graduation bay'. Here, over the next few weeks, they receive coaching support from both the training officer and the team leader for the section. The new entrants will take some calls, but these will be closely monitored or treated as joint calls. Their progress and performance will be assessed and, on occasions, the training officer will take the cohort of new joiners away to the training room.

Once the new joiner is fully competent, he or she will join the team and be given feedback by his or her team leader. At the customer centre, key performance indicators (number of calls, duration etc) are produced for each individual on a daily basis. They are consolidated monthly into an individual scorecard which also includes development needs. It is the responsibility of the team leader and their manager in conjunction with the training officer to ensure that these are met.

Case study 7.5 English language learning at Qatar Petroleum

Background context

Qatar Petroleum (QP) is a state-owned oil and gas supplier in the Arabian Gulf. In 2004, it produced just under 1 million barrels of oil and 3.8 billion cubic feet of gas. QP plays a very significant role in the State of Qatar as a dominant employer: some 7000 people work for QP (and several thousands more for its subsidiaries), in a wide range of job types from engineering through administrative, security, medical, training, marketing, etc. Significantly, more than half of these employees are non-Qataris recruited from all over the world.

In 2000, the State of Qatar announced the Strategic Qatarization Plan, with the objective of increasing the proportion of Qataris in employment in key sectors. English language learning was identified as a key component of the Qatarization programme, as the official business language of the petroleum industry is English. Accordingly, in 2002, QP established the English Curriculum Development Project to develop English language training materials, which according to the Strategic Qatarization Plan's English competence website:

> Cater to the competency-based training needs and to the specific cultural and professional requirements of the Energy and Industry sector in Qatar (www.ec.com.qa).

The programme

Gabi Witthaus, who has considerable experience in English language teaching and instructional design, heads a team of English instructors working as writers and editors and designers/multimedia specialists. The team's mission is to produce stimulating English language teaching materials that are relevant to people working in the energy industry.

The size of the programme is considerable. In the course of a year some 900–1000 employees and up to 1200 trainees (Qatari citizens who have left school and are undergoing a four-year work preparation programme at QP) will receive English training. Most of these learners are now using materials created by the Curriculum Development Project team.

The series of training programmes, branded as 'Power English', so far consists of four general English courses at different levels. Each level involves some 250–300 contact hours. The Curriculum Development team has also produced a number of short courses for people with job-specific language needs, for example 'Radio Communications for Process Operators', etc. All courses are supported by both print and multimedia materials. Feedback on the materials so far has been extremely positive, with learners, instructors and line managers particularly pleased about the way that English language learning has been contextualized within a familiar workplace setting.

Throughout all courses, rigorous assessment of competence takes place against specified criteria. Learners must demonstrate competence in all outcomes before they can move up to the next level.

Issues and delivery

Perhaps the greatest challenge for the Curriculum Development team is that, while the aim of the Power English courses is to teach general English for the workplace, the target audience comes from a wide range of job categories and line managers often want their subordinates to learn English for particular technical contexts. This issue is being addressed through the elective short courses targeted at learners with specific needs as mentioned above.

A second major challenge for the curriculum developers is finding the best way to produce stimulating, thought-provoking materials in an environment where the traditional learning culture involves a teacher-centred delivery mode and learners are not accustomed to taking full responsibility for their own learning. The team is addressing this challenge by developing high quality multimedia materials, including authentic video footage from various worksites, animated representations of processes within the petroleum industry and other high-impact presentation material, to stimulate discussion and higher-order thinking among learners. Team members have worked closely with subject matter experts from the line in order to produce these materials. Furthermore, since both the learning activities and the assessment tasks closely reflect the learning outcomes in the competency framework, there is built-in motivation for learners to apply themselves to the tasks in the training materials.

The third major challenge is identifying the role that technology can play in reducing the constraints of time and distance. For example Gabi recognizes that a number of learners are based in relatively remote locations (offshore, for example). It would be tempting to produce courses which could be delivered entirely through a PC but, in Gabi's view, these sort of learners are precisely the ones that need most face-to-face support, as they are often the ones that get the least chance to practise their English language skills at work.

According to Gabi Witthaus:

Language training needs interaction to be effective, so the predominant mode of delivery is instructor facilitated training of up to 15 learners in a group.

Accordingly, an instructor is designated to be based on site to support learners in remote locations wherever possible.

The support network

QP is committed to the development of its staff and an extended career development system is in place. As part of the Qatarization drive, all Qatari employees have 'Personal Career Plans'. Workplace Learning Coordinators in every department liaise with designated coaches (senior technicians and other first-line managers) to arrange for the necessary employee training on an on-going basis.

In formulating the Power English programme, the Curriculum Development team undertook an extensive needs analysis. The team has subsequently built on this initial needs analysis through site visits and a series of workshops with the coaches. These workshops would normally last up to half a day and have some 15 coaches present. They were designed primarily to inform the line about curriculum development work and get feedback from the coaches on draft materials. After seeing samples of the kind of English that learners are expected to understand and produce in the training centre, many coaches have said that they have a better idea of the level of communicative competence they should expect from their team members. In addition, the workshops provide an opportunity for coaches to share tips with one another as to how they help learners to use and retain their English language skills. In this way, a culture of post-training support for learners is gradually being built up throughout the company.

Looking at the future, Gabi Witthaus sees the development of the project in the following terms:

> *Power English has so far been successful in meeting QP's need for a dynamic English language programme relevant to people working in the petroleum industry in Qatar. With ongoing collaboration between the line and the curriculum development team, we are confident that we will continue producing learning materials that really make a difference to people's performance at work.*

References

[1]. Chartered Institute of Personnel and Development (2006) What it Means. London: CIPD. Available at: http://www.cipd.co.uk/mandq/standards/_means.htm

[2]. Jarvis, J. (2006) Training Budgets Squeezed by Poor Economic Outlook. Impact, 15, 13.

[3]. Reynolds, J. (2004) Helping People to Learn: Strategies for Moving from Training to Learning. London: Chartered Institute of Personnel and Development.

[4]. Argyris, C. (1994) Good Communication that Blocks Learning. Harvard Business Review, 7(4), 77–85.

[5]. Belbin, R.M. (1969) The Discovery Method: An International Experiment in Retraining. Paris: Organisation for Economic Co-Operation and Development.

[6]. Knowles, M.S. (1984) The Adult Learner: A Neglected Species, 3rd edn. Houston, TX: Gulf.

[7]. Senge, P.M. (1992) The Fifth Discipline: The Art and Practice of the Learning Organization. London: Century Business.

8

Support and Challenge

The previous chapter considered the role of the off-the-job or classroom course in 'supporting, accelerating and directing interventions that meet organizational needs' (to return to the first half of our role definition for the people development professional introduced in Chapter 1 (p. 18)). In some circumstances, one may say many circumstances, this approach is appropriate to the learner and the context in which he or she is learning.

Individual learning can take place in a wide range of circumstances. In almost all these circumstances learning can be facilitated provided those in a position to do so are willing to assist and have the necessary skills. Organizations are intervening by putting structures in place to ensure that this happens. This has been a feature of many of the cases considered to date. As Proposition 7 states: 'While off-the-job classroom-based training still has a place, it no longer occupies the central role in training provision as other forms of intervention are becoming more important'.

In an article written in 2004, Bob Garvey, of the Mentoring and Coaching Research Unit at Sheffield Hallam University, suggested that activities such as coaching, mentoring and counselling can all be understood to be 'helping activities' [1]. This term underlines the fact that individual learning can take place in a wide range of circumstances. In almost all these circumstances, learning can be facilitated provided those in a position to do so are willing to assist and have the necessary skills. Many organizations are intervening by putting structures in place to ensure that this happens.

In this chapter, rather than use the term 'helping activities', we will use 'support and challenge'. These describe a range of interventions which, through skilful mediation, encourage the recipient to find within himself or herself a way forward. In many cases, a desirable intervention will be a mixture of support (encouraging the learner to display confidence in their own capabilities and thus construct their own learning agenda) and challenge (demanding that a wide range of options are considered and the self-imposed objective stretches the owner). Support and challenge describe non-directive interventions: the recipient is not told what to do.

Such interventions can be delivered by a range of people in the organization. They certainly include an approach used in the classroom. Support and challenge is increasingly seen as a key development weapon to be used by line managers (see the Piccadilly case in Chapter 6 (p. 132)) and by peers in the workplace (see, for example, the Harvey Nichols case in Chapter 2 (p. 36)).

The first case study illustration in this chapter shows the broad range of approaches that can be used. DG REGIO, a Directorate of the European Commission, is seeking to extend learning beyond the training room. The specialist staff have considerable expertise, but travel extensively. They have limited time available in the office so a range of initiatives is needed to support individual development.

Case study 8.1 Developing on-the-job learning at the European Commission: the example of Regional Policy Directorate General

Background

Regional Policy directorate general (DG REGIO) is one of about 40 directorate generals of the European Commission. It employs some 650 staff who originate from all 25 member countries. Although in terms of headcount it is a medium-sized directorate general (DG), it is currently responsible for the second largest spending budget. To quote from an official publication:

> It allocates a major part of the funds granted to the Cohesion policy, which represents more than one third of the budget of the European Union to the reduction of the gaps in development among regions and disparities among the citizens in terms of well-being.

This is a high profile activity for the Community and the DG places much emphasis on the integrity of systems to ensure that the spend is appropriately directed and monitored.

DG REGIO staff have a range of technical specialisms, including policy expertise and finance. Many of them travel widely or spend extended periods of time in the Member States. Building good relationships with the governments of Member States and the Regions is recognized as critical to success.

The move from the classroom

In this environment, the training teams within the DG face a particular set of challenges. They have to deliver what is required to the individual against tight time pressures; many staff have limited time available for the office, let alone the training room. Any training must be of a high quality and trainers must be aware of the sensitive political environment in which DG REGIO operates. The training function must always look ahead to future demands: in 2007, for example, a new set of Member States will join the European Union. At the same time, new procedures and regulations for the structural funds, together with a new budget of about €300 billion for the next programming period 2007–13, are entering into force.

A key part of the response has been to take a range of initiatives designed to assist one-to-one training and learning and to create a coaching capacity. The initiatives in place will achieve both and promote more effective individual learning and develop a better culture to support learning.

However, there is still a place for the classroom. In the view of Marc Wauquier, the Head of Training, the classroom will remain the most effective method of delivering what is required or compulsory, for example in accountancy or policy and procedures. Importantly, the Deputy Head, Lena ter Woort, observes:

> *The classroom will need to become a different vehicle. It will become much more interactive, building on the joint knowledge in the training room. We will need to be much better at supporting the transmission of the knowledge and skills acquired back to the workplace.*

Whatever may happen to the classroom, the DG REGIO training teams agree that the development of one-to-one training and learning is critical. The individual learner's needs are very specific, the initial levels of knowledge can vary and much of the expertise is only available within the DG and must be delivered at the optimum time.

Some current initiatives

As has been noted, many of the initiatives are designed not simply to achieve an immediate objective, but also to build the coaching capacity within the DG. Much emphasis is therefore placed on providing one-to-one support at an early stage. In this way, the learner appreciates the benefit of the approach and his or her commitment increases.

Peer coaching

Peer coaching was formally introduced in January 2005. Its purpose is to offer each newcomer to the Directorate a coach drawn from within the existing staff. Ideally, the coach is appointed by the line manager before the new joiner starts his or her employment. The criteria for selecting a coach include a good working knowledge of procedures and tools as well as good interpersonal communication skills. The time commitment is estimated as an hour a day for two months. A recent review of the initiative indicates that it has been very well received. Recognized areas for improvement have been identified: coaches were not always appointed before arrival of the new colleague, which led to some coaches not being adequately aware of what was expected of them; some found it difficult to find the time to discharge responsibilities.

The three-way meeting

As part of a nine-step process, one of the induction steps is a formal meeting held between the new entrant, his or her line manager and a member of the training team. This normally takes place some three weeks after arrival. The purpose is to identify the most urgent training needs (across a wide range of competencies) and to determine how they may be met in the short and medium term. The training teams are seeking to develop a more formal individual training and learning plan to assist this process. Three-way meetings provide important input into the future training programmes and a possibility for continuous exchange with the managers of the DG.

Mentoring

The mentoring scheme was introduced at the same time as the peer coaching initiative. The purpose here is to provide long-term support beyond the initial induction stage. Participation is voluntary and, so far, some 25 staff members have agreed to undertake mentoring training and to act as a mentor. They are committed to meeting the mentee at least once a week over a six-week period and thereafter twice a month for at least six months. Many of the mentees come from the new Member States which entered the European Union in 2004. It is a valuable learning experience for both mentee and mentors, which facilitates diversity and indirectly benefits the organization.

Executive coaching

This initiative was introduced in 2004 and is aimed at senior and middle managers, who must, in advance, have participated in the Commission's Internal eight-day Management Training Programme. Some 30 out of 40 eligible managers have taken up the opportunity. The executive coaches are external consultants who are accredited by the Commission's central training unit and work as subcontractors for the Commission. The manager would expect to receive 12 sessions of 1½ hours. The early feedback from the scheme has been very positive. All the coaches meet with the training team and provide valuable input for the design of future training initiatives.

Network of key users

These are the technical specialists who support the major system changes. Their role is particularly important since, in 2002, a major shift in procedures took place away from paper-based towards electronic processes. The system changes were designed and implemented by external contractors, but 20 members of staff were identified as key users. They played an important role in providing input at the design stage.

Subsequently, their most important tasks are to support users on a one-to-one basis and to provide feedback on problems. In retrospect, Anne Verbist, a member of the Guidance and Informatic Training Team, recognizes that the initial training of the key users over-emphasized the technical features. Little attention was given to the need for key users to acquire the critical training or coaching skills. Equally, the need to acquire and deploy such skills was insufficiently taken into account in the choice of advisers by line mangers in some business units.

Network of trainers

While the key user initiative concentrates on information and system change, the network of trainers relates to the technical and policy issues which fall outside IT. The network now consists of some 41 members of staff – all of whom have relevant and important subject matter expertise (for example, in financial management, the European Structural Funds or audit). Most of their training is delivered to small groups, although they can be called on to give one-to-one support. The time commitment could range from as much as 15 days a year to as little as one and a half days.

None of these initiatives in themselves is out of the ordinary. What is unusual is the wide and ambitious range of activities, all of which are designed to place more emphasis on the individual learner through the provision of one-to-one support. Clearly, senior management commitment and understanding is essential as is their recognition that much effective learning takes place outside the training room. Considerable pressure is involved in terms of staff time. Some of the initiatives, for example, those focused on the effective use of IT systems, produce a very evident, immediate and often quantifiable business benefit. Others are directed to the longer term and to building capacity within the DG or the institution.

The training teams spend much of their effort reviewing and refining the initiatives. Continuous improvement is essential. A major issue is the need to ensure that there is a more consistent level of commitment and support across the unit. The least committed unit must be brought up to an acceptable level. There are also communication issues. As Marc Wauquier puts it:

> *People are aware of the initiatives that affect them immediately, but they do not necessarily appreciate the underlying strategy. It is difficult to communicate the whole piece.*

Lena ter Woort also identifies recognition and reward of those people who are acting as peer coaches and mentors as an issue. They can spend considerable time in these activities. Cash rewards would run counter to the remuneration strategies. Currently, efforts are in hand to ensure that contributors are recognized in the annual performance review.

Such problems are challenging. However, the training teams are confident that the emphasis on one-to-one training, learning and the development of a coaching capacity is the right strategy for the DG. As more people experience the benefits, support is growing and new approaches, for example, the introduction of action learning sets as well as job shadowing in a unit-to-unit exchange approach, become feasible.

Coaching

One form of 'support and challenge' has attracted considerable attention in recent years. We have witnessed an explosion in the use of the term 'coaching'. One recurring feature of the case studies through this book is the desire to get effective coaching support in place in the learner's place of work. Often the word 'coaching' is used loosely to describe any form of non-directive interventions delivered on-the-job. Sometimes the word 'coaching' is used to describe the interventions delivered by an external consultant. There has, for example, been an upsurge in executive coaching, where senior managers have an on-going relationship with an external adviser on a consultancy basis – with the cost of the provision met by the organization.

In a 2004 CIPD publication, coaching was defined as:

> *Developing a person's skills and knowledge so that their job performance improves, hopefully leading to the achievement of organisational objectives. It targets high performance and improvement at work, although it may also have an impact on an individual's private life. It usually lasts for a short period and focuses on specific skills and goals* [2, p. 19].

A CIPD factsheet [3] listed some generally agreed characteristics of coaching in organizations:

- it is essentially a non-directive form of development
- it focuses on improving performance and developing individuals' skills
- personal issues may be discussed but the emphasis is on performance at work
- coaching activities have both organizational and individual goals
- it assumes that the individual is psychologically well and does not require a clinical intervention
- it provides people with feedback on both their strengths and their weaknesses
- it is a skilled activity.

The factsheet went on to comment that:

> *It can be difficult to distinguish between coaching, mentoring and counselling which are all 'helping professions'. In practice, 'mentoring', for example, has come to be used interchangeably with 'coaching'. Traditionally, however, mentoring in the workplace has tended to describe a relationship in which a more experienced colleague used his or her greater knowledge and understanding of the work or workplace to support the development of a more junior or inexperienced member of staff.*
>
> *Similarly, it can be hard to draw a clear distinction between coaching and counselling, not least because many of the theoretical underpinnings of coaching are drawn from the worlds of counselling and therapy. For the purpose of managing coaching services, the key distinction to be drawn is that coaching is for those who are psychologically well; a coach should be able to recognize where an individual is so distressed by personal or social issues that he or she needs to be referred to specialist counselling or other therapeutic support.*

It also suggested that coaching is a particularly suitable development tool in the following situations:

- helping competent technical experts develop better interpersonal or managerial skills
- developing an individual's potential and providing career support
- developing a more strategic perspective after a promotion to a more senior role
- handling conflict situations so that they are resolved effectively.

The following two cases illustrate situations in which coaching is an appropriate form of intervention. At Economedia, a Bulgarian media group, coaching and mentoring were used to develop young talent where classroom training was not yet in place. This is described in Case study 8.2. At HSBC in Singapore, Case study 8.3, an initiative was introduced to support performance management in the organization by providing training in coaching skills for its senior managers.

Case study 8.2 Training new journalists at Economedia, Bulgaria

Background

Economedia AD is a new and rapidly expanding media company based in Sofia, the capital of Bulgaria. It was founded by two Bulgarian journalists who began publishing a weekly business newspaper 'Capital' in 1993. The number of titles has expanded and, in 2001, a business daily, 'Dnevnik', was launched. Output has been extended and the company now produces three newspapers and five magazines which concentrate on business issues in particular sectors (for example, retail, tourism and real estates); it also produces under licence Business Spotlight, a magazine for English language learning, and the Bulgarian edition of Foreign Policy.

On-line brands also feature prominently in the company's portfolio. These include Dnevnik.bg, Capital.bg and Careers.bg – the last is a site focused on HR management, education and job searching. The long-term strategy is to invest in on-line products and generate at least 20% of the company's income from the Internet. From the beginning of 2005, the company has been part of Verlagsgruppe Handelsblatt – the biggest business and financial media company in Germany. Verlagsgruppe Handelsblatt owns 50% of the shares and the other 50% are owned by Agency for Investment Information Ltd.

Some 300 employees are employed at Economedia of whom 65% are journalists – the remainder are involved in sales, management and administration. Printing is undertaken by a contractor. All of the employees, with the exception of one expatriate manager, are Bulgarian nationals. From the outset, the company policy has been to trust in young people and the average age of the team has been 24.

The human resource challenge

Nelly Hristova joined the group as the Sports Reporter for Dnevnik in 2001 and three years later moved on to become Human Resource Manager. Since 2004, the company has grown from 190 staff to its current level of 300 and the challenges of her job reflect this rapid growth. There is a need to design and implement some important personnel procedures, for example on remuneration, and to ensure alignment with the business. Most importantly, as Nelly Hristova says:

> There is a need to improve the management culture to become even more strategic and long term. We need more flexibility to respond to the challenges of new models which emerge and we need to manage change rapidly. We need to achieve more synergy in the use of our resources across the group.

One initiative that is going to be put in place is the use of an information management system to share details of career opportunities across the group. Economedia has a flat structure and people will need to move laterally through different jobs to develop.

However, in Nelly Hristova's view, the creation of a learning culture is of critical importance if the group can respond to new opportunities. Given the rapid growth, much of her efforts have been focused on developing the younger journalists.

Recruitment and the coaching initiative

It is Economedia's practice to recruit economic, politics and business graduates and to train them internally on-the-job as journalists. In Nelly Hristova's opinion, only one higher education institute in Bulgaria, the American University, offers a practical journalism master's course that would prove of real value. Economedia, therefore, offers 12 summer internships a year – six at Dnevnik and six at Capital – open to business and journalism students; this forms an important element in recruitment.

Given its rapid growth, on-the-job training has been variable.

Accordingly, in 2005, a structured mentoring programme was introduced in Capital. The Social Affairs Editor, Yana Buhrer Tavanier, agreed to take a cohort group of three to five young journalists and set them a series of job-related tasks. This pilot initiative lasts for up to three months for each of the groups. Tasks given to the trainees include structuring interviews and writing reports which would be of immediate benefit to the newspapers and magazines. Indeed, one of the tasks, reporting on the waste disposal/litter problems in Sofia, produced separate and very different items, which were published.

Yana Buhrer Tavanier has received no formal training in coaching but was chosen because of her professional knowledge and personal empathy. She makes the following observations on the challenge she has faced:

> The idea for this training came after we realized that most of the editors do not have the time or possibilities to pay the necessary attention to the new people in their departments, which is crucial both for the people that

start a new job and for the departments themselves. So far, the training has proved to be very useful. We work on a theoretical and practical basis, most of the stories we develop in the group are published in the paper and are well accepted by the readers. In this way, the trainees gain both the knowledge and the confidence they need to be good journalists.

Nelly Hristova has monitored the scheme and is pleased with results. Her challenge is now to identify other individuals who can act as internal mentors not only at Capital but also at Dnevnik and the other publications and introduce appropriate training. This will be delivered by an external consultant – probably from the management school.

Moving forward, Nelly Hristova feels that, in addition to structured mentoring, there is value in more formal subject-related training. She has engaged in some discussions with the Director of Holtzbrinck School of Journalism and is now seeking to establish an Economedia School of Journalism. This will employ some external consultants for the first year, for example Reuters' tutors, to design and deliver six modules of three days each. The subjects have been specified as investigative reporting; on-line reporting; power of visual journalism; company and markets reporting; financial reporting; European Union economics and politics reporting. The first two modules will be trialled in 2006 and the remainder introduced in 2007. The idea is to train in-company tutors for the second year of the school.

Nelly Hristova stresses that the formal training must be seen as a supplement, not an alternative to extended mentoring support across the organization. If the challenge is to improve the learning culture, a series of complementary initiatives will be required. She also plans to use the information management system for developing e-learning modules and share resources between employees.

All these initiatives are in place because we realized that it is more effective to train young people rather than buy stars. We prefer to recruit curious, intelligent, passionate, ambitious and dynamic people who want to develop, because their enthusiasm and ideas are helping the company to grow, develop and change too.

Case study 8.3 A coaching initiative at HSBC Insurance in Singapore

Context

The insurance activities of the HSBC Group employ over 6000 staff who provide a full range of life, general, medical insurance and retirement benefits products and services to individual and corporate clients in 35 countries and territories. HSBC Insurance (Singapore) Pte Limited is one of the smallest insurance subsidiaries in the HSBC Group, employing 200 full-time staff. It decided to introduce a coaching initiative in 2005 to support performance management in the organization, providing training in coaching skills for its senior managers.

As part of a global strategy, known as 'Managing for Growth', the environment in which HSBC Insurance operated was becoming much more results oriented. The programme was therefore designed to help managers and, in turn, their staff to achieve more stretching targets. It was expected to encourage more effective ways of communicating, encouraging managers to ask rather than tell and to support their staff in thinking things through themselves rather than expecting always to be told what to do.

The programme

Coach training was offered to 18 middle and senior managers who were the direct reports to the CEO or were in the level immediately below. No one was made to undertake the training – this was an invitation rather than a requirement – and each was given a trial coaching session to get a taste of what was involved before they made a commitment to it. Each then followed a programme delivered by Results Coaching Systems. This began with a three-day workshop, followed by eight weekly hour long telephone sessions and ending with a one and a half hour workshop. Each coach in training subsequently worked with one volunteer coachee, typically coaching them to achieve one personal and two work objectives.

At the end of the training, 12 went through an assessment, seven successfully achieving certification as level 1 coaches. This pass rate was considered acceptable, since the assessment was acknowledged as being rigorous. Moreover, the value of the programme was seen as being in managers developing coaching skills rather than in being assessed as being competent to be professional coaches in their own right.

Those coaches who completed the training are now about to start a second round of coaching practice, with one more volunteer coachee each. This will give them an opportunity to polish further their coaching skills. While they will have no formal support in reflecting on their learning here, they will have access to telephone support if they need it and there is now a network of managers trained as coaches which each can also fall back on for support. There has also been one 'lunch and share' session where those who had trained as coaches were able to reflect on the application of their skills.

Effectiveness

An evaluation study was commissioned from Results Coaching Systems to assess the impact the programme had had on the coaches and coachees involved and to identify any changes and impacts on the business. Those who had trained as coaches reported that they now felt more valued by their team members, that they were more confident in their management of staff and that coaching was fostering effective relationships with others in the organization. Their responses also suggested that using coaching skills in their work was having a positive impact on their own stress levels and also that they were using the coaching structure and framework for goal setting to improve their own personal performance. They commented that they were more aware of other people's thinking, more open to ideas, could confidently stretch others and were more generous with giving acknowledgement – important characteristics of a management style which can support performance improvement.

The greatest value of this coaching skills programme has been in enabling managers to use coaching skills to support their staff. Jason Sadler, Chief Executive Officer of HSBC Insurance (Singapore) Pte Limited, believes managers have derived benefit from their coach training and that the initiative has produced improvements in communication skills as intended. He has noticed a positive impact in managers' behaviours generally and particularly in behaviours in meetings; he is 'seeing people asking questions in a way that uses the guidance from the coach training'.

The coaching principles will now be rolled out to other heads of department through a coaching programme developed in-house. This in-house programme will be less intense and will specifically focus on supporting the development of leadership and management skills in the organization. The emphasis will be on helping line managers to use coaching skills in developing their staff, rather than in training them formally as coaches.

My thanks to my colleague Eileen Arney who produced this case study.

Action learning

At the same time as the rise of coaching, there has been a parallel resurgence of interest in the practice known as 'Action Learning'.

Reg Revans, the distinguished UK writer and academic who developed and promoted the concept some 50 years ago, argued that:

Action learning is cradled in the very task itself, asking whether that task can be done so that, merely by reflecting upon how it currently seems to be done, the very doing of it supplies the learning generally offered far from the scenes of managerial activity [4, p. 50].

The basic principles of action learning were recently outlined in the following terms by Professor Michael Osbaldeston of Cranfield School of Management [5]:

- participants tackle problems in real time
- participants meet in small learning groups ('sets')
- each set holds intermittent meetings over a fixed programme cycle
- problems are relevant to the participants' own workplace realities
- a supportive, collaborative learning process is engendered within a set
- process is based on reflection, questioning, conjecture and challenge
- each set is supported by a skilled facilitator ('set adviser')
- participants take action between set meetings to resolve their problem.

Participants in action learning groups or sets therefore pass through three stages. First, they are exposed to new ideas and knowledge (a cognitive phase); secondly, they are encouraged to internalize their new knowledge and change what they do (a behavioural stage); thirdly, they use their knowledge and skills to improve organizational performance (an application stage). Practices differ across organizations and some looser structures, called learning sets, are evident in practice. For example the use of facilitators may vary.

Two organizations which have incorporated action learning into development programme are the US candy manufacturer Just Born (Case study 8.4) and the international charity Christian Aid which has a UK base (Case study 8.5). Both organizations see facilitated learning sets and a project-based approach as a valuable element in their senior development plans. Support and challenge principles are capable of wide application and extension.

Case study 8.4 Developing leadership talent at Just Born

Background

Just Born's products are well known throughout the USA. The company manufactures candy, including Mike and Ikes®, Hot Tamales®, Peanut Chews® and a range of jelly beans. Its best-known product is a yellow marshmallow chick – Marshmallow Peeps®; 1.2 billion Peeps are produced in the course of a year.

Some 600 associates (the term used by Just Born) are employed at two factories and in management, administration and support roles. The largest of the factories is in Bethlehem, Pennsylvania and the second in Philadelphia, Pennsylvania.

Plant operatives are unionized and their progress is mainly determined by seniority. This case study concerns the process used to develop the 135 'support associates', who range from the most senior managers through to the most junior clerk.

HR processes and interventions are built against a background of strong commitment to learning and development from the top. While Just Born intends to continue as a family-owned confectionary company, it ensures that all associates receive opportunities to grow their leadership capability. Its stated mission is:

Aggressive growth and above average profitability through superior leadership.

One of the company's co-CEOs, Ross Born (a grandson of the founder Sam Born), in a recent interview for T+D magazine expressed his view that:

Learning is like breathing for us. We operate in a changing world. In our industry we have globalization; we have low cost competition; and we use a lot of technology. If you don't learn in this industry, you'll go out of business. Our competition is learning; we're learning all the time.

Alignment with the business

Meloney Sallie-Dosunmu, Just Born's Manager of Organizational Effectiveness and Talent, is a key member of the HR team. She works closely with five HR business partners who carry significant development responsibilities within their businesses. She describes her role as one of 'talent management with a focus on development'. Alignment is achieved through the cascade of Just Born's business objectives down through the operating departments. The processes involved are expressed in terms of a People Development System (PDS). This is designed to ensure that learning and development are aligned with the corporate strategy and that associates are equipped with the skills needed for future and current roles.

Two elements of PDS are of particular importance: a Performance Management Process (PMP) and a Career Development Process (CDP). Both involve an interview and agreement between the associate and his or her boss and written output. In the PMP discussion, associate and supervisor will agree up to four personal objectives and two competencies – the latter are skills or capabilities that the associate needs to drive or improve the personal objectives. A corporate competency glossary is available on the company's intranet to support these discussions. Once the competencies have been identified, the associate and supervisor are responsible for developing a simple learning plan for the year.

All support associates participate in the Performance Management Process which concentrates mainly on development in current roles. The Career Development Process focuses on future potential and is linked with Just Born's succession planning process. Most of the eligible associates undertake CDP discussions which are focused on future job interests and long-term career goals.

Meloney Sallie-Dosunmu, along with the other HR Business Partners, collates and records the output of the PMP and PDS discussions, while seeking to coordinate opportunities and movement across functions to build up the talent pool. Recently, for example, an associate transferred from finance to marketing, providing a visible example of the benefits of growing future potential from within the company rather than automatically looking outside. On occasions, she has to manage expectations and encourage a more realistic attitude towards career development. Together with the HR business partners, she supports the less experienced supervisors in their discussions. Effective processes are seen as essential for alignment with business goals. Mark McLaughlin, the Vice President for HR, puts it as follows:

The entire system must align, including even our annual merit process. Support Associates' merit increase is based on two sets of criteria. The first criteria, input by the supervisor measures achievement of their PMP objectives, delivery of daily job performance, achievement of PMP learning and CDP development plans and community volunteerism. The second criteria, input by the supervisor and two peers, measures team behaviour and results, customer service behaviour and results and the degree to which the associate walks-the-talk of our company philosophy. By aligning merit with the PDS, it ensures accountability and impact to our strategic objectives.

The High Performance Leadership Development Program (HPLD)

In 2003, Just Born introduced a significant leadership programme – the HPLD. Up to 30 associates in a given year will participate in the programme. The design of the programme has evolved over time, but has always been closely linked with Just Born's 'Wow ... Now' improvement process. This is a customized 'Kaizen' process which offers a systematic process to collect data and identify improvement opportunities, using a step-by-step approach.

Participants in the HPLD spend six months on the programme. They are developed in groups of 8–10. There is a classroom element to the programme: after initial orientation they begin with a three-day 'boot camp' and then meet once a month for modules of up to three-day tuition and discussion. Subjects include continuous improvement to systematic problem-solving and value (key element of Wow ... Now) through to the softer skills, for example, coaching. As the programme has evolved, so tuition has passed from external consultants to the internal Just Born HR staff.

HPLD is not, however, designed as a taught course. It is closely linked to the workplace and all participants undertake two projects over its duration. These are action learning projects, which contribute to the participant's development, but also provide a tangible business benefit to Just Born. The individual project must deliver $1300 to the business and the group project must deliver $10 000; these savings must be agreed and signed off by the finance department. Illustrative projects include:

- improvements in determining the weight allowance on customer ordering (this produced a saving of almost $400 000 for the company)
- better mistake proofing on bulk order delivery – benefit of $78 000
- improvements in production process on 8 oz candy bars – benefits of $30 000.

The responsibility for the action learning project rests with the individual. They must, however, identify an Executive Mentor at a senior level within Just Born and bring progress reports on their project to their fellow learners in the group. HR staff are available to act as facilitators and coaches to the group.

It is evident that alignment is a powerful theme running through all Just Born's development activities. Indeed, Meloney Sallie-Dosunmu expresses her biggest challenge in the following terms:

> We must always ask ourselves what we can contribute to the business. We must be aware of the current over-riding business challenges (which could, for example, be the promotion of a new brand) and ask how our learning efforts are assisting or could assist.

Adapted from an article that appeared in Training and Development, May 2006, by Bingham, T. and Galagan, P. with permission from the ASTD.

Case study 8.5 Action learning for management development – Christian Aid

Background

Christian Aid is the overseas development charity of 39 Christian (mainly Protestant) churches in the UK and Ireland. Its stated purpose is to:

> Strive for a new world transformed by an end to poverty and campaign to change the rules that keep people poor.

Unlike some charities that deliver aid directly, Christian Aid seeks to work in partnership and through local organizations.

> *Because we believe in strengthening people to find their own solutions to the problems they face, we support local organizations, which are best placed to understand local needs.*

Christian Aid employs about 750 staff; 500 based in the UK and 250 spread across 26 overseas offices in Africa, Asia, the Middle East, Latin America and the Caribbean. The number of staff in any country overseas can vary from 35 to as few as two. One of Christian Aid's major business objectives is to move the decision-making process as close as possible to the point of impact, which requires a strengthening of the management capability of all managers based outside the head office. This may also lead to a greater number of people being employed outside the head office and is part of a general process aimed at decentralizing decision-making and empowering managers at a local level.

The management development programme

Jimmy Naudi was appointed Christian Aid's Head of Learning and Development – a newly created role – in July 2006. However, he inherited, and is seeking to develop, a major initiative aimed at about 145 senior staff. In his words, this management development programme is designed to ensure that:

> *The right people with the right skills are in the right places. We need to be confident that our managers have the appropriate skills and awareness of Christian Aid without feeling the need to pass every decision upwards.*

The programme emphasizes self-awareness and the development of the 'softer' interpersonal management skills. Indeed, the management development programme begins with all participants completing a 360° feedback questionnaire which covers the following topics:

- Managing relationships – manages relationships both internally and outside Christian Aid. Gets the best out of staff and situations by effective management and support and helping people to contribute effectively to the organization's wider objectives.
- Leading and managing a team – manages performance effectively – encouraging strong performance and addressing poor performance in a timely and consistent manner.

- Decision-making and problem-solving – takes responsibility for solving issues and finding appropriate ways of overcoming them. Makes decisions appropriate to own level and situation.
- Strategy and vision – establishes strategic objectives, develops plans and prioritizes to achieve Christian Aid's vision. Challenges existing ways of working and provides direction.

Important organizational considerations also determine the programme's design. One is the need to create an on-going culture of mutual support, where managers from across the organization can seek guidance and advice from each other. They also need to be thoroughly aware of Christian Aid's philosophy, policies and strategies at all levels – particularly given the increasing local responsibility for decision-making. Christian Aid's management development programme is therefore based around action learning.

The structure of the programme

The programme is delivered to groups of managers who participate over a six-month period. So far, three groups of about 12 each have completed the programme and a new group of 23 has recently started it. The first three groups that piloted the programme were mainly based in the UK. But from now on the aim is to ensure that all senior overseas managers participate.

Currently, the programme consists of two three-day residential sessions. Both are held immediately after major Christian Aid events, such as Christian Aid Week or a significant Christian Aid campaign event, when overseas managers will be in the UK to participate.

All these group events involve some instructor-led elements. However, the group of participants agrees on the management themes based on their 360° Feedback Profiles. Programme participants are divided into small 'learning' sets of ideally six participants. A facilitator initially supports each set.

The group begins the process by sharing and considering the 360° feedback. Participants then choose a business issue that will be firmly embedded in the workplace, but designed to develop or enhance relevant skills. Project topics are always centred on interpersonal skills and recent examples have included:

- managing difficult relationships with colleagues, peers and direct reports
- influencing other policies outside the organization
- demonstrating effective leadership
- introducing a programme of change while maintaining team motivation.

At their first meeting, participants share their project and seek on-going advice and support from their learning set on how they should proceed. The set is expected to offer different ideas/suggestions and act as a sounding board for new and challenging ideas.

Clearly, different people will respond to action learning activities with varying degrees of enthusiasm. Some will evidently be holding back and not offering the support that they could, or be less forthcoming on the nature of their problem. This can be overcome by capable facilitation and establishing firm processes that encourage participation. Jimmy Naudi has produced guidance on creating such a process. As the group progresses, such processes become standard practice, almost habitual and the need for an imposed structure and facilitator disappears.

The project's progress is then kept under continual review within the learning set, through e-mail or telephone conferences before the next group meeting.

Some issues

Jimmy Naudi is a firm believer in action learning. He feels that it fits well with Christian Aid's management philosophy of self-directed problem-solving within a supportive framework. In his view, it is essential that those in more remote locations across the world are not at a disadvantage in terms of access and support.

Some problems have arisen and some changes have been required. On one occasion, for example, the participants were guarded about sharing their 360° feedback in front of the whole group, so one-to-one sessions were required. However, the fundamental model will remain unchanged.

The ultimate test of success will be the extent to which the learning sets become on-going mutual support groups beyond the life of the programme and that managers are more effective at leading and managing their staff and operations.

The attraction of action learning and, indeed, with all 'support and challenge' or 'helping activities' is that they can be customized round the specific circumstances of the individual learner in the context of the organization. The down-side, however, is that they are resource-intensive – or, putting it simply, expensive. When introducing such initiatives it becomes even more important to consider and demonstrate the value that they bring to the organization and the individual. Value, evaluation and validation will be considered in Chapter 10. Next, however, we will consider the impact that the new opportunities offered by technology have had on our work in recent years.

References

[1]. Garvey, B. (2004) The Mentoring, Counselling, Coaching Debate: Call a Rose by any other Name and perhaps it's a Bramble. Development and Learning in Organizations, 18(2), 6–8.

[2]. Jarvis, J. (2004) Coaching and Buying Coaching Services. London: Chartered Institute of Personnel and Development. Available at: http://www.cipd.co.uk/NR/rdonlyres/C31A728E-7411-4754-9644-46A84EC9CFEE/0/2995coachbuyingservs.pdf

[3]. Chartered Institute of Personnel and Development (2006) Coaching. London: CIPD. Available at: http://www.cipd.co.uk/subjects/lrnanddev/coachmntor/coaching.htm?IsSrchRes=1

[4]. Revans, R. (1998) ABC of Action Learning: Empowering Managers to Act and to Learn from Action. London: Lemos and Crane.

[5]. Osbaldeston, M. Action learning. Presentation prepared and given at the CIPD Annual Learning, Training and Development Conference, 12–14 April, 2005.

9

Embracing Technology

'Support and challenge' and its component elements have been a feature of training and learning for as long as learners have existed. The next proposition, however, is one which would not have appeared in a list prepared a decade ago. Since then we have seen the emergence and the absorption of e-learning.

> **Proposition 8**   Technology is becoming an important enabler in people development, but there are many conceptual and practical issues to be resolved surrounding its implementation.

The term 'e-learning' first emerged in late 1999. Suppliers of computer-based training were full of optimism and were considering the implications of delivery through the web. The US-based supplier, CBT systems, rebranded themselves as 'Smartforce – the e-learning company' and held a satellite broadcast to announce the change a month later. However, if distributed technology products (CBT discs and CD ROMs which do not depend on the connectivity of computers) are included, it could be argued that e-learning stretches back several decades. The current CIPD definition of e-learning is 'learning that is delivered, enabled or mediated by electronic technology, for the explicit purpose of training in organizations' [1].

Subsequently, the progress of e-learning has been gradual rather than spectacular. In the corporate sector, e-learning has almost certainly advanced most in the USA and the figures set out in Table 9.1 are drawn from the ASTD's annual 'State of the Industry' survey [2].

It is possible to chart the progress of e-learning across three distinct phases. First, there was a need to move beyond the initial hype. In its early phases, e-learning was shamefully oversold. One of the main arguments advanced was that it was possible to save the travel and accommodation costs associated with residential courses – never mind whether anyone learned anything! When it came from the suppliers of

Table 9.1 Per cent of training delivered by learning technology

1997	9.1
1998	8.5
1999	8.4
2000	8.8
2001	10.5
2002	15.4
2003	23.6
2004	27.0

Source: ASTD State of the Industry Report

e-learning such over-promotion was not surprising. However, the difficulties were compounded, certainly in the UK, by an uncritical attitude from Government (who saw e-learning as a cheap way of increasing the amount of training) and some industry commentators.

The second phase was one in which a number of critical issues were identified. Let's take the obvious: the computer literacy or sophistication of the learners themselves. One story sticks in the author's mind. A UK retailer (who has asked to remain anonymous) decided to introduce e-learning at their stores. They ensured that PCs were available and sent out CD-ROMs accompanied by detailed instructions on their use. The following week they received a plaintive telephone call:

It says in our instructions that you should look on the desk-top. We have no desks at the store so have placed the PCs on tables. What should we do?

The third stage, which is where we are now, can be described as developing best practice. To mark the fifth anniversary of e-learning in 2004, the CIPD held an on-line poll to monitor progress, identify problems and offer some thoughts for the future. The overall view is that, while there is still much practical work to be done on implementation, e-learning is now accepted as an essential feature of training delivery.

One of the comments submitted by a respondent offered a good summary of the current position:

E-learning in its early years did suffer from being over-hyped. However, I now feel that it is suffering a hangover from this phase. The potential for e-learning is huge, but we still have too many people who are frightened of this technology. Training and learning does not need to be about stand-up trainers in training rooms and it is also not about technology. It is about meeting the needs of learners as efficiently and effectively as possible.

Two studies are presented in Case study 9.1 and Case study 9.2.

Reuters is a knowledge-intensive organization providing news and information for clients across the world. The workforce consists mainly of knowledge workers or 'symbolic analysts' to return to the categorization introduced in Chapter 2.

The Hilton Group, the hotel chain which has already been the subject of a case study in Chapter 6 (p. 127) also have a very dispersed workforce (in the personal services category). Here well designed and effectively supported e-learning is seen as a key element in the company's development and retention strategy.

Both are large organizations who have thought through their e-learning strategy and are prepared to commit the attention and resources to make e-learning effective. One thing that we have learned is that e-learning is not a soft or easy option.

Case study 9.1 E-learning for journalists at Reuters

Background

Reuters is a knowledge-intensive organization which provides up-to-date news and financial information to clients across the world. Currently, Reuters employs 15 000 staff (of whom 4000 are based in the UK). The main journalism function (known internally as Editorial) – which is the subject of this case study – employs 2300 people (mainly text journalists, but including video-journalists, photographers and graphic specialists) who work in 197 bureaux in almost as many countries.

In 2001, Charles Jennings joined Reuters as a consultant and subsequently became Global Head of Learning. As a former University Professor in Electronic Communication, he has a strong awareness of the potential of e-learning. The first bespoke module, on legal defamation, was introduced in 2002. Today, there are some 35 bespoke modules available on Editorial topics and this area has witnessed the most successful uptake of e-learning within Reuters. Each month more modules are added to the portfolio. Although e-learning has been successful, it still only accounts for 5–10% of total training time spent at Reuters. It is not surprising, therefore, that much of the current focus is on ways of embedding the use of e-learning in the organization and making its use more widespread.

Why e-learning?

Nigel Stephenson, Reuters Editorial Training Manager for Europe, Middle East and Africa, puts the case for e-learning as follows:

> Cost is undoubtedly a factor but so are a number of practical considerations on access to courses. Many bureaux are small with two or three

staff or even a single member. Releasing them for off-the-job training can be difficult in terms of sustaining the operation. In addition, journalists work at high speed and are under time pressure – 'tell me what I need to know about this subject?'

Course-based events remain a feature of Reuters training but, in Nigel Stephenson's view:

The classroom is not the best place for information, when it's available in advance as a download. The classroom is good for tips and war stories, skills and sharing experiences.

Although the e-learning modules produced for Editorial have been designed primarily for stand-alone use, they have been incorporated as pre- and post-course activity in course design. For example, participants in the basic journalism course (which every new starter should attend) are required to have undertaken the following e-learning modules before they enter the classroom:

Headlines

- story structure
- legal defamation
- hoaxes
- filing drill
- grammar
- interviewing.

The e-learning modules in the 'Editorial' series are similar in style and use a standard template. They are between 20 and 40 minutes in length and encourage the learner to progress through text and undertake a series of quizzes and tests. Techniques extend beyond 'tick the correct answer' and include 'drag and drop' and 'matching' games. However, the fact that some learners will access the material from countries where there is no broadband has meant that media-rich alternatives have been avoided.

The production process begins with the training specialists within Editorial specifying their requirements, which is then used to produce the detailed content. This is handed over to the central Reuters e-learning team who commission an instructional designer to write the storyboard. The final product is produced by a software development house at an estimated cost of £2000 per module.

Progress to date

Reuters Editorial have now reached the stage where they feel that e-learning is a cost-effective way of promoting the relevant learning. Immediate feedback on modules has been positive and their use is growing. The site has been extensively marketed using announcements on the Editorial website, e-mails to regional groups, colour fliers using titles and sales pitches on conference calls.

The Reuters training team recognize that there are a number of technical problems to be overcome: user-access can be difficult; there is a lack of easy fit with other systems (for example, the enterprise and customer relationship management systems); and some users report that the technology can be a bit chunky. However, Richard Taylor, the Global Head of Training for News and Data, emphasizes that once they get in there they find something of value. No major revision to module design is under consideration, therefore the challenge is to ensure that the e-learning produced is embedded in organizational practice.

A particular success has been achieved in the Asia region. Here, an established Regional Training Manager agreed a target with the Senior Team that staff should undertake an average of four modules in the course of the year. This figure was exceeded, though in part this may reflect a ready cultural acceptance in the region of the need to achieve centrally set targets. Progress towards these targets was included as an element in the appraisal of local managers. Building on this success, in January 2005, the News Management Executive team has set a target of three modules per person.

However, as Richard Taylor is keen to emphasize:

Ownership for individual performance and learning must rest with the line management. The training function, through their supply of material and use of channels, must not set out to disintermediate that process.

The future of e-learning

A number of initiatives are under way at Reuters. To extend the range of material available in Editorial, a content swap has taken place with the BBC.

Virtual classroom-on-line seminars to update worldwide staff on changing applications (particularly around technology) are used extensively throughout Reuters – one is taking place practically every day somewhere in the world.

The next step, once the existing content has been embedded, will be to create better links with knowledge management. This is a critical element in Charles Jennings' agenda as he seeks to move the function from volume to value. Some parts of the business are currently piloting the use of on-line performance support tools, mainly round the customer relationship management system. These are accessible panels which will offer on-line advice on technical activities that the user encounters during his or her day-to-day work. The potential of such just-in-time learning could be considerable and learner acceptance is under review in the pilot.

Case study 9.2 Embedding e-learning globally at Hilton University

Background

The Hilton Group is committed to offering learning opportunities to its team members irrespective of location; in 2002 it established an e-learning platform, Hilton University. In part, this followed recognition that, given the geographical dispersal of the operation, there were limits to what could be achieved through the provision of residential courses. To quote from a Company vision statement:

> *Whether people are working in a small hotel in Madagascar or a major hotel in London or Paris, we want to offer them the same learning opportunities – irrespective of background, gender and ethnics. We take the view that e-learning is the ideal method to achieve this ambition.*

From the outset it was felt that, provided it was properly embedded and supported, e-learning was particularly appropriate for the hotel environment. People could learn in their own time and, in short study periods, acquire relevant information to help them do their jobs and develop personally.

The next section outlines the approach that was used to ensure that e-learning would be effective and the subsequent section describes the results and implications of a survey of learners undertaken in 2005.

The approach

The Hilton University Learning and Development team have taken a number of steps to ensure that e-learning is of benefit to the organization and is valued by the individual learner. These initiatives can be grouped under the headings of access, support and relevance. Much of the local interpretation and delivery of these initiatives lie in the hands of the Regional HR and Management teams.

Maarten Staps, the International Learning and Development Manager, talks of 'five building blocks of the learner experience': hardware; software; connectivity; learning zone; and service.

Access

Clearly, any shortcomings in the technical requirements (hardware, software and connectivity) will be all too evident and cause frustration to the learner. Here, it is important to emphasize that content needs to be accessed by learners in more than 80 countries. The intention is that learning zones, equipped with computers, headphones, printers and Internet connection are made available at all hotels, even the smallest.

Service

Service is about personal support. Every hotel has an HR manager; most have an e-learning champion and/or a learning manager – though the individuals concerned will be combining this responsibility with another job. The precise responsibilities of those supporting roles are determined locally – it is considered wrong to be too prescriptive, but the clear intention is that the individual learner receives support as well as access opportunities.

Relevance

Currently, the University is organized into seven faculties: management, finance, operations, business development, human resources, executive education and research and an IT professional development programme. Hilton International have found much value in making generic material available but, as the University develops, are increasing the provision of bespoke or customized learning activities. Across the generic range of content, the most used materials include time management, communication skills and the finance courses; the popularity of these items is thought to reflect the need to acquire new skills as learners advance to a management position beyond a specialized functional role in a hotel. Customized and bespoke material covers 'Hilton specific' areas, for example e-commerce and distribution, reservations, account management and marketing.

The e-learning material is delivered through a public website – www.hilton-university.com to enable learning at any pace and in any place and is supported by a learning management system. As a result, the number of people who access e-learning across the company is known exactly. Some of these users are encouraged to participate by line managers, perhaps at the time of their annual development review; some e-learning is required before team members attend residential courses; However, most of the learners select their own courses out of a library of more than 600 courses. Hilton International is satisfied with this profile at this time. In the words of Andrea Kluit, Hilton's Director of International Learning and Development:

> *E-learning requires considerable self-discipline in a hotel environment and the good news is that so many people are doing it. It has by now become an integral part of our learning and development activities worldwide.*

The survey

By late 2004, there was a recognized need to improve the technological infrastructure for the Hilton University. Learners were gaining access through a number of different systems and there was a need to achieve consolidation through the introduction of a single learning management system. The implementation of the system was considered an appropriate time to gain information on the learner perspective – access, usability and quality of experience and their perceptions on the value and relevance of the learning activities available to them.

Accordingly, between April and May 2005, an Internet survey was sent to 4500 learners worldwide – over 1800 submissions were returned, a completion rate of some 40%, which is good for a survey of this nature.

The overall headlines were encouraging. On most areas there was a positive message: for example, over 70% strongly agreed with the statement, 'After the login it is easy to find learning activities which satisfy needs'. Most importantly, over 90% of respondents strongly agreed or agreed with the statement that, 'the courses help with my personal development'. Even more encouragingly, over 70% strongly agreed or agreed with the statement, 'what I learned yesterday in my learning activity, I use today at my work'. This is a remarkably high figure for learning transfer – even taking into account the element of self-selection among some of the Hilton University learners in the first place and those who were sufficiently committed to return the Internet questionnaire.

Almost 90% strongly agreed or agreed with the statement, 'I am happy with Hilton University' and 98% with the statement, 'If a friend or colleague asked me if I could recommend Hilton University, I would say yes'. One important question, given the challenge of staff retention, was 'the opportunity to develop myself through Hilton University is a factor in me deciding to continue my career in Hilton'. Here, 37% said yes and 50% said, 'it isn't the (decisive) factor but it is important to me'.

The future direction

As a result of the survey and the overall impression on e-learning's value and acceptability, Hilton feels certain that e-learning will continue to play an important role in the learning, training and development of its team members.

Plans for expansion include the provision of more customized or bespoke learning activities. The 2005 survey will be regarded as an initial benchmark to ensure that access and support improve. Other targets relate to volume expansion – a greater number of learners and more use of the range of learning activities are desired.

Another set of ambitions surround the use of technology as a collaborative tool for learning. The current system has asynchronous discussion forums to allow community discussion and support – the 2005 survey indicates that these were found useful by the learners. However, there is some education to be done before the organization and the individual take full advantage of the potential offered by this facility.

The Hilton University and its scale, scope and ambition is unique within the hospitality sector. To appreciate fully the level of enthusiasm and commitment of those involved, it should be remembered that the entire project was conceived and implemented at a time when the hotel industry was going through one of its most turbulent periods.

The University is currently starting to use a Virtual Classroom solution which will soon be fully integrated into the Learning Management System – to improve the seamless provision of all sorts of learning activities to the learners. The Hilton Learning and Development team are optimistic that developing technologies will emerge further to enhance the learning experience.

Some principles

Anyone who has watched the progress of e-learning must be depressed about the past but optimistic about the future. There is much more that can be achieved and will be achieved than has been evident to date. However, if we are to progress, people development professionals must not allow themselves to be seduced by the technology – or more correctly seduced by the potential of the technology.

The suggestion here is that five principles should underline any strategy for e-learning. It will be seen that these are consistent with the themes advanced throughout this book. They are:

- Start with the learner: recognize the limitations of the population that you are trying to reach.
- Relevance drives out resistance: if the e-learning material is seen as relating to something that matters in the organization, people are more likely to try to use it.
- Take account of intermediaries: this is simply a matter of reinforcing the lessons of the previous chapter on support and challenge. Much learning requires an intermediary to advise and direct the learner. This is just as true of e-learning; it will not be successful if taken in isolation from other learning.
- Embed activity in the organization: this is a subtler point, but follows from the previous one. E-learning modules should be seen as one element in an organizational

learning strategy; where possible their use should be linked with instructor-led courses and other human resource management systems (for example, performance appraisal).

■ Support and automate: this final catch-all point reinforces and underlines the others. E-learning does not offer us the opportunity to automate all our learning processes, instead, it is a powerful new element in a wider strategy which requires support for learners in the context in which they learn.

In short, recognition of the limits of e-learning is an essential part of any strategy for its application. The next case study on language training in India, Case study 9.3, provides a good illustration. It also introduces the term 'blended learning' which has become popular in the e-learning context.

Case study 9.3 E-learning for language training in India – Liqvid

Background

English is a primary language for the urban elite in India; it is the second language for a large population of educated city dwellers who have contributed significantly to the global competitiveness of the country. Indeed, it has been widely recognized that the ability to communicate in English has become one of the biggest factors determining the economic growth of the nation.

One consequence is a rising demand for training in the English language. This can arise from college students who would like to improve their employment prospects, through to organizations who employ significant numbers of people who need to communicate regularly using English.

Liqvid employs some 100 people and is based in a suburb of Delhi. It produces customized e-learning products for clients and has developed a range of products which support English language training in India. Their main product, English Edge, was developed by licensing content from BBC Worldwide, in October 2003 and formally launched in October 2004. This was the first time that BBC Worldwide licensed content for a CD-ROM-based Instructor-led language course, bespoke to a particular country. The course is based on content from the BBC World News English course and contains BBC news footage that Liqvid has combined with local content to provide a bespoke course for the Indian market. The issues involved in adapting the product for Indian users provide some useful insights on the attractions and problems in using e-learning.

The learning challenge

According to Rajiv Tandon, the Liqvid Vice-President in charge of the customization and distribution of English Edge, there are a number of issues facing Indians who aspire to attain proficiency in spoken English. The first is pronunciation and people from various parts of the country face unique region-specific challenges. Ideally, therefore, the teaching approach adopted should reflect the particular difficulties faced by the learners. The second is the fact that many learners 'think Indian and speak English'. They will translate phrases that are common in their languages into something that appears clumsy in English – for example they will ask: '*What is your good name?*' which is a literal translation from Hindi. A third area concerns grammar: mistakes that can arise in the use of tenses, definite and indefinite articles and prepositions, among others. The fourth area concerns listening and comprehension – there is a need for the learner rapidly to appreciate the nuances of spoken English delivered in a variety of different accents.

Together these constitute a demanding set of learning needs. Moreover, the learning product will be used in some very different contexts. In some instances, college students will be accessing Liqvid's products along with their regular domain-specific courses. In other cases, they will be accessing the material as part of a corporate training programme. Recently, for example Liqvid has entered into an arrangement with Frankfinn – India's largest cabin crew training provider for aspiring air-hostesses. 'English Edge' will be available at the 68 Frankfinn training centres and become a compulsory course for all students and an integral part of their long-term diploma.

Given this range of potential users, Liqvid places considerable emphasis on the need for instructor support of learners. This they describe as blended learning. Part of the delivery package involves extensive trainer manuals designed to support trainers and learner courseware to sustain individual learners. According to Rajiv Tandon, most implementations are 50% computer-based training (CBT) and 50% instructor-led training (ILT). Instructor support is important in India in two respects. First, instructors can motivate learners and encourage them to continue and persevere in the event of difficulties. Secondly, since technology-based learning is a new concept, there is a need to encourage learners to try CBT.

While the instructor is important, in Rajiv Tandon's view, the products will always be enriched as technology develops and will also be deployed in self-learning modes. At present this is evident in three separate features of English Edge.

Product enhancement

The first important feature is the use of the BBC News English as the underlying product. This contains news items and current affairs clips. As such it is up-to-date and can engage the adult learner and be seen as relevant to their needs.

The second feature, which is a result of the growing sophistication of the technology, involves audio recording and pronunciation comparison tools. These allow the learner to listen to the right pronunciation and compare this pronunciation with that delivered by the learner. The comparative information is presented in the form of sound waves shown on the screen – these highlight the difference between the target pronunciation and that produced.

The third feature is the use of interactive learning activities. These include on-line quizzes and on-going assessment tools which can, as with the case of Frankfinn, contribute to the overall certificate. In the view of Rajiv Tandon, 'progress can be a powerful incentive'.

To date much of the English language training in India has been directed at motivated learners. The model, as can be seen, recognizes the limits of technology and depends on the supportive interventions of the instructors. Such interventions become more important for less motivated and less confident learners.

There is scope for future product enrichment using technology, but there are limits to such enrichment. However, Rajiv Tandon is optimistic:

> *Technology can enable ordinary trainers to create an extraordinary learning experience and hence will be ideal for markets like India, where the availability of high quality training resources in remote locations is a problem.*

One of the most thoughtful of writers on e-learning has been Professor Allison Rossett of the University of San Diego. Writing with Rebecca Vaughan Frazee, she defined blended learning as follows:

> *Blended learning (BL) integrates seemingly opposite approaches, such as formal learning, face-to-face and online experiences, directed paths and reliance on self-direction, and digital references and collegial connections, in order to achieve individual and organizational goals*

and identified three different models of blends:

> *An Anchor Blend starts with a defining and substantive classroom event, following by independent experiences that include interaction with online*

resources, structured workplace learning activities, online learning and ref-
erence, diagnostics, and assessments.

The Bookend Blend is characterised by a three-part experience: some-
thing introductory; an essential, substantive and meaty learning experience,
online or F2F, [face to face] and then something that concludes and extends
the learning into practice at work.

The Field Blend is most distinct from training-as-usual. It is employee-
centric, with each individual surround by many kinds of assets and continu-
ous choices about when and where and whether to reach for them [3].

To re-emphasize, what is important is to remember that e-learning is a learning activity. Learners learn in different ways and in different contexts. This demands a thoughtful and considered perspective, as the approach currently being developed by IBM and set out in Case study 9.4 illustrates.

We may not have seen the best of e-learning yet, but it is here to stay.

Case study 9.4 Technology and learning: an IBM perspective

For several decades, IBM have had a considerable impact on the place of technology in learning. In 1999, for example, IBM introduced Basic Blue for Managers, a core training programme which was implemented in the company throughout the world [4]. This programme went on to win awards and gain wide recognition within the training and learning industry. Particular emphasis was placed on a phased approach which combined e-learning simulations, in-field experience, workshop sessions and post-course technology-enabled collaboration; subsequently 'Basic Blue' has been cited widely as an example of effective blended learning [4].

Increasingly, IBM are developing consultancy solutions and services and these include an integrated suite of tools known as 'Workplace Collaborative Services-Learning'. What is of interest in the context of the broader discussion is the underlying model they have established and their views on the way in which the interface between learning and technology is developing and will continue to develop. A starting point is recognition that learning will be affected by a combination of factors including commercial and business considerations, work and lifestyle preferences and technology. For example, when challenged that much technology-enabled learning will only be attractive to global organizations with widely dispersed populations, IBM's learning solutions team point at the increasing attractions of home-based working for smaller and domestic organizations.

Further, IBM are keen to emphasize that technology is an enabler not a total answer. As Joe Fitzpatrick, a Programme Director Learning at the

Company's Dublin Software Laboratory, puts it: 'if someone buys our products and believes that the software alone will solve all of their learning issues then we know that we are heading for problems'.

The learning model

The premise behind the IBM approach is learning and work will increasingly converge to a single on-going activity rather than distinct processes. Generally, in today's organization three distinct types of learning can be identified.

Formal learning

This type of learning takes place separately from work. It can include classroom courses or simulations; it is often prescribed and sometimes based on a curriculum and results in certification.

Enabled learning

This describes learning that is experienced as part of work. It can involve collaboration with others in the workplace; self-motivated or directed search and discovery can be constituents in enabled learning and there are strong links with knowledge management.

Embedded learning

Here, learning is entrenched within work. Learning arises from, or is triggered by, the workflow itself – so the learning opportunity is timely and the content relevant. The term 'activity centric learning' is used by IBM, but they emphasize that this sort of opportunity does not simply arise in routine processes but can occur across a range of workplace activity where there is technical or intellectual content. The challenge, of course, is to get the right information in the right form at the right time.

It is important not to see 'formal', 'enabled', 'embedded' as alternatives or indeed, as a progression. There will, for example, always be a requirement for formal learning where compliance needs arise (for example, to meet health and safety objectives or external regulation). IBM's approach is to create an effective range of technology-based tools that will be available to assist all three forms of learning to take place. Such tools will include learning management systems and course catalogues to support formal learning;

collaborative and search tools to support enabled learning; and transaction and user process tools (linked with business process management more generally) to support embedded learning. In the words of Tyler Tribe, the Global Product Manager of Learning and Team Space Workplace:

We need to offer a range of solutions and let the organization determine which is most appropriate for them at the stage they are at. They need to look at how their people learn and how they can assist in developing skills within cost and time constraints.

In most IBM client organizations, the emphasis is still on the support of formal learning. However, IBM see considerable potential in collaborative learning. For example, in many enterprises there has been a growth in instant messaging. Some of this activity has a learning component beyond the immediate exchange of information. This suggests there is fertile ground for collaborative learning and here web conferences or virtual classrooms are likely to grow in importance. In other organizations the cultural acceptance of collaborative learning could be more problematic.

References

[1]. Chartered Institute of Personnel and Development (2006) E-learning: Progress and Prospects. London: CIPD. Available at: http://www.cipd.co.uk/ subjects/ lrnanddev/elearning/elearnprog.htm
[2]. Sugrue, B. and Rivera, R.J. (2005) State of the Industry 2005: ASTD Annual Review of Trends in the Workplace Learning and Performance. Alexandria, VA: American Society for Training and Development.
[3]. Rossett, A. and Frazee, R.V. (2006) Blended Learning Opportunities. New York: American Management Association. Available from: http://www. amanet.org/ blended/index.htm
[4]. Lewis, N. and Orton, P. (2000) The Five Attributes of Innovative E-learning. T+D, 54(6), 47–51.

10

Delivering Value

This chapter considers the final proposition, which is set out below. It covers an important topic: 'evaluating training' and 'assessing learning' were both identified in the research outlined in Chapter 5 (p. 97) as significant challenges facing people development professionals. We will describe some important work in progress, but offer less firm conclusions or recommendations than in other parts of the book. As a profession, our ideas on measuring value have left much to be desired. There have, however, been exceptions and some excellent work is starting to emerge; much of this is built round an understanding of how stakeholders perceive the value that learning brings to the organization.

> **Proposition 9** It is important to demonstrate the value to be derived from people development activities, but traditional hierarchical training evaluation may not be the most appropriate method.

This ninth and last proposition is the one that has attracted much energy and excitement in the profession. Unfortunately, we have produced more heat than light. The proposition is carefully drafted. It encourages us to think about the value rather than 'proving'.

Some of the most interesting recent ideas have been developed by the ASTD and Tony O'Driscoll, one of their Research Fellows, described the challenge facing the profession in the following terms:

> *As more and more organizations consider human capital development to be an integral part of their business strategy, the demand for learning value measurement can be expected to increase significantly. Unfortunately, the learning function does not have a strong track record in aligning with the strategic needs of the enterprise, optimizing the allocation of scarce resources to address the priority needs of the business, and demonstrating value in terms of business outcomes as opposed to training activity* [1, p. 2].

In his analysis Tony O'Driscoll drew much inspiration from the work of Wang [2] and Russ-Eft and Preskell [3].

In short, there is so much to be done. In order to appreciate the importance of the new approaches that are emerging, we will need to understand the limitations of the traditional approach to evaluation. To begin, however, we will look at the concept of value more generally.

Value

The Partnership Model was introduced in Chapter 4 (p. 76) and expressed diagrammatically important elements of the developer's role in promoting learning in his or her organization. It emphasized the need for all parties involved in learning to recognize the role and play their part. 'Deliver and validate' was indicated as a key activity.

The use of the term 'validate' was deliberate. It is defined in Chambers dictionary as 'to make valid, to ratify, to confirm, substantiate'. This is the critical challenge. The role of the people developer has been defined as supporting, accelerating and directing learning. There is a requirement to see that these efforts are valid and this has two aspects. First, there is a need to ratify or confirm that these interventions deliver value to the organization. Secondly, that the resources that are to support these interventions are deployed effectively. The questions here are: 'are we putting our efforts towards the right objectives?' and 'when we have identified these objectives, are we operating with maximum effect?' Both are legitimate and important questions and can be brought together as validation. The ultimate objective for learning, development and training is to bring value to the organization. However, for many trainers the focus is on 'evaluation', something that is intended to 'prove' the value of a course or event and, by implication, justify their existence as a function.

Moreover, the choice of the term value reflects a tendency across the whole range of HR activities. One of the leading US commentators on human resources, Dave Ulrich, put value as the centre piece of his 2005 book co-authored with Wayne Brockbank [4]. Importantly, he reminded us that value is defined by the receiver, not the giver.

Value is defined by the receivers of HR work – the investors, customers, line managers, and employers – more than by the givers. HR is successful if and when its stakeholders perceive that it produces value. Delivering what matters most to stakeholders focuses on the deliverables (outcomes of HR) rather than on the doables (activities of HR). We suggest that these realities differ for internal and external stakeholders [4, p. 11].

This quotation from Ulrich and Brockbank could helpfully serve as text for this chapter. The problem is making the sentiment a reality. As will be seen later, an ASTD/IBM study sought to identify different perceptions of the stakeholders on value. This produced some valuable insights for the profession. Before outlining this work, it is important to discuss what might be described as the orthodox approach to evaluation. Traditional trainers of a nervous disposition are advised to stop reading here!

Traditional evaluation practice

In 1975, Donald Kirkpatrick wrote a hugely influential book for the ASTD [5]. In this and subsequent work, he developed what is now known as the Kirkpatrick model which proposes four levels of evaluation:

- Reaction – how well did training participants like the programme?
- Learning – what knowledge (principles, facts and techniques) did participants gain from the programme?
- Behaviour – what positive changes in participant's job behaviour stemmed from the training programme?
- Results – what were the training programme's organizational effects in terms of reduced costs, improved quality of work, etc?

Over the years, there has been discussion on whether a fifth level – return on investment (ROI) – should be added or whether it is a re-expression of the fourth level.

A whole industry seems to have developed round ROI. At seminar after seminar new ways are presented for isolating the impact of a training intervention from other activities which are taking place at the same time. The assumption seems to be that if you assemble information from multiple sources, analyse it correctly and package it appropriately, the Chief Executive will undergo a 'Road to Damascus' conversion. He or she will see the light and your role will be enhanced; training and learning will be recognized as key business drivers and your future will be assured!

No disrespect is meant to Donald Kirkpatrick in advancing the argument below. He has made an enormous contribution to the profession and it is a reflection of his coherence that his approach still dominates our thinking 30 years later. However, a lot of change has taken place over that period – not least the shift from training to learning. So, as we enter the 21st century, three observations should be made on traditional evaluation.

First, this model of evaluation does not happen in practice. Successive surveys show that, in most cases, little evaluation takes place beyond Kirkpatrick level one (the end of course reactionnaire). According to data from the ASTD's Benchmarking forum organizations: 91% of programmes are evaluated at level 1 (reactions), 54% at level 2 (learning), 23% at level 3 (transfer) and only 8% at level 4 (results and impact) [6, p. 50]. In the UK, the CIPD 2006 Annual Learning and Development survey showed that, while nearly all organizations evaluate their training and development activities in some way, only 36% seek to capture the effect on the organization's bottom line, with fewer still undertaking a return on investment evaluation (18%) [7]. The Italian study undertaken by the AIF and outlined in Chapter 1 (p. 19) reported that, while initial reactionnaires are used by more than 80%, evaluation of the effective transfer of learning to the workplace is more of an aim than reality (32% of the sample say it happens but only for some interventions) [8].

Secondly, in a lot of cases it could not happen. In a lot of cases it is impossible to assess the effect of a training intervention and attribute without any doubt the business benefits. A review of the multiplicity of case studies presented in this book will highlight numerous similar examples, particularly in soft skills training, where there are unquestioned effects on organizational morale which could not be captured quantitatively.

Thirdly, in many cases (but not all), it should not happen in practice. It is simply not worth the resources that would be spent on higher level evaluation. There is no demand for such figures: there is simply no 'pull' from the organization. We need to ask why this is the case.

Moving forward

So how can we move beyond the mind-set of 'proving' – assembling after the event information and presenting it to another stakeholder in the organization to demonstrate how effective our work is? How can we break out of what has become an increasingly sterile debate? In the remainder of this chapter, two approaches will be considered. The first for convenience will be called 'aligning perceptions of value' and the second 'metrics and scorecards'. They are complementary rather than competing approaches and hopefully will assist the people development professional in determining a strategy for validation that will work in their organization.

First, however, we will introduce a case illustration, set out as Case study 10.1. This describes a major sales training initiative at Levi Strauss Europe. What is important here is to recognize the importance of front-end alignment with the business. In the view of the Director of Talent, Learning and OD, this obviated the need to 'prove' the effectiveness of his training team.

Case study 10.1 The Levi Strauss & Co. Way to Sell: training's contribution to a business problem

Background

Levi Strauss & Co. is a manufacturer of casual wear and is one of the best-known brand names in the world. Its core product, Levi's® 501® jeans, has almost iconic status. The company also manufactures and distributes the well-known Dockers® clothing and the range of Levi Strauss Signature® brand products which are sold largely through hypermarket chains. With headquarters in San Francisco, Levi Strauss & Co. employs around 9000 people across the world.

Levi Strauss Europe (LSE) employs just over 4000 people across 21 countries; 2225 are employed in manufacturing in Poland, Hungary and Turkey. The remaining employees, just over 1800, are professional staff and support staff involved in three main activities: brand management; supply chain management; and sales. The 423 sales staff, the subject of this case study, are organized in eight major market groups across 21 European countries. Although the product range is similar, the challenge can be very different. The Spanish market for example is dominated by one large department store – El Corte Ingles and some of the UK sales force are concentrated on key accounts (for example, Selfridges or Debenhams), while others could be selling to hundreds of small independent retailers.

The sales challenge

Fashion is a fast-moving and aggressively competitive market. In late 2002, when David Macdonald, Director of Talent, Learning and Organizational Development, joined the company, it was recognized that the sales operation needed to become more consistent in its approach and perhaps more disciplined about process. Subsequent progress has been driven by sales growth targets.

At the outset, although it was recognized that a step change in sales effectiveness was needed, there were differences of opinion as to 'current state'. Key managers differed on their perspective of the state of the sales operation and sensitive handling and negotiation were necessary. The absence of an agreed framework for judging effectiveness led to the development, by Levi Strauss Europe's Learning and Development team in conjunction with the consultancy group Hunter Roberts, of a diagnostic instrument known as $4 \times 4 \times 4$. This embraces four definitions of capability (process, resource, organization and people), four disciplines of selling (account planning,

195

account management, selling basics and selling apparel) and four 'times in the season' (launch, selling, replenishment and preparation for sales launch). The diagnostic is based on fundamental principles of effective sales, but is firmly grounded in the approach required in Levi's® markets. For example, the importance of different pressures and practices needed at different times in a very short sales cycle is emphasized. In this way, the diagnostic secured acceptance in the business and by the most senior executives in LSE. One of the major reasons was that the diagnostic allowed the Company to get a consistent view of the current state that everyone would recognize as reality.

The Hunter Roberts consultants used the $4 \times 4 \times 4$ diagnostic to observe sales practices across Europe and reported in summer 2002. Much of the output must remain confidential for commercial reasons. However, among the findings were identified opportunities to improve sales practice across a wide range of activities. Importantly, there were inconsistent results reporting and forecasting procedures. The skills problem was therefore just one dimension. A significant proportion of the sales force had never received any training and were using practices which they had developed themselves – some of which were inappropriate or unsatisfactory.

Sales foundations training

There was therefore a need to build, install and embed the basic standards of good selling. This sentiment had powerful support at the top. The project that was developed – directly influenced by (and with the personal ownership of) the President of Levi Strauss Europe – was called the 'LS & Co. Way to Sell' and the goal statement, coined by the President, was 'famous for selling in three years'. As David Macdonald puts it:

Ownership of anything like this should never rest with human resources.

The training contribution has been developed and refined over time. The approach in the first year has been based on four Sales Foundations modules. In turn, they deal with processes and disciplines; basic skills and the sales call structure; styles and flexibility (how to sell to different types of customer); and a final module which uses a full day role play to pull together all of the skills and disciplines learned in the first three. This event (Sales Foundations part 4) also serves as an embedding tool by allowing clear insight into whether or not learning has successfully taken place. The classroom elements last one day per module and were initially taught by the specialist sales training organization, Spence Associates, and LSE Learning and Development. It was important throughout to build a perception of ownership as lying with true sales experts, rather than internal Learning and Development.

Many of the processes introduced in the Sales Foundations curriculum are mandatory. It is hard to see how this would be acceptable without strong commitment from the sales force themselves – they could not be 'imposed' by human resources or training. David Macdonald emphasizes that the problem has never been one of variable buy-in – generally, there is considerable enthusiasm for the new approach. Questions, however, surround the skills and capabilities of a very diverse workforce operating in different circumstances and conditions.

For this reason, the Sales Foundations programme is cascaded through the eight major market groups by the senior sales professionals themselves. The Sales Director will be joined by two or three of their best performing sales managers and their Human Resource Director. This small group of four or five people will be responsible for training the other sales staff in their market group. Thus, some 35–40 people will attend the modules and will then accept responsibility for arranging its delivery to the full 400 sales staff across LSE. Moreover, the modules must be delivered at the phase of the sales cycle when they are likely to be most valued as this improves retention. The underlying principles (which are reinforced through the issue of laminated cards) must therefore be sufficiently straightforward so they can be delivered locally under different circumstances.

The 'LS & Co. Way to Sell' is work in progress. Early in 2006, all four modules of the Sales Foundations programme will be repackaged as 'sales foundations in a box' – a flexible delivery package that will allow Sales Directors to roll out key parts of the training in as little as an hour at one time. A more sophisticated, higher level programme – 'The Way to Sell' – and master classes will be introduced in 2006. The underlying principles of the sales training approach will remain unchanged. There will be very short sessions; the material will be cascaded down through local sales management; material will be made available in different forms, ownership will rest firmly with the sales force.

Judging effectiveness

There are a number of practices in place which have been developed by the training department to reinforce its initiative. Some of these could be described as 'evaluation by intervention'.

First, as part of the improvement in sales procedures, the Sales Directors are introducing a dashboard of key metrics. These will be the key figures that determine top line effectiveness: volume of units shifted, revenue, penetration in key designated markets etc. The effectiveness of the sales force and their deployment of relevant skills will be a major contributor to this dashboard.

Secondly, in January to March 2005, a series of telephone interviews with sales staff were undertaken. In total, just over 20 calls were made to ask programme participants what they found useful, which of the tools they were using and how the programme and its application could be improved. Importantly, and this is a powerful endorsement of the perceived relevance and importance of the initiative, these calls were made by four of the most senior managers in Levi Strauss Europe including the President and the Vice-President for Commercial Operations.

Further, all 14 members of the European Leadership team, the most senior staff, are carrying laminated cards with key questions on the programme. As they visit the major markets they question the sales staff and provide feedback to the training function. Sometimes this feedback is positive: 'there is a great deal of interest and acceptance in this region'. Some will be negative: 'there doesn't appear to be a clear message getting across here'.

Generally, the initiative to check has been well-received. However, David Macdonald has not been overly concerned to apply traditional training evaluation techniques to determine effectiveness. As he puts it:

We do not feel the need to prove the effectiveness of the training team. What any internal client is interested in is the results of the sales team. If you can build something that will affect their top-line results the sales force will monitor and measure it themselves.

Aligning perceptions of value: the ASTD/IBM study

In October 2005, the ASTD published the results of a joint study undertaken with IBM. Their aim was to examine the alignment of views of CXOs (Chief Officer Level Business Executives) and CLOs (Chief Learning Officers) on the strategic value of learning. How do mind-sets of the CXO and CLO compare? The result of their study offered important insights on our ninth proposition. The study is described fully in an article in the ASTD's journal, T+D [9]. Importantly, it showed that, if the CEO has a high level of trust in the CLO, elaborate metrics become less important. Indeed, the most powerful conclusion is the one that is reproduced below:

To align more closely with CXOs, CLOs should place more emphasis on up-front strategic alignment with organisational outcomes rather than measurement of value contribution [9, p. 78].

The approach used was to undertake in-depth discussion with C (Chief)-level executives in 26 separate organizations. At each organization, one senior executive outside the learning function and the CLO were asked the same six questions which were:

- How does the learning function provide strategic value to your organization?
- How does the learning function's strategic activity translate into business results?
- What is your involvement in the learning investment process?
- How do you know the learning function is maintaining ongoing alignment with your strategic business needs?
- How do you measure the learning function's value contribution to your organization?
- How do you know the learning function is performing as efficiently as possible?

All six questions are critical to the success of the learning, training and development effort. Any people development professional could do worse than start with that list and seek the views of influential managers within his or her organization. Significantly, only the fifth and sixth questions fall into the domain that forms the traditional debate on evaluation.

The responses to the two sets of interviews were compared to see where perceptions aligned and where they did not. To quote the summary of the research that appeared in T+D:

The findings suggest that there are significant opportunities to align more closely with C-level expectations and aspirations, to make learning more strategic and central to the ongoing success of the enterprise [9, p. 70].

The study provides useful information on a whole range of issues that are important to this book. Some insightful extracts are set out in Table 10.1.

Table 10.1 Some findings from the ASTD/IBM study

CLOs should:
- Simultaneously anticipate and respond to enterprise, business and individual development needs
- Balance metrics and ROI data with anecdotal evidence, particularly stakeholder perceptions
- Combine top-down and bottom-up investment planning processes and emphasize the alignment of learning goals with business goals
- Be proactive in facilitating the formulation of strategy for the business and identifying opportunities for performance improvement
- Continue to focus on process improvement, service-level agreements, standardization and leveraging technology and outsourcing to maintain or reduce learning function costs, while increasing operational efficiencies

Measures of value

One of the new elements in the debate on value, therefore, emphasizes alignment of perceptions. How do the key stakeholders, outside the learning, training and development function perceive the value that learning brings to the organization? A second element also looks outside the function. This time it considers how organizations report on value. Here again, there is much new thinking: two of the most important strands concern the growing importance of human capital and an earlier debate on balanced scorecard. There is much literature available in the public domain on both, so here we will simply offer a brief overview.

In the UK, a Government Initiative in 'Accounting for People' described human capital as an approach to people management that treats it as a high-level strategic issue and seeks systematically to analyse, measure and evaluate how policies and practices create value. The intention behind the initiative, as its name implies, was to seek more effective reporting measures. What was accepted was that the value of a company was increasingly reflecting its intangible assets (people, patents, systems, relationships, etc) rather than the physical assets (plant and machinery). To quote from one of the CIPD publications:

> The CIPD has located human capital as one of three factors that make up intellectual capital, the other two being organizational and social capital. Organizational capital is capital owned by organizations. Examples are patents, copyrights or knowledge stored in knowledge management systems. Human capital is the skill experience and capacity to develop and innovate, that is owned by individuals. Social capital represents the structures, networks and procedures that enable the individuals to acquire and share their capital. These can include training programmes, discussion forums, the design of jobs themselves, and people management processes [10, p. 6].

Although the emphasis has been on financial reporting, the whole debate is encouraging for people development. In the service-led knowledge-driven economy, human resource practices will drive value and people development practices are among the most significant drivers. As a result reporting on such systems has moved up the agenda.

The interest in balanced scorecard is another manifestation of the same set of concerns. This approach was originally formulated by the US academics and consultants Robert Kaplan and David Norton in a Harvard Business Review article in 1992 and developed later in a book [11, 12]. Their starting point was a recognition that financial/accounting indicators were insufficiently comprehensive, therefore:

> The Balanced Scorecard complements financial measures of post performance with measures of the drivers of future performance. The objectives and

measures of the scorecard are derived from an organization's vision and strategy. The objectives and measures view organizational performance from four perspectives: financial, customer, internal business processes and learning and growth [11, p. 8].

Subsequently, countless organizations have adapted the balance scorecard approach; almost all have adapted the perspectives and redefined the elements to support their own circumstances.

The point of this discussion on measures of value is to indicate that such issues are very much on the organizational agenda. The most senior managers and their strategic advisers are considering how to value (and potentially report on) human capital. Managers at all levels are designing and reporting on scorecard measures.

The question, then, that people development professionals should ask themselves is how they should align and support such initiatives. Some illustrations of current thinking follow.

Metrics and scorecards

This second approach which will move us forward, therefore, focuses on the right measurement and on people development activities and integrating them with company scorecards. Practitioners are beginning to give serious attention to such possibilities.

In a 2006 article in the ASTD's journal T+D, Tony O'Driscoll argued:

Today, most training measurement is leveraged to justify investments that have already been made. Executives who are considering placing more investment in learning will not be willing to wait until after the program is paid for before finding out if their investment yielded value. Instead they will push us to provide a dashboard of leading indicators – metrics that suggest that an investment in learning may be warranted as part of an overall strategic investment management system [9, p. 45].

The emphasis will therefore shift from evaluating programmes to using data on a continuing basis. As Brenda Sugrue, The ASTD's Head of Research, put it in the same article:

It is common now to have comprehensive dashboards and scorecards that allow learning executives to see – at a glance – the current status as well as the planned destination of the learning expenditure, content usage, and progress towards business metrics that were identified as targets for particular learning investments [9, p. 46].

The ASTD are therefore currently developing the scorecard approach and launching it as a commercial WLP (workplace learning and performance, see Chapter 3, p. 56) scorecard product.

Before we get too enthusiastic on developing metrics, it is worth remembering the importance of perceptions. In the 2006 T+D article, Tony O'Driscoll commented:

> *In some instances perception data may be sufficient or at least a large component of the evidence for learning's value contribution. . . . No financial gymnastics are required. If the purpose of a specific leadership development intervention is to address attrition by providing managers with empathy and career coaching skills, perception data on employee satisfaction and attrition data may be more than enough to track* [9, p. 50].

In a different context, at the CIPD's 2006 Human Resource Development Conference, Siobhan Sheridan, a Human Resource Manager at Capital One, presented a powerful critique of the traditional approach to evaluation. Her comments are summarized in Table 10.2.

Table 10.2 Demonstrating value at Capital One

We evaluate to demonstrate value, but we did not use evaluation measures in isolation to do so. At Capital One, we have a balanced business scorecard approach which includes key measures drawn from our evaluation process and elsewhere. The scorecard is agreed in advance each year with our key stakeholders to ensure that it induces the things that they perceive as adding value.

- The problem we face is that our internal clients would perceive value only if it contained the same high level of analytical rigour that we demonstrate throughout Capital One. We contracted for analytical resource to support us. We looked for evidence to a level that was acceptable to our client rather than seeking to control to a level of proof.
- In my experience, I have found it quite rare to come across instances where natural control groups can be found. In an organization like ours, the level of analytical ability is so highly developed as to be able to find the slightest chink in research design and exploit it to argue that its research conclusions are invalid. So why even put us on a pedestal to start with – a conversation about protocol tends to draw out the desire for all of top analysts to prove us wrong. Whereas a conversation about evidence is much more satisfying for all.

Drawn from the 2006 HRD Conference presentation delivered by Siobhan Sheridan

Capital One is the one of the largest credit card companies in the UK. It has built much of its success on the rigour of its analysis in assessing the credit worthiness of potential clients. Hence, it has many staff with strong mathematical and quantitative skills.

Siobhan Sheridan's argument illustrates the problems of seeking to attain total 'proof' of the effectiveness of training and the need to seek evidence that appeals to the client. In her words:

> *too often we use evaluation as a way to seek to isolate the combination of the learning and development function from all else round it. The most successful studies where I have been involved have all recognized that learning and development can only be successful in the context of the overall system.*

Undoubtedly, a thoughtful choice of metrics and their contribution to overall business performance mechanisms can contribute to a solution to the 'evaluation problem'. However, the future does not lie in 'proving' the value of training. We must be focused on delivering business benefits.

Interestingly, in undertaking the case studies of good practice that appeared throughout this book, evaluation was scarcely mentioned and did not seem to be an issue. The implication must be that a good intervention speaks for itself. This does not mean that resources should not be monitored and controlled, but that the emphasis should be placed on delivering value that benefits the organization.

We will therefore conclude the chapter with a case illustration. Case study 10.2 describes the activities of Jardine Aviation Services at Hong Kong Airport. They are essentially about time to competence: bringing new staff to a level of effective performance in a way that absorbs the least resources of time and money. It illustrates the two most important principles for delivering value: get the alignment right and manage the resources available for training and learning efficiently.

It is to stress the importance of both of these principles that the use of the term 'validation' rather than 'evaluation' is advocated. More generally, to summarize the chapter, it seems that, currently, the benefits of 'evaluation' lie more in the process than the outcome. It can enable the people development professional to undertake a constructive dialogue with other stakeholders in the organization. It seems evident that the most important stakeholder group, the most senior management, are much more interested in alignment of the training effort than in the minutiae of delivery. This, therefore, is the most productive area for dialogue. Once again, this chapter illustrates the need to avoid a trainer-centric approach to our work. The concerns of the organization matter more than the concerns of the training department.

Case study 10.2 Time to competence at Jardine Aviation Services

Background

The Jardine Aviation Services Group (JASG) is a subsidiary of the Jardine Matheson Group (see Case study 6.1, p. 117) and provides services for clients at Hong Kong International Airport. JASG employ some 2000 staff at the airport and they divide across two separate companies: Jardine Airport Services, with some 1200 staff, deliver passenger services including check-in and reception (landside) and aircraft reception (airside). These airport services staff have a high level of education, with a good proportion of graduates – they are in constant interaction with the client's customers. The second company, Jardine Air Terminal Services, has 800 staff. Here, the activities are operational – the moving of ramps and land stairways and loading and unloading of freight and luggage. The staff are less qualified and the job involves a mixture of equipment handling and manual work. JASG passenger and airport services are supplied to 20 different airlines.

The timing of the work is determined by flight patterns. As a consequence, there are a lot of split shifts; staff are needed in the morning and evening with down-time in between. Staff attrition is therefore a problem and there is a continuous requirement to bring new staff up to the required level of competence in the shortest possible time. This is particularly true in the case of passenger services: travellers have a clear expectation that the person they are dealing with knows the answers and can work the systems – irrespective of the complexity of their enquiry.

The training challenge

In these circumstances, Ben Li, the JASG Learning and Development Manager, faces continuous demands for training new joiners and in providing basic operational training. The latter requirement can arise at short notice when a new client airline is secured. Ben Li estimates that, in 2005, training for new joiners and operational training (mainly for passenger services) accounted for over 90% of his training effort.

A major concern for Ben Li is to free up resources to invest more time and energy in management training. He can take advantage of a strong commitment to training and learning from his CEO. Four major areas where the human resources and the learning and development functions can contribute to the business have been identified. These are: ensure a sufficient supply of talented staff; identify and develop a JASG talent pool; facilitate process improvement through training and skills practice; keep management up to date on all compliance issues.

JASG are participants in the Jardine Group's staff planning and management development systems and also undertake their own soft-skills and management training. However, the immediate requirements of new starter training and operational training must be satisfied and Ben Li's challenge is to deliver this in the most efficient and cost-effective manner.

New joiner and operational training

The knowledge and skills required of a passenger services agent can be divided into three categories. First, there is a need to understand basic check-in procedures. These are generic systems and processes: with some minor exceptions they will apply across all airlines. Secondly, there is a need to know the requirements of specific client airlines – for example, details of their frequent flier programmes. Thirdly, there is a need to apply the IT software: the basic passenger handling and check-in systems. The second and third categories are constantly changing and the JASG agent must be able to meet the requirements of a whole number of client airlines – often working for several clients in the same day.

Ben Li and his team have developed a nine-week basic induction programme. Details for the programme for passenger services are set out in the table below.

Week	Programme
1	Induction, fare and ticketing (4 days)
2	Basic check-in product (4.5 days)
3	Passenger handler, other airline product (4 days)
4	On the job training
5	Passenger handler – other airlines (2–4 days)
6	Dangerous goods and security (1 day)
7	Basic customer service skills (2 days)
8	On-the-job training
9	On duty

It can be seen that the primary means of delivery is the classroom. New joiners are divided into cohort groups (these can range from 3 to 18 depending on the number of joiners, though generally the figure is at the top end) and receive instruction from a trainer. In Ben Li's view that remains the most efficient approach. However, he has in hand, or is in the process of developing, a number of initiatives to improve the effectiveness of the training process. These include:

- The use of line trainers. Currently, some 15 staff have been identified and developed in this way. They could work in either passenger or airport services but have management responsibility for operational aspects of the service provided for client airlines; they will have the skills and motivation to act as classroom instructors and also teach on-the-job.
- Establishing a network of coaches. So far, 150 have been thus identified; they participate in a 'train the trainer' session and receive a small enhancement of salary. Currently, there are plans under discussion to formalize the coaching system, which may include the systematic collection and review of feedback from trainers and supervisors on the performance of the coach.

One other potential area for process improvement, which could facilitate shorter time to competence, is the use of e-learning. Ben Li's view is that e-learning could be of most value in the first stage generic requirements in passenger services. Production of acceptable material would require a tight specification by JASG's learning and development team before issuing a contract to a software house. Such e-learning would be deployed as a precursor to the classroom and would be closely integrated with instructor-led training – a blended approach.

The induction training for operational staff is also tightly specified. However, the requirement of the job varies considerably. Loaders, for example, need 5 days classroom or simulation training and 4–10 days on-the-job training. Equipment operators need 3–5 days classroom followed by 5–10 days on-the-job. Ramp workers may only need a day in the classroom and conveyor belt operators a day and a half. For all these people an area of the airport is set out for simulation training, where equipment can be deployed in a controlled environment. As can be seen, on-the-job training is a key part of the process. At the end of the training period, all operational staff are tested and certified in the requirements of the job.

Moving forward

As is evident, much of the learning and development efforts are concentrated on the day-to-day operations. The majority of JASG's employees are involved in routine activities, though there is a continuing need to update knowledge and skills as processes change. However, there is a recognized requirement to build a more effective management culture. When a contract for services is agreed with an airline, JASG becomes, for a period, a sole supplier. There is a danger that complacency can set in rather than a desire to seek process improvements. Hence Ben Li's determination to put more of his efforts into proactive leadership and management development.

References

[1]. O'Driscoll, T. (2005) Valuing Human Capital and HRD: A New Millennium Requires a New Approach. Unpublished paper.

[2]. Wang, G. (2003) Valuing Learning: The Measurement Journey. Educational Technology, 43(1), 32–37.

[3]. Russ-Eft, D. and Preskell, H. (2005) In Search of the Holy Grail: Return on Investment Evaluation Human Resource Development. Advances in Developing Human Resources, 7(1), 71–85. Available at: http://adh.sagepub.com/cgi/reprint/7/1/71.pdf

[4]. Ulrich, D. and Brockbank, W. (2005) The HR Value Proposition. Boston, MA: Harvard Business School Press.

[5]. Kirkpatrick, D.L. (1975) Evaluating Training Programs. Alexandria, VA: American Society for Training and Development.

[6]. Davenport, R. (2006) In God We Trust: All Others Bring Data. T+D, 60(4), 44–51.

[7]. Chartered Institute of Personnel and Development (2006) Learning and Development Annual Survey Report 2006. London: CIPD. Available at: http://www.cipd.co.uk/NR/rdonlyres/97BE272C-8859-4DB1-BD99-17F38E4B4484/0/lrnandevsurv0406.pdf

[8]. The research 'Indagine sugli Investimenti Formativi nelle Grandi Aziende n Italia – 2005' was undertaken by dell'Associazione Italiana Formatori and by the University 'Cà Foscari' of Venice, under the leadership of Ulderico Capucci. (see www.aifonline.it)

[9]. O'Driscoll, T., Sugrue, B. and Vona, M.K. (2005) The C-level and the value of Learning. T+D, 59(10), 70–77.

[10]. Chartered Institute of Personnel and Development (2006) Human Capital Evaluation: Getting Started. London: CIPD. Available at: http://www.cipd.co.uk/NR/rdonlyres/CA1F572C-11A7-45C7-A62B-EE9C88CB7124/0/humcapeval0306.pdf

[11]. Kaplan, R.S. and Norton, D.P. (1992) The Balanced Scorecard: Measures that Drive Performance. Harvard Business Review, 74(1), 75–85.

[12]. Kaplan, R.S. and Norton, D.P. (1996) The Balanced Scorecard. Boston, MA: Harvard Business School.

PART 4

The broader picture

11

The Modern Challenge: A Summary

In the previous two parts of this book, we identified the new context in which people development must take place. We have conducted this discussion round nine propositions and considered their consequences for our profession.

The core argument has been that new competitive models demand a different approach to the acquisition of knowledge and skills. Importantly, the emphasis has shifted from training to learning and the role of professional development becomes learner- rather than trainer-centred. This necessitates creating a different set of relationships with managers and employees across the organization. This was expressed diagrammatically as a partnership model in Chapter 4 (p. 78). Although the interventions must depend on the nature of the business, the role of the people development professional has become one of 'Supporting, accelerating and directing learning interventions that meet organizational needs and are appropriate to the learner and the context'.

People development has been introduced and justified as the preferred term to describe the job role. Training should no longer be seen as a discrete set of activities round a course or similar event. The activities required to bring about more effective learning must involve the wider human resource and management community; they do not just lie in the domain of the trainer. The job is no longer centred on what happens in the training-room – though off-the-job classroom training still has an important role to play. Instead, the people development professional must address and overcome a series of inter-related organizational challenges and thus create a more effective learning culture. Some of the challenges are set out in Table 11.1. This draws on the idea, introduced in Chapter 4 (p. 83), and based on a model developed at the Ashridge Management Research Centre, that a clear ladder of progression is involved in building a learning culture. It will be seen that this idea offers useful insights in the discussion of the international dimensions that will take place in the last three chapters.

Table 11.1 Progressing towards a learning culture

Characteristic behaviours of parties at each level of sophistication	Fragmented	Formalized	Focused
Employer (i.e. Senior Management)	No link perceived between business success and learning. May support individual requests for learning opportunities on an ad hoc basis	Supports professionals by actions such as signing off training policy, approving budget. May introduce development planning or carry out succession planning for the Board	Supports and challenges to ensure learning takes place to support organizational strategy and to develop talent for the future. Well aware of learning, training and development initiatives
Line Manager	Does not see learning as his/her responsibility though may respond to individual ad hoc requests	Meets with HR to discuss training needs of self and own team. Takes part in formal appraisal processes, coaching and training programmes	Ensures that self and all team have the means to acquire the knowledge and skills to achieve targets. Initiates (with HR) processes to ensure that learning takes place where needed. Supports a range of learning opportunities for staff
Individual learner	Acquires the skills and knowledge required for job role and waits to be told what is next. The more ambitious may look for opportunities for learning to follow personal aspirations, learning in	Needs identified at appraisal with manager. Takes part in courses offered as part of the formal organizational plan. May learn on- or off-the-job	Learns as part of role development guided by line manager and HR. Has formal development plan and discusses past and future learning at appraisal. Takes part in formal and informal learning, with line manager, others, on- or

People development professional	own time and sometimes at own cost	Supports individuals or line managers who seek them out. Delivers statutory training courses and evaluates reactions	Develops and communicates training plans to meet the needs identified at appraisal. Ensures that training is delivered efficiently and meets the identified needs	off-the-job. May also act as coach or mentor to others	Consults with senior and line managers on the best ways to meet learning needs. Ensures that all have formal learning plans, that line managers and others have the skills to coach or mentor. Supports learners and encourages the adoption of new learning methods. Ensures that learning happens at optimum times and locations. Evaluates learning and organizational outcomes

This table was produced by Jennifer Taylor, a Member of the CIPD Vice-President's Learning, Training and Development Panel

Some trainers may well be uncomfortable with the term people developer or people development professional. Others may wish to suggest alternative titles. Whatever the job title, however, it seems that some new vocabulary is required. Table 11.2 sets out some of the terms that have been introduced to date in the course of this book.

Table 11.2 Some new vocabulary

Intervention: the learning that the organization requires will not necessarily happen as a consequence of day-to-day activity (see Chapter 3, p. 41)

Contingent: the appropriate intervention will depend on the circumstances of the organization (see Chapter 3, p. 41)

Alignment: brings interventions and contingency together – a critical role for the development professional is to ensure that the resources committed to the learning, training and development effort reflect and reinforce business priorities (see Chapter 3, p. 41)

Partnership: all parties must understand what is required and have the necessary skills (see Chapter 4, p. 78)

Time to competence: ensure that critical groups of staff acquire the knowledge and skills to meet business needs in the shortest possible time (see Chapter 6, p. 126)

Support and challenge: encouraging the recipient to display confidence in their capabilities and to construct their own learning agenda and also to demand that a wide range of options are considered and objectives are stretching (see Chapter 8, p. 156)

Validation: to confirm, corroborate, substantiate, support; ensure that the intervention achieves its objective and delivers value to the business (see Chapter 10, p. 203)

At all stages of the argument, some illustrative good practice interventions have been presented as case studies. It can be seen that, given their different circumstances, people development professionals may be implementing initiatives which focus on the problems identified in the different cells included in Table 11.1. For this reason, it is better to talk of 'good practice' rather than 'best practice'. It is not possible to recommend a single blueprint to describe what a people development professional 'should be doing'. To do so would be unhelpful. One is reminded of the aphorism coined by the US writer H.L. Mencken: 'For every complex problem, there is a solution that is simple, neat, and wrong'. Essentially, the main advice to the practitioner must be to trust your judgement, show confidence in yourself and formulate your own way in your organization.

Nevertheless, it is possible to offer some observations on what those who are adopting good practice are doing. They are:

- showing a clear understanding of the business drivers in their organization
- helping their organizations add value and move up the value chain
- establishing a clear vision and strategy for people development
- involving others and engaging stakeholders in a transparent way
- having both a good overview of what is needed to advance in the long term and also of the short-time priorities
- using processes and techniques appropriately
- applying metrics to demonstrate value.

And above all:

- understanding the legacy that learners bring with them and adjusting their interventions accordingly.

12

Culture and Learning

In this chapter and the next, we shall consider the following question: does the approach to people development that we have described in this book apply across the world? We will ask whether a global model is emerging.

This is an important question. It is of immediate relevance to those people developers who have responsibilities for programmes that operate across different countries in a multinational organization. It also has wider importance as the global economy demands effective development practices in emerging economies.

So far, the case studies in the book have been presented without undue emphasis on the national context in which the organization operates. The focus has been on the training and learning problems that have been identified, the approach adopted and the interventions made by those responsible for people development. We now need to ask if radically different approaches will be needed (or will emerge) in different countries throughout the world?

There is good news and bad news here. Let's start with the bad. It is easy to drift into cultural stereotyping and this can sometimes take a comic form. At a US training conference held in 2003, I purchased a cultural guide on business in Britain. This had been published in 2000. To avoid embarrassment I will not name the source.

In that guide I learned that we British do not like speculative thinking or theorizing (so much for Isaac Newton and Tim Berners-Lee). I also discovered that we enjoy socializing during tea time where we snack on teas, scones and buns (none of the CIPD staff could recall an occasion when they participated in such a ritual). As far as business etiquette is concerned, I learned that first names are rarely used, that in formal introductions we move from the highest-ranking to the lowest and a man should wait for a woman to extend her hand first. As for my nation, the Welsh, it appears that decisions are made more slowly than in England. Since we won the 2005 European national rugby championship by demonstrating impressive speed of ball distribution before a tackle, this last particularly rankled. Crude stereotyping does not help and may offend. It reminds one of the winning entry in a UK competition for unhelpful advice to foreign visitors. This ran: 'On boarding a bus or tube in London it is expected that you shake hands and introduce yourself to all the existing passengers!'

The good news comes from two sources. First, there is a growing amount of information which is generated from research and is providing us with valuable insights and ideas on national culture. However, as will be shown, this research does not readily produce easy answers, still less immediate templates. It is helpful to repeat an argument presented early in Chapter 1. It would be nice to have a sound body of well-researched, academically-sound, information in many of the areas we discuss, but neither the information base nor the shared vocabulary of understanding is available at present. Therefore, people developers will need to apply their skills and judgement in the situations that they face. The second source of good news is that this is precisely what is happening in practice. So, before considering some of the underlying arguments, research and models, this chapter will begin by presenting two case studies.

The first case, set out in Case study 12.1, outlines the work of Ingersoll Rand University. Here, a globally agreed set of learning priorities is being delivered across the very large Asian Region. The second case concerns cross-cultural training. One of the organizations that impressed in its approach to this topic was Pfizer Research – the subject of the Case study 12.2. Both the cases emphasize the practical steps that 'thinking performers' (see Chapter 7, p. 136) can take to 'manage' cultural differences.

Case study 12.1 Implementing a global HRD-strategy at local level: Ingersoll Rand University

Background

Ingersoll Rand is a global conglomerate which was created by a merger between two well-established US companies. Corporate headquarters are in New Jersey and there are some 40 000 people employed throughout the world. They are deployed across a number of divisions, including construction equipment, industrial solutions (for example, air compressors), climate control (refrigeration and air conditioning), security systems and a division that makes a well-known golf-cart. Over 6000 of these staff are employed in the Asia Pacific Region with significant concentrations in seven major counties. Some 3000 are in China and 1200 in India.

Among the major business challenges facing Ingersoll Rand is the need to create a culture of development and competitive leadership skills across the world. The major vehicle in place to achieve these objectives is Ingersoll Rand University, which was established in year 2003. Kong Chin, who was born in Burma but spent his childhood in the USA, is the University's Director for Asia Pacific. He is based in Shanghai and is supported in his work by two professional and two administrative staff.

Implementing the corporate skills objectives

Corporate priorities are determined at an Annual Leadership Conference which all of the most senior managers attend. At this conference, one or two key leadership skills are identified and these must be developed across the group at all relevant levels. In recent years, these have included Channel Development (which develops distribution routes to sell company products); Sales and Marketing (which is especially important in emerging markets) and Operations Excellence (which aims to improve efficiency and productivity of the factories). Kong Chin sees his job as containing two main elements. First, he has to participate in the detailed consideration of curriculum design that arises as a result of the choice of key skill needs:

I have to participate in a lot of conference calls at night.

Secondly, he has to construct and deliver interventions in the region to implement the skills development agenda. The number of critical learners who need to acquire the skills identified will vary according to the priority chosen. Most of the activity to date involves taught courses; there is no infrastructure in place at this stage to ensure that other forms of learning intervention take place. Much of his local effort, therefore, is concentrated on the selection and deployment of external consultants to localize and deliver events. Where possible Kong Chin will try to separate out the regional training needs analysis, which will be undertaken by one consultancy, and delivery, which will be undertaken by another. Generally, Ingersoll Rand University will try to find a global delivery partner – one consultancy or associate – that can deliver a consistent programme across the world. However, this is not always possible and Kong Chin regards the choice of consultant for delivery as critical: he checks their background, meets them personally and observes the way that they deliver in the classroom.

In his words:

I must have someone who understands the mind-set of the learner.

One of his frustrations is that he cannot ensure the optimum level of service across a widespread region. At present, for example, it is difficult to get material translated into Japanese. Further human resource management infrastructure needs to be improved if the desired levels of human resource development is to take place.

Regional and cultural differences

Kong Chin perceives very real differences in learning styles across the region. He believes that cultures have different personalities. He also feels that the Confucian tradition has an effect on behaviour in Asia and it influences learning preferences, as does the method of teaching experienced at school.

Broadly he divides the countries in his region into four groups:

- North Asia (which includes China, Korea and Japan) – Learners are very content orientated. They seek and need hard information and are less interested in other activities – motivational speakers using the US approach, for example, will not be well-received.
- South Asia (which includes Hong Kong/Singapore/Malaysia and the Philippines) – These countries are a lot more open to the international culture and learners are receptive to diverse approaches to learning. Training events can include a range of activities beyond instruction and these can be extended beyond the classroom – for example to include action learning.
- India – Any trainer used must be experienced and credible. Learners will be demanding and seek to engage in dialogue and debate and extend beyond the narrow subject areas.
- Australia and New Zealand – For all practical purposes the participants here reflect a Western or European tradition and customization of material developed in the USA requires less adjustment.

Although local circumstances and individual learners can vary considerably, Kong Chin has found the differences described above in meeting the main challenge of his job which he describes as:

Determining how we fulfil a globally agreed competency model at local level.

Case study 12.2 Encouraging collaborative research across cultures in Pfizer

Background and context

According to its corporate publications:

Pfizer is a research-based global pharmaceutical company that discovers, develops, manufactures and markets leading prescription medicines for humans and animals.

Some 105 000 people are employed, of whom approximately 14 000 work in Pfizer Global Research and Development (PGRD). The largest R&D presence is in the USA but some 2600 are employed in Sandwich in South-East England and some 400 at Nagoya in Japan. This case study concerns learning interventions designed to underpin essential collaboration between research and development colleagues at these two locations.

Collaboration in research across the globe is critical to Pfizer's business. It can take from 10 to 15 years and expenditure of in excess of $1 billion to bring a product from idea to new marketed medicine. Pfizer is a global organization and it needs to leverage its worldwide resources. Given necessary economies of scale, a regional model does not work. Japan is particularly important in this global context – the country is the second biggest market for pharmaceutical products in the world. Pfizer has been a presence in Japan since 1953 and the Nagoya site specializes in early stage and exploratory research. Once identified, its experimental medicines will be tested and trialled elsewhere, including Sandwich.

To quote from the PGRD President in his introduction within the UK PGRD booklet on communicating with Japan:

Effective communication lies at the heart of the Pfizer values and leader behaviours and is crucial to our ongoing success. Time and energy are required to address problems and come to common ground around the best possible solutions. Maximum interaction is therefore critical when we are communicating with colleagues, from other countries and cultures.

Culture organization and language training

For over a decade, collaborative skills have been supported by training interventions. In Sandwich, this support has taken the form of a one-day course on 'Partnering with Japan'. In Nagoya, the focus has been on language training, organized by Human Resources, supported by a team of freelance trainers.

Both sets of interventions continue in place, but recognition of their limitations has led to extended and new approaches. What was on offer in the UK was an overview of Japan and Japanese customs. However, the often stereotypical view of the Japanese did not reflect the reality of the research scientists working in Nagoya. These are graduate scientists, intelligent and aware; they are innovative and share ideas. Many have chosen to work for Pfizer because it is a vibrant international company. Senior leaders are drawn from both the local and global talent pools. Consequently, the business practices are a complex mix of cultures and customs; neither stereotypically Japanese, nor completely westernized.

In 2005, to illustrate the differences between the stereotypical view of Japan and the way that people in Nagoya behave, Tim Kendall (English Language Training Coordinator in PGRD Nagoya) undertook a short exercise in which he asked colleagues in Nagoya to consider some questions regarding business culture. Respondents were asked what they believed would actually happen within their own working environment and also what they perceived to be the traditional Japanese stereotype. Two examples of questions that gave a clear indication of significant mind-set and cultural differences are set out below.

Participants were asked:

What will normally happen in a meeting if some of the participants are running late?

1. The meeting will always start on time as scheduled.
2. Participants will wait until the late arrivals arrive if they are high ranking.
3. Participants will always wait for those running late.

Eighty-two per cent of respondents in Pfizer Nagoya marked choice 1, with the remainder marking 2 for their own working environment. However, when participants were asked their views regarding a more traditional Japanese working environment, 100% marked choice 2, thus highlighting the weight of importance that a high ranking colleague may have within a more traditional Japanese setting.

Participants were asked:

When a Japanese colleague says that your idea or proposal might be a bit difficult to succeed in Japan, it is best to:

1. Ask 'Why?'
2. Ask 'what can be done to make it succeed?'
3. Realize that they are saying 'No' and give up.

Of the respondents, 68% marked choice 1 with a further 32% choosing 2 for their own Pfizer environment. In complete contrast, 97% of respondents marked 3 as their choice when considering the situation in a traditional Japanese business environment.

Taken together, all the evidence led Pfizer to conclude that solutions to issues are an important part of decision-making within a western business environment and because colleagues in Pfizer work in an American company their mind-set is significantly impacted by this action. In addition, Tim Kendall undertook a series of interviews with participants in the questionnaire. This suggested support for these conclusions, but that there were significant differences between the views of colleagues that joined Pfizer during the past 12 months; those that had joined more than 12 months ago; and those that had only worked in the Pfizer environment.

At Nagoya, the challenge was to develop English language training beyond 'text-book' understanding. In particular, to be effective partners in global R&D teams, it was considered necessary to enhance skills in effective oral communication (including clarifying, questioning and debating, where cultural norms may impact two-way dialogue), especially where that communication is via virtual means, telephone, teleconference, e-mail and e-Net-meeting.

Moving forward

Such initiatives in isolation would lead to improvements. However, in 2005 following a short review of trainers involved in cross-cultural working and the part that learning and training could play in reducing cultural barriers, Tim Kendall (PGRD Nagoya) and Jane Waters (PGRD Sandwich) were charged with developing joint initiatives.

The first step was for Jane Waters to identify more clearly who in Sandwich would benefit from cross-cultural training. It may seem obvious in retrospect but the best information was held in Japan. Language training in Nagoya was most sharply concentrated in those who worked closely with fellow scientists at Sandwich. They were able to supply details on whom they interacted with and the nature of this interaction. This allowed the Sandwich learning and development team to ensure the right people attended the classroom training event and at the right time. A second step was to use those people who had participated in a secondment in Japan to assist in taking the design and input of the classroom training (together with a third party vendor, able to bring wider, multi-industry cultural training knowledge into the design).

Additional outputs have been guides – both for Japan and the UK – which are tailored to the specific situation of the company. Some of the material is generic and covers what would be expected, however, the illustrations capture eloquently the reality of the relationships and potential pitfalls aiming to be overcome by training and support. To quote from the guide for the UK:

> I appreciate that UK and US colleagues usually make an effort to speak clearly at the beginning of meetings, but they tend to speed up and use more colloquial expressions when we get into deeper discussion. (Attributed to a Manager, PGRD, Nagoya)

and

> I was surprised when, during one teleconference, my colleagues in the UK called for a 30-minute lunch break. It was 01:00 in Japan and I felt that

my considerations were not fully considered. (Attributed to a Researcher, PGRD, Nagoya).

The training activities in Sandwich and Nagoya will continue. The continuing challenge is to keep them relevant as cultures continue to be modified by globalization influences. Another objective is to achieve greater leverage and value for the organization by extending support to US colleagues working with Japan.

However, interestingly this does not mean that there is no place for the more generic cultural orientation/awareness event. John Castledine, PGRD's Director of Learning and Development, points out that UK staff who spend time in Japan (or elsewhere) do not interact solely with their PGRD research counterparts at Nagoya. They have business contacts with customers/suppliers and thus experience a wide range of cultural influences, which are better approximated by accepted cultural 'stereotypes'.

Moreover, John Castledine believes that the learning and development function, in its collaboration, needs to model what it is seeking to promote in the rest of the company. Only by ensuring L&D professionals are ahead of the organization in their ability to partner effectively across cultures can the organization discover the steps needed to establish and prioritize the learning activities needed to support on-going effective cross-cultural collaboration.

Convergence or divergence?

The chapter will continue with a wider exploration of the topic of culture. We will structure the discussion by considering two positions. For convenience they are labelled divergence and convergence.

A convergence view argues that, since training, learning and development is a derived activity, all that matters in the long term will be what is required to achieve business success or service delivery. Although consumers will display different levels of sophistication, mainly but not exclusively connected to their disposable income, the indications are that they will ultimately demand the same products, goods and services. At its simplest, shops, hotels and resorts will be the same throughout the world. Given this, the interventions designed to ensure that employees acquire the relevant knowledge and skills will depend primarily on the sector and the nature of the business and prior awareness and experience of the workforce rather than their national background.

A divergence view, by contrast, starts from the premise that citizens of different countries have different personality characteristics which are related to different cultures; hence they will need to be managed in different ways and will learn in different ways. Given that, it is important that interventions designed to ensure that employees acquire the relevant knowledge and skills are flexed to take account of the personality/learning preferences prevalent in the country or region of operation.

We will consider in turn the case for convergence and for divergence. The discussion of the latter topic will introduce the complex, but important, area of cross-cultural psychology. In the next chapter, we will, through the use of case studies, consider further how some people developers who manage cross-cultural initiatives are adjusting their programmes to cope with the pre-dispositions of learners from different countries.

Taken together, the analysis in both these chapters will lead us to offer some comments on the future role of people developers. This discussion will be continued in Chapter 14, which will consider the particular case of China.

A case for convergence

In 2005, the US journalist Thomas L. Friedman wrote an influential book with the intriguing title 'The World is Flat' [1].

Friedman did not seek to make a case for convergence. He merely drew attention to what he saw as an inevitable trend in the globally competitive economy – one which will be particularly acute in the knowledge-intensive industries. Indeed, he began his deliberation at Infosys in Benguluru, the subject of a case study included in Chapter 3 (p. 47). Some extracts from his book, which are chosen because of their relevance to the convergence argument, are set out in Table 12.1.

'The World is Flat' is a thoughtful, compelling work about geo-politics. The key implication for our enquiry is captured in the final quotation in Table 12.1. Those cultures that embrace the new tools of collaboration will compete in similar ways for similar markets. Although Friedman mainly concentrated on the outputs produced by knowledge workers, his argument can be generalized across all sectors. If, and admittedly it's a big if, consumers demand the same goods and services, the best techniques of production and management will be communicated and transmitted across the globe.

Cross-cultural psychology

The challenge to the convergence view is quite simply stated: it is that people from different cultural backgrounds will behave in different ways. An investigation of the extent to which this is true lies at the heart of the subject known as cross-cultural psychology. In a comprehensive, but accessible book, Professor Peter

B. Smith and fellow authors, use the following terminology:

We shall . . . refer to individuals as having a particular 'cultural orientation'. By this phrase we shall mean a propensity to interpret their surroundings in a way that is consistent with one or other of the dimensions of culture that we shall be exploring . . . Speaking of individuals' 'cultural orientation' acknowledges the continual interplay between a culture and the individuals who are socialized by it and in turn sustain it. This interplay is of particular interest to these who define themselves as 'cultural psychologists' [2, p. 31].

and

While cultural psychologists emphasize the way that the individual and culture are inextricably interwoven, cross-cultural psychologists see benefits in using different terms to characterize the perspective of individuals (cultural

Table 12.1 The world is flat [1]

'The world is flat.' As soon as I wrote them, I realized that this was the underlying message of everything that I had seen and heard in Bangalore in two weeks of filming. The global competitive playing field was being levelled. The world was being flattened (p. 8).

But I was also excited personally, because what the flattening of the world means is that we are now connecting all the knowledge centres on the planet together into a single global network, which – if politics and terrorism do not get in the way – could usher in an amazing era of prosperity, innovation, and collaboration, by companies, communities, and individuals (p. 8).

It is this triple convergence of new players, on a new playing field, developing new processes and habits for horizontal collaboration – that I believe is the most important force shaping global economics and politics in the early twenty-first century. Giving so many people access to all these tools of collaboration, along with the ability through search engines and the Web to access billions of pages of raw information, ensures that the next generation of innovations will come from all over Planet Flat. The scale of the global community that is soon going to be able to participate in all sorts of discovery and innovation is something the world has simply never seen before (p. 212).

As the world goes flat, and more and more of the tools of collaboration get distributed and commoditized, the gap between cultures that have the will, the way, and the focus to quickly adopt these new tools and apply them and those that do not will matter more. The differences between the two will become amplified (p. 410).

Reprinted by permission of International Creative Management Inc. and Penguin Books Ltd from The World is Flat: the Globalized World in the Twenty-First Century, Thomas Friedman, pp. 8, 212, 410. Copyright © Thomas Friedman.

orientation) and to characterize the extent to which their understanding of events around them is shared by others (culture) [2, p. 32].

We will proceed by citing two perspectives in this area which have had considerable influence on practitioners – the work of Geert Hofstede and of Fons Trompenaars.

The Hofstede perspective

Geert Hofstede is one of the most respected names in cross-cultural psychology. A native of Holland, he became interested in national culture differences when he worked for IBM Europe. Here he founded and managed the Personnel Research department. This research led to the publication, in 1980, of 'Culture's Consequences'; and a second edition of what had become now a hugely influential work appeared in 2001 [3]. The subtitle of the book is 'company values, behaviours, institutions and organizations across nations'. The choice of values as the first term is not coincidental. His research suggested that it is values that underpin differences.

The quotations that are presented below are drawn from the second edition of the book which begins by reproducing the preface to the 1980 edition. This underlines Hofstede's view on the importance of the topic:

The survival of mankind will depend to a large extent on the ability of people who think differently to act together. International collaboration presupposes some understanding of where others thinking differs from ours [3, p. *xv*].

He defines culture as 'collective programming of the mind' and argues that:

People carry 'mental programs' that are developed in early childhood and reinforced in schools and organizations . . . these mental programs contain a component of national culture. They are most clearly expressed in values that predominate among people of different cultures [3, p. *xix*].

He initially came to this conclusion as a result of an extensive survey of IBM employees across 72 countries; later his research was extended beyond IBM. This all led him to suggest that there were five dimensions where country cultures differ. These five are often cited and widely accepted as a framework for considering national cultural differences. They are:

- power distance – the extent to which the less powerful members of an organization accept and expect that power is distributed unequally
- uncertainty avoidance – the extent to which a culture programmes its members to feel uncomfortable in structured situations
- individualism or collectivism – the degree to which individuals are supposed to look after themselves or remain integrated into groups, usually around the family

- masculinity or femininity – the distribution of emotional roles between the genders
- long-term or short-term orientation – the extent to which a culture programmes its members to accept delayed gratification of their material, social and emotional needs [3, p. *xix–xx*].

Geert Hofstede accumulated powerful research evidence: he argues that each of the five dimensions is empirically verifiable and each country can be placed in a position along the two poles of each of the five dimensions. This obviously has important consequences for encounters between cultures as the title of his book indicates.

Hofstede's perspective covers a wide range. For example, when considering 'organizational development' (OD) interventions he argues that:

OD was never very successful in Latin countries (high PDI), [power distance index] which lacked the equality ethos needed for such programs. Latins believe less in the possibility of people's self-development. They will easily interpret interpersonal feedback competitively, unless it comes from a person seen as superior [3, p. 390].

In a 2005 book, co-authored with his son, Gert Jan Hofstede, the practical implications of his approach are extended and made more accessible to practising managers (the message is updated for the intelligent lay reader). At heart, the argument is that values more than practices are the stable element in culture; that there are differences in the thinking, feeling and acting of people around the world. 'There is a structure to this variety that can serve as a basis for mutual "understanding"' [4, p. 2] – and by implication assist in determining the management action that is appropriate in any given situation.

One other element of Hofstede's thinking is important in the context of this book – this concerns the relative permanence of the differences. To quote from 'Culture's Consequences':

The evidence . . . showed that there was no international convergence of cultural values over time, except towards increased individualism for countries having become richer. Value differences between nations described by authors centuries ago are still present today, in spite of continual close contacts. For the next few hundred years; countries will remain culturally very diverse. [3, p. 454].

The work of Fons Trompenaars

Much of the focus of Fons Trompenaars' work is on corporate culture. His argument is based on 15 years of academic and field research and experience gained in 900 cross-cultural programmes in 18 countries. In the introduction to his influential book 'Riding the Waves of Culture' [5, p. 1] he puts forward the statement that, 'it is my belief that you can never understand other cultures'

[5, p. 1]. He formed such a view at an early stage as the son of a Dutch father and French mother. He, too, is sceptical of the view that 'internationalisation will create, or at least lead to, a common culture worldwide' since, *'There, are indeed, many products and services becoming common to world markets. What is important to consider, however, is not what they are and where they are found physically but* what they mean to the people in each culture [5, p. 3].

Assessing this underlying meaning is a challenging task since, 'the essence of culture is not what is visible on the surface. It is the shared way groups of people understand and interpret the world' [5, p. 3].

Trompenaars adopts a practical perspective, arguing that every culture distinguishes itself from others by the specific solutions it chooses to problems. These problems can arise from relationships with other people, from the passage of time and those which relate to the environment. Analysis of these areas has led him to identify 'seven fundamental dimensions of culture'. These dilemmas are described fully in 'Riding the Waves of Culture' and their consequences considered.

There is no one best way of managing, but difficult dilemmas of international management can be 'mediated' (to use his preferred term).

While you cannot give universal advice *that will work regardless of culture, and while general axioms of business administration turn out to be largely American cultural axioms, there are universal dilemmas or problems of human existence* [5, p. 164].

Importantly, Trompenaars argues that: 'while nations do differ in *how* they approach these dilemmas, they do not differ in needing to make some kind of response' [5, p. 164]. Indeed, 'in the final analysis, *culture is the manner in which these dilemmas are reconciled, since every nation seeks a different and winding path to its own ideals of integrity'* [4, p. 165]. Much of his work concerns corporate culture, where he has articulated four different models of culture and his view is that national cultures vary substantially on their relative preference for the four cultures.

The work of Hofstede and Trompenaars, have had considerable influence on practising human resource managers. The points they both raise indicate that there are some serious issues here which could have a significant influence on the future path of learning, training and development in the world. Cross-cultural psychology is, indeed, an important area of research and a relevant international project will be briefly outlined next.

Personality profiles of culture

In the early 1990s, two US psychologists, Robert McCrae and Paul T. Costa produced an instrument or inventory, the Revised NEO Personality Inventory (NEO-PI-R), to assess adult personality across these five dimensions or domains. Following an extended period of research and discussion internationally, what has become known as the Five-Factor Model of Personality has become accepted as a powerful construct in our understanding of personality. I am grateful to Professor Peter B. Smith to reproduce a summary table from his recent book as Table 12.2 in this volume.

Table 12.2 Dimensions and facets in the Five-Factor Model of Personality

Costa and McCrae's Five-Factor Model provides a synthesis of broad overarching dimensions each of which is defined by a series of more specific facets that are, in turn, made up of items reflecting individual traits. We may expect evidence for cultural generality to be strongest at the level of dimensions, with greater cultural specificity attending the meaning of individual facets and especially of individual items. The facets making up each dimension give some indication of its meaning.

Agreeableness	Conscientiousness	Neuroticism	Extraversion	Openness to Experience
Trust	Competence	Anxiety	Warmth	Fantasy
straightfor- wardness	Order	Angry hostility	Gregariousness	Aesthetics
Altruism	Dutifulness	Depression	Assertiveness	Feelings
Compliance	Achievement striving	Self- consciousness	Activity	Actions
Modesty	Self-discipline	Impulsiveness	Excitement seeking	Ideas
Tender mindedness	Deliberation	Vulnerability	Positive emotions	Values

Reproduced with permission from Smith, Bond and Kagitcibasi [2, p. 134].

Two questions which are a current focus of research are:

- Is the five-factor model a sufficiently robust and valid construct to assess personality across all national cultures?
- If so, what differences in personality can be identified in different cultures in different countries?

These questions are being explored in a project known as 'Personality Profile of Cultures'. This is an international project with 77 contributing members across the globe and is described more fully in an academic article by Robert McCrae [6]. The article describes the project which is based on individual personality ratings undertaken by college students in 51 cultures. As the author points out at the beginning: 'There is enormous appeal in the idea that cultures have distinctive personalities' [6, p. 407]. Despite reservations that necessarily arise from the complexity of the problem under investigation, the broad conclusions are that the five-factor model dimensions are universally replicable and, despite many cautions:

Aggregating individual personality scores is a useful way to characterize cultures. At present, one can be fairly confident about generalizations that characterize large regions of the world: In particular the evidence that Europeans, on average are more extraverted than Asians or Africans is quite strong [6, p. 421].

In Chapter 14, this area of research will be considered further in the context of learning, training and development in China.

The work that is emerging from cross-cultural psychology has considerable value for the people development professional, as do the implications of the well-respected models. Take, for example, the work of Hofstede. Each of his dimensions provides ideas and insights that could influence training delivery and learning in very practical ways. Working in collectivist cultures, for example, it would seem appropriate to place more emphasis on team or group learning activities and be cautious about handling individual feedback. Learners from cultures with high power distance may expect and welcome more directive training in the classroom. Certainly, it will be seen from some case illustrations considered in the next chapter that practitioners recognize and act on an assumption that people of different nationalities may need to be treated differently.

However, some caution is necessary. There is a logical chain involved, where every link needs to be considered, before we come to an unequivocal conclusion in support of the position which was previously described as divergence. The chain runs as follows:

- different national cultures are associated with different personalities
- those different personalities will affect the way that people learn
- we can identify and produce practical information that is of operational value on the different ways of learning
- thus informed, we would then know enough to adjust our approach so that we both train and support in different ways according to the culture.

At present, there are important questions to be asked at every link in the chain. There is evidence of differences in personality types between nations but they are modest. Many other factors, particularly the economic and historical, influence how workplace cultures arise and develop. The research that has been encountered in the course of this book does not specifically explore the area of learning at work. The section in Chapter 5 (p. 106) on learning styles showed that we have insights, but certainly not well codified and structured information, on individual learning styles and preferences.

Respecting culture

As in the case of Pfizer Research, many of the organizations interviewed in the course of this book undertook or commissioned programmes of cross-cultural training – these are generally programmes designed to sensitize learners to the existence of cultural differences and modify their behaviour accordingly. All who used them found these programmes a useful element in their training offerings. All agreed that they needed to be treated with due consideration of the context, rather than regarded as a convenient sheep-dip (a trough through which everybody should pass through to be disinfected!).

Another important area of interest is the growing literature on 'cultural intelligence'. This recognizes that some individuals have a knowledge or skill-set that enables them to adapt more quickly and perform more effectively in cultures other than their own. Extracts from a particularly accessible article are included in Table 12.3.

Table 12.3 A perspective on cultural intelligence

The term was defined in a 2004 Harvard Business Review article by P. Christopher Earley and Elaine Mosakowski [7] as follows:

But occasionally an outsider has a seemingly natural ability to interpret someone's unfamiliar and ambiguous gestures in just the way that person's compatriots and colleagues would, even to mirror them. We call that cultural intelligence or CQ. In a world where crossing boundaries is routine, CQ becomes a vitally important aptitude and skill, and not just for international bankers and borrowers. (p. 139)

And

Cultural intelligence is related to emotional intelligence, but it picks up where emotional intelligence leaves off. A person with high emotional intelligence grasps what makes us human and at the same time what makes us different from one another. A person with high cultural intelligence can somehow tease out of a person's or group's behaviour those features that would be true of all people and all groups, those peculiar to this person or this group, and those that are neither universal nor idiosyncratic. (p. 139)

The good news is that to an extent, this is a trainable skill.

Although some aspects of cultural intelligence are innate, anyone reasonably alert, motivated, and poised can attain an acceptable level of cultural intelligence. (p. 140)

As a profession, we must hope we see the continuing emergence of well-founded frameworks from the area of cross-cultural research. However, they will only take us so far. People developers will need to be sensitive to the immediate task in hand and should not expect to be able to rely on easy-fix templates. Encouragingly, the case studies in this and the next chapter demonstrate that this is what is happening in practice.

Moreover, an acceptance of cross-cultural differences could easily drift into unhelpful, indeed damaging, generalizations. Writing in a very different context and for different purposes, the Nobel prize-winner in Economics, Amartya Sen, pointed to the danger of what he called singularization. In the course of his book he described this as follows:

> the odd presumption that the people of this world can be uniquely categorized according to some singular and overarching system of partitioning. Civilizational or religious partitioning of the world population yields a 'solitarist' approach to human identity, which sees human beings as members of exactly one group [8, p. xii]

and

> (singular affiliation) takes the form of assuming that any person preeminently belongs, for all practical purposes, to one collective only – no more and no less. Of course, we do know in fact that any real human being belongs to many different groups through birth associations and alliances [8, p. 40].

In other words, to return to the sensitive approach demonstrated at Pfizer, the learner is a many faceted individual. Pfizer's learners, to draw on Case study 12.2, are research scientists who have many and varied other affiliations and preferences – as well as being citizens of Japan.

The exploration of the convergence–divergence question leads, as would be expected, to a conclusion that the most sensible position does not lie at either extreme. However, the discussion has shed some important light on the place of learning, training and development in the global economy. This discussion will continue in the next chapter, when we will further consider some practical examples of the strategies that people developers are using in the international context.

References

[1]. Friedman, T.L. (2005) The World is Flat: the Globalized World in the Twenty-First Century. London: Penguin Books.
[2]. Smith, P.B., Bond, M.H. and Kagitcibasi, C. (2006) Understanding Social Psychology across Cultures. London: Sage.

[3]. Hofstede, G. (2001) Culture's Consequences: Comparing Values, Behaviors, Institutions, and Organizations across Nations, 2nd edn. Thousand Oaks, CA: Sage.

[4]. Hofstede, G. and Hofstede, G.J. (2005) Cultures and Organization: Software of the Mind. New York: McGraw Hill.

[5]. Trompenaars, F. and Hampden-Turner, C. (1993) Riding the Waves of Culture: Understanding Cultural Diversity in Business. New York: McGraw Hill.

[6]. McCrae, R.R. and Terraciano, A. (2005) Personality Profiles of Culture: Aggregate Personality Traits. Journal of Personality and Social Psychology, 89(3), 407–425.

[7]. Earley, P.C. and Mosakowski, E. (2004) Cultural Intelligence. Harvard Business Review, 82(10), 139–146.

[8]. Sen, A. (2006) Identity and Violence: The Illusion of Destiny, pp. xii, 40. Reprinted by permission of W.W. Norton & Company and Penguin Books Ltd. Copyright © 2006 Amartya Sen.

13

The International Dimension

One of the central themes of this book is that it is practitioners who will determine the future progress of people development. In this chapter, we will therefore offer some illustrations from organizations that are seeking to develop multicultural workforces. We will then offer some concluding observations on cultural convergence and divergence.

Over an extended period, the CIPD has undertaken research on the topic of International Management Development (IMD). In 2005, the CIPD published a guide which explored IMD from the joint perspective of individual managers. Among the conclusions were the following:

- While there are clear cultural differences in perceptions of leadership across the world, the Global Leadership and Organizational Behaviour Effectiveness (GLOBE) project has identified the most effective leadership styles across all countries as to be: charismatic, team-oriented and participative.
- Organizations are actively trying to retain 'high-potentials' in an increasingly competitive global marketplace. Initiatives include talent management, internal electronic job posting and dual-responsibility for career planning.
- IMD initiatives should form part of an integrated talent management strategy. This will include global employer branding for recruitment and selection and reward packages, as well as IMD processes.
- Creating a set of international leader competencies that define the key behaviours required in order to be effective at the most senior levels in the global organization is a first step in developing leaders for most global organizations.
- The international leader competency framework needs to be integrated into recruitment and selection, reward and development processes across all global units through a culturally sensitive consultative process [1, p. 41].

This list reflects many of the activities and initiatives discussed in the first three parts of the book, while stressing the need to proceed with sensitivity. This is reinforced in the set of case studies which follow, all of which concern the delivery of training, learning and development initiatives to people of different national backgrounds. These case studies are taken from:

- The UK National School of Government (Case study 13.1)
- The European Commission (Case study 13.2)
- Ernst & Young (Case study 13.3).

Case study 13.1 International training and consulting – the UK National School of Government

Background – the international dimension

The National School of Government was launched in June 2005 as a centre of excellence for people development, professional training and skills consultancy for the whole of the UK public service. Its well-established top management development events, professional qualification and CPD programmes, skills development training and organizational change services are informed by the best international and domestic strategic thinking and delivered in partnership with leading practitioners and institutions, such as Harvard.

The National School of Government is at the heart of UK Central Government; it is committed to securing demonstrable improvements in public sector performance. Some 250 staff are employed: they are mainly located in Sunningdale in the UK Home Counties, south-west of London. The National School delivers training courses, learning support, leadership programmes, research and consultancy. The National School's open courses and customized provision for public and private sector clients are well respected in the UK and internationally. These are delivered to some 30 000 students in the course of a year (amounting to just under 90 000 annual student days). The most popular topic areas include leadership, project management and policy development: a wide provision of specialist and soft skill training is on offer, as are programmes leading to certification and higher level qualifications.

About a tenth of the output of the National School is delivered outside the UK or by hosting study tours – in 2004 this was about 400 events. The overseas activity has mainly consisted of course delivery and consultancy, often following success in a competitive tendering process. These have led to long-term contracts – perhaps two years or more – sometimes delivered on a partnership basis with counterparts in other countries. Today, they are moving away from open market bidding processes and, instead, concentrating on work that is directly commissioned by stakeholders and reflecting current government priorities, especially in countries deemed important by the Department for International Development and the Foreign and Commonwealth Office.

A particularly high-profile project was the National School's (then known as the Civil Service College) training of new government staff in the South African Republic in the mid-1990s. In support of the UK Government's desire to assist emerging democracies, many of the recent contracts have been delivered in the former Yugoslavian countries and in the countries that have recently gained accession to the EU. The National School has delivered programmes and consulting in Africa, Eastern Europe, India and China and has experience of operating across the world.

The approach to local delivery

Given this background, staff at the National School are well placed to comment on the different considerations that apply to training in different countries.

Graham O'Connell, a learning and development consultant in the School, expresses the challenge in the following terms:

> *Different countries do have very different ideas about the concept of learning. In most of the countries in which we operate there is a more evident association between training and education. Sometimes different motivational drivers exist: training and learning can be seen primarily as a route to promotion and less about competence. With our courses and events there is a general eagerness on the part of the learner; many of them see training as a precious resource and they seek maximum advantage from the opportunity it presents.*

However, Graham O'Connell emphasizes that some surprising differences can emerge and anyone who operates internationally must remain open and avoid accepting easy generalizations. In the Czech Republic, for example, he encountered excellent facilities and equipment (such as dedicated training rooms with interactive electronic whiteboards and the latest Microsoft applications on their PCs; though syndicate rooms were in short supply as traditionally the training rooms were lecture rooms), but the awareness of broader learning issues was not high. In China, there was a high degree of openness to new ideas and an acceptance of the value of experiential learning, while still expecting a high proportion of formal instruction. In South-East Asia, there is greater respect for seniority which means that junior staff will be less willing to ask the first question.

Generally, however, Graham O'Connell and the members of the National School who deliver programmes overseas emphasize the importance of a pragmatic approach. It is a matter of adjusting the delivery style to the audience that is encountered rather than seeking a template or pattern to apply to training delivered in a particular country or group of countries.

For example, he offers the following comment on training in Kosovo:

Back in the training room we were exposing the group to an increasing array of participative activities. For some this was their first experience of training after years of oppression where even basic education was denied. For others, it was a substantial departure from the traditional, yawn-inducing lectures they had been brought up on. Their willingness to learn was not a surprise, but their eagerness to try out new approaches was delightfully unexpected. A few old hands stuck to what they knew best, but many of the more progressively minded took to training very well – unlike some British managers.

What is needed, in his view, is a mind-set of 'no assumptions in advance – you have to use your judgement as you go along'. When a new contract is secured, the first step is to see what experience can be gained from other National School staff (or elsewhere in the government structure) and assemble research information from public sources. However, there is little published information of value on the practicalities of training in different countries.

In Graham O'Connell's words:

You can't help other people learn unless you're prepared to learn yourself. It's therefore a matter of practice built on experience – it's all about seeking to pick up the nuances of behaviour as they occur. We aim to work with the grain of local tradition as well as drawing on best practice from around the world.

The overall advice is: know your customer and seek to build through relationships. Do the research in advance and consciously try to learn about their culture.

Case study 13.2 Multinational training at the European Commission

Introduction and background

In 2006, some 28 000 staff were employed at the European Commission. They were drawn (in fairly even proportions) from the citizens of the 25 member states. Together, these staff had 21 'mother-tongue' languages, though the languages most commonly used in the daily work of the Commission are English and French. Norman Jardine, the Head of Learning and Development in the Commission's Directorate-General for Personnel and Administration (DG ADMIN), not surprisingly faces a major challenge in delivering effective learning to this diverse client group. Previous cases on training and learning at the European Commission have been included as Case study 1.1 (From training to learning) (p. 9), Case study 5.1 (Developing the interpreter service) (p. 102), and Case study 8.1 (DG REGIO) (p. 157).

Language

The need to deliver training and learning in several languages and in a form that is easily comprehensible to people who have 19 other first languages, is the most immediate and practical problem.

Ninety-five per cent of the classroom training is outsourced and it is essential that the same message is delivered in sessions held in English, French and other languages. At the operating level, the central training team have to check content ensuring that the translation of written material is precise. More importantly, however, there is a considerable up-front effort involved in this selection of outsourced trainers – their ability to operate in both languages is critical. One consequence for training design, according to Norman Jardine is, 'that you must deliver a simple message to a complex and demanding audience'. What is meant here is that there must be no ambiguity of meaning – all staff must leave the seminar with a clear and consistent understanding – but the session must be delivered in a way that engages an intelligent and confident audience.

These skills must be deployed at both the delivery and the design stage. Norman Jardine offered the following observation:

Language is important. Your perceived personality, your perceived competence and your perceived value is limited by your capability in the language. Our classroom trainers must take account of this; they must vary the pace, check understanding and recognize that some participants will find participating and contributing more demanding.

A related issue is language training itself which, according to the Commission's 2006 Strategic Training Framework:

Will continue to occupy a privileged position in the Commission on account of its multilingual and multicultural character.

In 2005, DG ADMIN offered some 900 separate courses in 28 languages which attracted 13 500 participants.

Multinational and multicultural issues

Norman Jardine recognizes that nationality and culture are closely connected. He uses two separate terms, multinational and multicultural, in part to illustrate the way in which simple stereotyping can detract from the effort to create effective strategies for dealing with the complexity. He offers the following illustration:

> *Most trainers rely heavily on US models – motivation theory would be a good example. These models are often perceived as Anglo-Saxon and their use frequently leads to demands for a consideration of alternatives developed elsewhere. This demand has become even stronger since the accession of the ten new countries in May 2004.*

Coping with the challenge

Norman Jardine is by no means dismissive of models or frameworks which assist in understanding cultural differences. However, they do not feature extensively in the training programmes offered by DG ADMIN. In the induction course, there is a session on working in a cross-cultural environment. An outsourced contractor offers a one-day course on working in a multicultural environment.

Norman Jardine sees it as important to avoid stereotyping and not to make assumptions:

> *background and life and work experiences are bound to lead to different starting points and different receptiveness.*

Adjustments must be made by those responsible for designing and delivering training and this is part of the professionalism of the job.

The importance of the choice of outsourced trainers has been outlined above. One of the criteria is that the consultants should be able to demonstrate, in concrete and practical terms, how they can run a session in a way that takes account of different starting points. In the classroom sessions, trainers can expect more challenges from participants who are coming from different sets of prior experiences. Trainers must allow more time for intervention; they must 'slim down' the basic message so that it is clear to all participants.

This all requires 'craft skills' – a particular part of trainer competence – and success is about professionalism and competence.

Case study 13.3 Global leadership development at Ernst & Young

Background

Ernst & Young delivers Assurance and Advisory, Tax and Transaction Advisory services for clients across the world. Each country has its own partnership structure and hence a measure of autonomy and self-determination. In total, over 107 000 people are employed in more than 600 locations in 140 countries. There are 7000 partners worldwide.

Ernst & Young Global Limited, which has its headquarters in London, undertakes a role in global support which includes supporting those human resource practices where some consistency of approach is required. Mike Mister, Global Director Executive Development, is responsible for facilitating the design and deployment of structures that will help drive some consistency into those practices that relate to the management and interpersonal development of partners.

The approach

Given the independent structures and sensitivities to the regulatory environment, globally-imposed solutions would not be effective. The emphasis is on creating a shared understanding of what is desired and how this can be achieved. There is also a strong recognition of understanding the importance of local delivery.

These principles guide the work of global learning and development. At each stage, development takes place through a series of interventions and these can be grouped in the following categories:

- Personal awareness: what processes should be in place to generate self-awareness and how should it be delivered and facilitate personal development? Mechanisms include multisource feedback and career planning discussions – linked in turn to the partner performance management system.
- Learning: this category includes structured off-the-job training programmes and other interventions whether delivered externally or internally.
- Experience: there is a general acceptance that most 'partner learning' occurs on-the-job and results from the roles that they fulfil and the challenges that arise as a consequence.
- Enablers: these concern the relationships that are developed, particularly coaching and mentoring and also the opportunity to develop skills capabilities outside the working environment. Some country practices, for example, have developed relationships with charitable organizations who can offer partners different perspectives which contribute to their development.

An examination of these four categories reveals the extent to which the global-local responsibilities must vary. The business school relationship and the development and delivery of some off-the-job courses and evident illustration of 'learning', is one area where ambitions and intentions are readily aligned and a consistent approach established. 'Strategic Leadership for Partners', for example, is a 5½-day course delivered by Harvard faculty: each year one programme is run in the USA and one in Switzerland. A slightly longer programme is run in association with the Kellogg Business School. A new programme for experienced partners to help them to continue to deliver at the highest level has been co-developed by the Netherlands, UK and Belgian practices and will, in due course, be available worldwide. Mike Mister describes his preferred approach to course provision as 'adopt and go', so he needs designs that can be implemented, with minimal changes, worldwide.

By contrast, 'experience' and 'enablers' can usually only be identified and delivered in the local country. What can be offered at a global level is guidance or a structure on how these can be made most effective as mechanisms for particular learning. The 'personal awareness' category is the one that is most sensitive to the country culture; here only a broad approach can be specified and the key mechanisms identified.

Gaining support worldwide

In Mike Mister's own words:

> *We have some phenomenally capable learning and development people across the world and we need to capture their ideas as well as gain their support. The issue is not simply about framework and processes; it is about collaborating around action and commitment.*

Given this background, considerable importance is placed on facilitating a network of learning and development specialists who operate in their own countries around the world. This involves the Global Learning & Development Team, the designated Area Chief Learning & Development Officers in the seven areas and the learning and development specialists in the countries who are focused on Partner Development. Importantly, this network is seen as a crucially important contributor to the design of partner development strategy. The network meets around three times a year, but Mike Mister travels extensively to different areas to ensure experiences are shared and the network coordinates.

Progress in implementing the desired structures and processes in individual countries depends on the following factors:

- Are there people locally, the learning development specialists or consultants, who can understand and deliver what is needed?
- Are the resources available?

- Is the business ready for this aspect of development?
- Culturally will it fit with what is understood to be helpful and appropriate at the moment?

Mike Mister recognizes a progression through levels of 'development maturity' and his challenge is helping accelerate deployment of activities in one area, without slowing down global progress overall.

Cultural issues

In his role, Mike Mister is well placed to offer comments on cultural differences as they affect personal development. His starting point is a clear recognition that it is much easier to achieve an understanding of the 'harder' more technical skills than the softer interpersonal skills. As has been noted, the technological methodologies (for example in audit) have become global and business strategy processes and challenges are the same throughout the world.

Two examples highlight different attitudes in soft skills intervention. The first concerns the use of multisource feedback – where partners use feedback on their performance and capability collected from their boss, peers and subordinates (and in some cases clients) to generate self-awareness. In Mike Mister's experience, the introduction and acceptance of such a system is comparatively easy in Northern Europe. In some countries, a complex system will produce a reaction in the form of a demand and requirement for something which delivers what is required in the form of a short summary of the essential points. In other countries, however, using such feedback would present a considerable challenge. A tradition of respect for elders means that subordinates could find it difficult to be candid about a boss's weak points and the boss could find it difficult to accept such feedback from subordinates. A second example concerns outdoor training as a development activity. Mike Mister says that such interventions are still popular, but one factor that impacts the effectiveness of the experience is whether the country has a tradition of compulsory national service. Outdoor activities requiring energy and interactivity are considered far less fun if the participants have been compelled to participate when younger, together with the perception of relevance and the skill with which the process reviews are conducted.

In Mike Mister's view, an appreciation of cultural sensitivity and the implications this has for managing progress, is something that can only be acquired through experience and observation over time. This challenge is to try to operate the requirement for global partner development in a way which is culturally neutral but still effective and impactful.

You need to know how people from different national cultures would expect you to react to different situations – for example, how you deal with unacceptable service in a restaurant or relate to colleagues when working away from your home country. Only in this way will you gain the credibility to achieve results through a global network.

Coping with different cultures

The three cases that have just been presented have much in common with others that have appeared earlier in the book. It seems that, when developers deal with multi-cultural workforces, there are a number of strands that can be identified in the approaches they adopt.

First, there is an underlying assumption that people may learn in different ways and that these differences may reflect national backgrounds or traditions – generally described as culture by practitioners. None of the development professionals interviewed seemed to find this threatening or alarming. It was simply a factor that they had to take into consideration.

Secondly, language is an issue. In his book on cross-cultural psychology, which was cited earlier, Peter B. Smith had argued:

Although first language speakers of English frequently fail to appreciate it, language use is by far the most important influence on the outcome of cross-cultural interactions. Language fluency determines power relations and influences the degree to which persons like one another. Language can be used to define one's identity in relation to others. The absence of a shared language severely constrains the success of a cross-cultural interaction. However, use of a shared language does not ensure that one understands the other party's goals or perspectives [2, p. 220–1].

The third and arguably most important common thread is that the people development professionals in the organizations concerned have developed strategies and tactics to cope with cultural differences. Moreover, they can articulate them persuasively. These strategies and tactics allow them to cope with the challenge of delivering common programmes (or programmes with similar objectives) to learners of different nationalities. This was also evident in the course of discussions undertaken with those responsible for human resources and/or training at Hilton Group Hotels in various locations in Europe. These are set out in Case study 13.4.

Case study 13.4 Developing the multicultural workforce at Hilton hotels

London

Hilton London Metropole, in the Edgware Road, near Paddington, is a very large hotel with 1054 bedrooms – it is also the biggest conference hotel in Europe. Some 500 staff from 68 different countries are currently employed at the London Metropole; just under a fifth of the staff are British citizens and the remainder are spread across a range of countries in Europe, Africa, Asia and the Antipodes. Given this, language is evidently a practical consideration. At their all staff communication/training days, key information is presented in English, Portuguese and Russian or Lithuanian. Fire training is undertaken in five languages.

Debbie Hayes, the HR Director, believes that a full range of modern training techniques, using a variety of approaches is needed to engage the learner and increase motivation to learn – but this is not a function of the learner's nationality:

> *People learn differently, irrespective of the nationality, so we must be ready to adjust according to our learners' requirements. It will be the same in any organization.*

Leeds

There are some 206 bedrooms in the Leeds City Hotel, making it a medium-sized hotel for the group. The number of staff varies according to activity, but would normally stand at about 200. Of these staff, some 60 are non-UK nationals – 20 would be from emerging European countries (Poland and Lithuania would be particularly well represented) and there is a large contingent from India. In total, about 20 nationalities are represented in the workplace.

The different nationalities working at Leeds City mean that Elaine Cawley, the Area Manager for four Yorkshire Hotels (Leeds, Bradford, York and Sheffield) and Leonie Smith, HR Manager for Leeds City, face a number of additional challenges. Language is an issue and, at the very least, a different pace and, on occasions, support from a member of staff who is fluent in the participant's language is required at initial training: 'We find someone else in one hotel who can interpret'. Sometimes training must take place on a one-to-one basis. Photographs are used in housekeeping for people with language difficulties or learning difficulties. A sensitive subject concerns standards of personal hygiene and grooming and these must be dealt with by the supervisors supported by HR. Leonie Smith recognizes some differences that reflect different countries: 'laid-back' and 'degrees of commitment' can be associated with different backgrounds and origins, but these are dealt with on an individual basis as part of day-to-day performance management.

Moreover, local differences can matter. As Elaine Cawley puts it:

Within Yorkshire people can be different. Sheffield traditionally had a massive steel and coal industry which has now disappeared. When we were staffing the new Sheffield hotel, we embarked on a heavy recruitment programme. We were interviewing people who had never worked or whose parents had not worked for some time. We were interviewing ex-steel workers who had been made redundant many years earlier. These people were simply not as motivated and needed to regain (or discover) the work ethic. Some who joined, worked two days in a week and then wanted a rest. There were, however, positive features: many of them were very appreciative of the opportunity to get back to work. You can pick up signals at induction, it can be difficult to motivate and energize people who are not used to work – they take a long time before they will participate actively.

Dublin

Hilton Dublin has 192 bedrooms and 130 staff across a range of hotel activities; some half of those staff were born outside Ireland. The most common nationalities are Polish, Slovakian and Hungarian, with some Chinese.

Joanne Mulvey is the HR Manager; she is supported by a full-time HR officer and a part-time HR assistant. Given the number of non-nationals employed at the hotel, Joanne Mulvey is involved in training a considerable number of people whose first language is not English. This she sees as a practical issue. It may take some people longer to demonstrate their TBS competencies (see Case study 6.4, p. 127) if their spoken English is not good. Limitations in written English can cause problems in some job roles. HR and management staff must demonstrate flexibility and try to support staff appropriately: within accommodation, for example, there are a number of supervisors who are proficient in languages and they can be called on to assist in the training room. Beyond the language issue, Joanne Mulvey has not identified any issues (cultural or otherwise) which have required her to make operational adjustments in the way her programmes and procedures are delivered.

Brussels

Joelle Hellinckx is Director of Human Resources for Hilton Brussels. Three hundred and sixty staff are employed across the two 431 room properties.

245

About 40% of the staff are Belgian nationals, some 15% French, 12% Moroccan, with a significant number of staff from the Philippines – there is a wide spread with 25 different nationalities represented in total. There were few staff from the new accession countries of Eastern Europe at the time of the interview, since they are unable to secure work permits, though the situation will change in May 2006.

On issues of training and learning in a workforce drawn from a large number of countries, the following observations were made. Coping with languages is undoubtedly an issue. All welcome days need to be delivered in both English and French, which takes time. All supervision training takes place in English, but Hilton Brussels have identified a successful training company who deliver a course specific to the hospitality industry in French. However, beyond this, Joelle Hellinckx does not see nationality as an issue and all staff are subject to the same performance management issues and can take advantage of the same development opportunities.

Learner receptiveness and labour legacy

In Case study 13.2, Norman Jardine, the Head of Training at the European Commission stated, 'the background and life and experiences are bound to lead to different starting points and different receptiveness'. It is evident from a review of all the cases in this book that such starting points are implicitly and explicitly taken into account by people developers when planning their interventions. They regard this as a critical part of their skill-set. Among the most important life experiences are those that occur in the later years of schooling and those that bridge the transition to work.

The bridge between the late school/college has become an important focus for Government policy. Most governments have some policy framework which is designed to develop workforce skills and thus take the nation up the value chain. These can involve creating incentives for employers to invest in skills training; advocating skills policies; intervening to create a national qualifications structure (often based on a competency analysis).

The extent to which Government policies provide an effective framework for skills development is an important consideration for the development professional. It is one, but only one, determinant of the background and receptiveness of the learner. It is of considerable relevance at the induction stage.

If a new joiner has relevant prior experience of the work that they will encounter, this can greatly reduce the necessary 'time to competence'. Government efforts to improve the pool of labour is obviously also of benefit to recruiting organizations. Some illustrations may assist. Case study 13.5 sets out the employability skills policies adopted by the Government of Singapore. Two more specific examples are drawn from the hospitality industry. The first (Case study 13.6) concerns the personal experiences in Germany of Andrea Kluit, the former Director of International Learning and Development, Hilton International. The second (Case study 13.7) describes the links between the Industrial and Vocational Training Board of Mauritius and the hotels on the Island.

Case study 13.5 Employability skills in Singapore

The Singapore Workforce Development Agency (WDA) was established as a statutory board under the Ministry of Manpower in September 2003. Its mission is: 'to enhance the employability and competitiveness of employees and job seekers and to build a workforce that meets the changing needs of Singapore's economy'. The WDA's efforts are focused on the citizens and other permanent residents and it seeks to build up the Island's human capital and its capacity to compete in the world economy.

When the WDA began operations in September 2003, the economy was, in Singaporean terms, showing relative stagnation and unemployment had risen to over 4% from a norm of 2% or less for many years (unemployment peaked at 5.8% in early 2004). Much of the early emphasis was therefore on short-term strategies to get people back into work. Over the subsequent three years, unemployment has reduced to about 2.9% and the WDA is now concentrating on longer-term solutions to address structural problems in the workforce which could act as barriers to productivity and growth.

Singapore has seen a decline in low-value added manufacturing production (for example, household goods and textiles); most of these jobs have transferred to lower-wage countries, for example, China and India. Demand in the service industries has grown. Since Singapore is not rich in natural resources, it can only achieve sustained competitiveness through realizing its human capital more effectively. However, as Gog Soon Joo, Director of the WDA's Quality Assurance Division puts it:

We need to develop in niches or sectors where our advantage cannot easily be copied elsewhere. For example, we do not need just to develop expertise in finance, but become particularly strong in risk management.

A particular problem that Singapore faces is that about a quarter of the current workforce have lower than secondary education. This group of workers, many of whom are now in their late 40s and 50s, are most susceptible to structural economic changes. At a time of economic change, WDA is reaching out to this group of workers by putting in place relevant training programmes to prepare them for conversion into emerging jobs in new or sunrise sectors or to prepare them with skills upgrading to take on more highly skilled jobs in their existing sectors. Two main vehicles are currently in place to manage the transition in the labour force. The first is the development of national industry skills frameworks, so that the right training programmes are available to support up-skilling and re-skilling, and the second is the 'Place and Train', which is a conversion training-cum-placement programme to help workers get into jobs.

The WDA has developed an integrated system known as the Singapore Workforce Qualifications system (WSQ). This system focuses on job competencies that encompass employability, occupational and industry skills. The cornerstone is a set of generic and portable skills that are applicable across all industries. These are:

- Workplace literacy (WPL) and numeracy (WPN)
- Workplace skills:
  - Information and communication technology
  - Initiative and enterprise
  - Communication and relationship management
  - Problem-solving and decision-making
  - Lifelong learning
  - Global mind-set
  - Self-management
  - Work-related life skills
  - Health and workplace safety

Above these basic employability skills, each industry framework identifies job specific skills and industry specific skills.

A particularly important achievement over the last year has been acceptance by the Institute of Technical Education (ITE), the national further education institute to adopt WPL and WPN as alternatives to qualifications gained in the education system for entry into its vocational certificate and trade courses. This is important in supporting more varied career development pathways.

A pool of about 200 generic competency statements act as a 'source code' for the Employability Skills. This 'source code' can be deployed in particular configurations and modules at various levels, operations, supervisory and managerial, to help workers move from industry to industry as these skills sets are portable. The challenge is adapting these competency statements to the needs and specific circumstances of different job families in different industries – the problem of 'contextualization' of essentially generic skills.

Indeed, as the WDA plans gain momentum, implementation becomes their main area of concern. The WDA does not run training programmes itself but seeks to build up the professional training infrastructure on the Island. It is funding capital projects for education institutes and private training providers and making these training places available through funding models which support employer-based as well as individually initiated training. WDA's Deputy Chief Executive, Dr Gary Willmott, sees a lack of trainers with a strong background and capability in competency-based training and assessment and with an ability to contextualize training programmes to specific needs, as a major challenge for workforce development.

Case study 13.6 Vocational training in Germany: some personal views from Andrea Kluit

There are various different approaches to ensure that the transition from school through learning to real work is as smooth as possible and each country finds its own way to do so.

Germany has chosen a dual system of vocational training, whereby theoretical knowledge is gained in vocational schools and practical training takes place directly at the place of work. This combination guarantees the internationally recognized high level of qualification of German craftsmen and skilled labourers.

The occupations for which training is provided in the dual system are determined in close cooperation between central government, the federal states and industry and employee associations alike, which means that the contents are geared to the requirements of the labour market. The dual system is financed by the companies involved (trainees' allowance) and by the state (covering the costs for vocational schools). Most of the learning takes place on 3–4 working days in companies, only 1–2 working days of a week are spent at school; another model is organized in a way that the learners go to work 5 days a week and then have three periods of 4–6 weeks within a year where they attend school.

Depending on the occupation and the age and qualification of the trainee, training takes 2–3 years, at the end of which the learners have to undergo a formal certification process, which consists of a theoretical written and a practical part, usually supervised by the relevant vocational school as well as the local chamber of commerce.

Vocational training in Germany is currently provided in more than 350 recognized occupations, in the public sector as well as by the independent professions. The dual system is constantly being advanced further to include new occupations and modernized training for existing professions. Over the past few years, new occupations for which training is required have emerged specifically in the fields of IT and the media.

To highlight the particular advantages of the system, I would like to explain it using my own career path as an example. After passing my A-levels at the age of 19, I was not really inclined to go to university, as I could not see the relationship between the theories taught at the campus and real life work; therefore I chose a rather practically orientated route. I applied for an apprentice in hotel management in a German hotel. I deliberately chose a hotel that was part of an international group since I wanted to go outside of Germany in my later career and felt that this would be easier once I had this company on my CV. I worked four days a week in various departments of the hotel and attended school on the fifth day.

As an apprentice, I really started learning from scratch and then gradually worked my way up – I first polished glasses before I was allowed to see the first guests, I worked early, late and weekend shifts. The great thing about this way of learning was that I got to know all aspects from start to finish. Also, an important learning point for me was that I got used to work with different people from different cultures at an early age. This especially strengthened my ability to accept people in different circumstances and in various capacities in my later career.

The apprenticeship trains a person's resilience in terms of dealing with sometimes unusual or even unfavourable work as well as with regards to people. It develops one's stamina and teaches not to throw in the towel at an early stage. I progressed through various fascinating departments and learned how to deal with guests, colleagues and superiors alike, whatever the situation. Finally, I finished my tuition, passing my exams, overseen by the German Chamber of Commerce. Soon after, I started working as a Human Resources coordinator and soon developed myself quickly through the ranks in HR and Learning & Development. With hindsight, the dual vocational system has been very successful to me as it enabled me to experience different situations that later returned in my career, improving my self-confidence in dealing with different matters.

Part of my later role was to set up an exchange programme where my Company sent hotel apprentices, serving in their second year of training, to other hotels in different European countries. Due to great success, the programme grew dramatically and the students partaking in the scheme, returned with concrete confirmations of jobs with their new work environments.

To conclude, Germany's dual vocational system teaches both social and personal behaviour patterns along with relevant technical and practical job skills and that make the young professional's transition from formal training into a genuine work situation much easier. Often, apprentices who are in the final stages of their training are already offered a full-time position with their current employers, facilitating the transition even more [3].

Case study 13.7 Developing skills for tourism in Mauritius

Mauritius is an island in the Indian Ocean with a population of 1.2 million and a workforce of 545 000. Historically, it was best known for its sugar cane production, subsequently textiles became increasingly important. Both of these sectors have seen, and will continue to see, job losses and there is a determined effort to build up the tourist industry. Currently some 60 000 people are employed in textiles and 22 000 in the sugar industry. Tourism on the island now accounts for 25 000 direct jobs and is increasing rapidly – about twice as many indirect jobs are created for every direct job, making it an attractive form of employment creation for the Government.

A target of two million tourist visitors per year has been set for 2015. It is estimated that 800 000 people visited Mauritius in 2006. If this target for tourism is achieved, it is expected that 55 000 people will be directly employed in tourism and 110 000 indirectly. There is a major challenge in ensuring that sufficient people will acquire the necessary skills to fulfil these roles. The Mauritian Government have created a policy framework and a number of institutions to develop the skills base – with the Industrial and Vocational Training Board (IVTB) responsible for skills training.

The role of the IVTB

The IVTB was established by legislation in 1988 and became operational the following year. At that time it was given three broad areas of responsibility – each area applied across the entire spectrum of the private sector. First, the IVTB acted as a regulator of the training industry – training providers were obliged to register with the IVTB who would ensure that programme design and delivery met acceptable standards. Secondly, the IVTB acted as a facilitator of training by managing the training levy system that had been introduced. The basis of the system was that each private sector organization would pay 1% of payroll into a central fund and a grant refund from the levy collected would be reimbursed if they provided approved training for their workforce. The third role for the IVTB was to deliver training as a provider in its own right.

In 2002, the Mauritian Qualifications Authority (MQA) took over responsibility for the regulation of training providers. It has also assumed responsibility for the development and maintenance of the national qualifications framework. In the following year, the Government Council established the Human Resource Development Council (HRDC). This body has assumed responsibility for translating broad economic policy into skills requirements and analysing skills in sectors. These changes have meant that the IVTB is now concentrating entirely on the delivery of training. Although it operates across all sections, given its central importance to the future economic prosperity of the island, tourism is a particular area of focus. Indeed, the IVTB established a hotel school as long ago as 1990.

Training for tourism

The IVTB delivers three types of training for the tourist industry:

- Training, linked to the award of an accredited qualification within the national skills framework overseen by the MQA
- Training linked to a national apprenticeship scheme
- Short-courses specifically designed for client groups.

It is the first category that is becoming more important as efforts are being made to encourage more Mauritian nationals to acquire qualifications. Such qualifications include a national certificate at levels 2 and 3 and the more prestigious higher national diploma. It can take a student between one and three years of study to obtain one of these qualifications, depending on the level. The apprenticeship scheme involves a student spending four to five days of the week in the hotel and the fifth or sixth at the hotel school.

A considerable amount of training is delivered in-house at the larger international hotels on the island. Otherwise, virtually all the training for tourism in Mauritius takes place with the approval, or directly through, the IVTB. Currently, the IVTB has an annual capacity of 1800 places on accredited courses; to meet the projected manpower needs of the tourism industry, the number of places will need to almost double to 3500.

Understandably, Roland Dubois, the IVTB Director, sees building the capacity of the organization while maintaining quality as a major challenge. He observes that women are under represented in the trained workforce. Another frustration in his job is the inevitable poaching of trained staff from one hotel to another and the fact that many Mauritian trained staff leave the country to work in hotels in other countries. However, he says that an approach based on a commitment to training is essential for the island's future:

Only competent human resources, the only asset that we have, can help to propel Mauritius to the high end of the middle income group.

Some conclusions on culture

The exploration of the convergence–divergence question in the previous chapter led, as would be expected, to a conclusion that the most sensible position does not lie at either end of the spectrum. However, the discussion has shed some important light on the place of learning, training and development in the global knowledge and service economy.

The first conclusion is to reinforce what has been evident throughout the case studies. Organizations across the world are competing or seeking to deliver services in similar ways. The acquisition of relevant knowledge and skills by employees allows the organization to deliver services more effectively. If the organization is competing in the private marketplace, it will permit it to deliver higher value products. The aspirations or intentions of the people development professional are fundamentally the same throughout the world – and so far, all the evidence is that the processes adopted are also the same. The same competency lists (admittedly sometimes using a different language) are developed in different countries. There is no evidence of training courses, support and challenge interventions, or e-learning being deployed in a fundamentally different way because learners come from different cultural backgrounds.

However, if intentions and aspirations are the same, they must be executed in some very different contexts. This will become increasingly evident when we consider current practice in China. The key point is that learners come from different starting points and bring different baggage (for want of a better term) to the learning environment.

National culture is, however, just one of many variables that affect starting points and receptiveness. There is a danger of the word 'culture' being asked to do too much work. 'Context' is arguably a preferable term: those responsible for supporting, accelerating and directing learning must be able to adjust round the context in which the learners operate. Another term which could be used to describe the prior experience of groups of learners is labour receptiveness or legacy. Here, we should use a broad perspective which extends beyond Government policies on vocational skills.

'Culture', therefore, should be seen as an operational concept. It is one of the contextual factors that influence the way we should approach the delivery of training and learning.

One further important conclusion emerges from this discussion. Our consideration of learning, training and development in the multicultural context has underlined the importance of the people developer as an intermediary in the learning process. Whatever the context, it is the task of the people development professional to deliver the knowledge and skills agenda in a way that takes full account of the context – the broader legacy that the learner brings with them. It also suggests that our profession must be prepared to carry greater responsibility in the future. We have obligations to the organization and the individual to interpret what is required and deliver effectively in rapidly changing circumstances.

All this was elegantly captured in a detailed study in 2002, undertaken to investigate learning and teaching practices at the Cisco Network Academy program [4]. This is a public-private partnership between the IT Company Cisco, Governments and educational institutes, which teaches students how to design, build and maintain computer networks. Data were gathered using a web-based questionnaire and interviews with 300 students and 100 instructors involving 57 academies in 11 countries in Europe, the Middle East and Africa. Most interestingly, pedagogical practices were examined in each of the countries visited and their subsequent impact on how the curriculum was taught was assessed.

The findings offer a wealth of information on how culture and context can affect learning and teaching. The main conclusion offered good news to those of us who are involved in training delivery. The instructors made the programme culturally and pedagogically relevant for their students. They were the ones who assisted the students in their preparation for work in their own country by ensuring that the programme related to their country's infrastructure and standards. They also made any adaptations to the presentation of the curriculum to ensure that the approach taken fitted the usual learning environment.

To quote from Dr Michelle Selinger, the Cisco Systems Education Specialist who undertook the study:

Instructors should be fully aware that they are the most important element to the success of the program.

Good news for the profession indeed!

References

[1]. Harris, H. and Dickmann, M. (2005) International Management Development. London: Chartered Institute of Personnel and Development. Available at: www.cipd.co.uk/onlinedocuments
[2]. Smith, P.B., Bond, M.H. and Kagitcibasi, C. (2006) Understanding Social Psychology across Cultures. London: Sage.
[3]. Deissinger, T. (1997) The German Dual System – A Model for Europe? Education + Training, 39(8), 297–302.
[4]. Selinger, M. (2004) Cultural and Pediagogical Implications of a Global E-learning Programme. Cambridge Journal of Education, 34(2), 223–239.

14

Is China Different?

The emergence of the Republic of China as an active participant in the world economy is the economic story of our times. It has been the subject of a never-ending stream of analysis delivered in books, journal articles and newspaper columns.

Our concern here is more specific. What can we learn from the challenges that China will face in putting effective learning, training and development in place? Will people development in China be fundamentally different and if so why?

In early 2006, upward revisions of China's Gross Domestic Product – particularly the previously under-valued service sector – revealed it to be the fourth largest economy in the world. This had followed an extended period of unprecedented growth, underpinned by far-reaching and continued reforms which had begun in the late 1970s. Before the reforms, the economy was dominated by large state-owned enterprises (SOEs), which were concentrated on industrial production. In December 2001, following lengthy and demanding negotiations, China was admitted to the World Trade Organization (WTO). After admission, China undertook a massive overhaul of trade and business regulations to conform to WTO standards.

There have been far-reaching consequences of these reforms. First, the dominant SOEs will be expected to change in character. Secondly, there has been the emergence of a small but growing private sector. Thirdly, there has been the growing influence of multinational firms operating in this country. Each of these developments will have a profound influence in the pattern of learning, training and development. However, and here we are signalling our conclusions at the outset, whatever the sector, the role of learning, training and development will be fundamentally the same. Through increasing the knowledge and skills of the workforce, effective people development will allow the organization to compete more effectively by producing higher value products or delivering better services. The objective will be the same as everywhere else in the world, but the context in which learning and training is to be delivered will be different. In particular, the prior experiences of the learners (the labour legacy, using a broad definition) will create different starting points and different levels of receptiveness.

This is illustrated simply in the first case study, on the Hilton Hotels in Beijing and Shanghai, set out in Case study 14.1. Here, the aim is to bring staff up to the required standards, the time to competence, using an identical Technical and Behavioural Skills framework to that in place elsewhere in the Hilton Group. However, local labour market conditions (particularly in Beijing), present a considerable challenge.

Case study 14.1 Recruitment, attrition and training at the Hilton Hotels: Beijing and Shanghai

Background

The Hilton Beijing is a 375 room hotel, making it medium sized for the group. It is situated in the 'new diplomatic' area of the City and has just completed a major renovation of rooms, restaurants and bars, event facilities and public areas including the hotel lobby. There are just over 600 team members at the hotel. Almost the entire workforce is Chinese nationals. There are currently 13 non-Chinese team members on the payroll and all of them work in senior or middle management positions. Work permits are required for expatriate managers and these are difficult to obtain. Moreover, the hotel has a deliberate policy of developing its local workforce.

The Hilton Shanghai is a very large hotel: it has 720 rooms and an extensive conference and banqueting facility; 1200 staff are employed across eight major departments. All except some 20 of the staff are Chinese nationals – the exceptions are a number of management staff and four management trainees from overseas in an internship.

Recruitment and retention

At Shanghai, Ester Zheng, the Director of Human Resources and Development, regards recruitment as her major problem. Overall turnover rates are 7%, which is less than other hotels in Shanghai. This reflects a positive brand image for Hilton and the company's commitment to development – this is demonstrated in good results from staff surveys. However, the situation is particularly acute in the food and beverage department where staff need to have a standard of English which allows them to talk to guests and to be well presented. Hours of work are long and the salary of junior food and beverage attendants does not compare well with other departments in the hotel. There are a number of routes to recruitment, including websites, newspaper advertisements and links with hotel schools. The most important source of recruitment comes from websites and applicants who approach the hotel themselves.

Similarly in Beijing, Emma Ma, the Hotel's Human Resource Manager, and Marcia Stubbings, the Assistant Human Resources Manager who is in charge of Learning and Development, consider that team member attrition is the major problem that they face. The demand for team members who are able to work in international-standard hotels far exceeds the supply. Such team members not only need English language skills and good standards of personal grooming, but also an awareness of and ability to meet the requirements of international clientele. Experienced personnel will move to jobs in other hotels and often their ambitions for advancement exceed their capabilities. As a result, attrition rates at the Hilton Beijing can be quite high. This is both expensive in terms of resources and damaging for team members' morale. It will take some time for the labour market to adjust and, with the Beijing Olympics due in 2008, hotels are expanding and demand for suitable workforce is intensifying.

A number of strategies are in place to meet this operational challenge. At Shanghai, about 50–60 trainees are recruited into an internship programme at the hotel each year. They can start at various times in the year since initial orientation sessions are held once a month. Most of the trainees come from Shanghai, so have been living in a city which is open to international culture. However, few of these new joiners will have prior work experience in hotels – they could be shop assistants or part time tutors or retail attendants.

The Beijing Hotel has implemented a scheme which involves the recruitment of up to 70 trainees a year, who then undertake a year of training. The Hotel recruits three-quarters of this trainee population from the Shanxi Labour College located in Xian, which is 12 hours away by train from Beijing. Trainees are also recruited from hospitality and catering schools elsewhere in China, including Beijing, but as Emma Ma puts it:

> *The rapid growth and resulting shortage of skilled personnel in all industry sectors in the major centres has led to skewed expectations of the young generation. They no longer wish to enter the service industry as a first choice and are very particular about the jobs they will take. Those in rural areas are keen to take the jobs, but lack the educational background and awareness of the international approach required.*

The trainees from rural centres have not had the exposure to the demands of an international hotel. They will not have taken a meal in a western-style restaurant or experienced the accompanying service. In part, this raises practical issues in delivering a training programme – the culinary skills taught at rural centres often focus on Chinese rather than western cuisine and service delivery. As Marcia Stubbings puts it:

> *Trainees from secondary cities tend to have a less developed awareness of some common etiquette and therefore may need to be reminded to avoid certain behaviours when in the lobby or guest contact areas.*

As a result the city-based students tend to progress more quickly during their training period.

Training at the hotels

Once the trainees have joined, they spend two days in orientation, which is mainly focused on giving the trainee an exposure to the Hilton company culture: what is expected of them and the support they receive. They then spend a period of two to four weeks on initial training: in most cases half of this time is spent in the classroom and half in an operational department, closely supervised by a manager or a skills trainer. This is then followed by a period of rotating assignments. During this period they have to complete the TBS training (see Case study 6.4, p. 127). The TBS forms have been translated into Mandarin Chinese and this is the preferred version in some departments, for example, housekeeping. At the end of that period, successful trainees are offered jobs; some may decide to return to their home town or village.

It can be seen that on-the-job training is critical to trainee progress. Both hotels have similar mechanisms in place to ensure that there is effective delivery of support for learning in the workplace. At Shanghai, for example, each department has one to two departmental trainers and some skills trainers depending on the size and they will all have secured certification following a train the trainer course. There is also a network of 62 skills trainers across the Hotel. Ideally, the HR department would like 10% of total staff to be skills trainers. These staff are certified to deliver the brand standards and departmental skills and knowledge training.

Training to learning

The HR and training staff at both hotels regard the Chinese trainees as passive learners compared to other nationalities. In their view, Chinese learners like to take notes and are less likely to interact or ask why. They ascribe this to the instructor-led pattern of Chinese education. Indeed, Rachel Deng, the Shanghai Training Manager, describes her mission at the hotel as seeking to:

> *Help the learners find their passion.*

She does, however, detect marked regional differences in approach among the trainees and adjusts her style accordingly. Unsurprisingly, trainees from Shanghai are seen as the most sophisticated and confident learners.

At Beijing, both Emma Ma and Marcia Stubbings emphasize that all trainees, but especially those from rural areas, are eager to learn and to seize the opportunity to acquire the relevant skills. Generally, they regard Chinese learners as well motivated but somewhat passive in their approach. They ascribe this to the fact that they are products of an education system which is firmly instructor-led and does not encourage interaction. However, they respond rapidly and become receptive to more participative methods. As Marcia Stubbings observed:

> *After our initial induction session, one Chinese trainee said to me: 'It's amazing – I never knew learning could be like that. I had fun'.*

Unsurprisingly, Marcia Stubbings sees a key demand of her job as adjusting her approach to the learning needs of trainees from different parts of the country.

Why should learning in China be different?

It is not surprising that, after taking account of the different starting points of the learner, the approach used at the Hilton Hotels in China is fundamentally the same as that applied elsewhere in the Group. The product demanded by the consumer, in this case the guest, is a global product.

This is by no means incompatible with the suggestion that Chinese people learn differently. So we must ask if there is something in the Chinese character and traditions that cause them to learn in different ways.

There are two undercurrents in the research literature that offer some indications that this might be the case. The first is the work on Chinese Personality assessment and the second is a consideration of the idea of 'guanxi' – a concept which is firmly embedded in the Confucian tradition.

In Chapter 12 (p. 229), the Personality Profiles of Culture project and its consideration of the universal applicability of the 'Big Five' was outlined. Researchers at the Chinese University of Hong Kong, especially Professor Fanny Cheung, have produced evidence to suggest that an indigenously-developed assessment of personality measured features which were not uncovered by tests developed in the west. This instrument is known as the Chinese Personality Assessment Inventory (CPAI) [1].

The additional dimension concerned interpersonal relatedness.

This factor, which was originally labelled as the Chinese Tradition factor, consists of the indigenous personality scales developed specifically for the

CPAI, including Ren Qing (relationship orientation), Harmony and face. In addition, this factor is loaded negatively by Flexibility. The characteristics associated with these personality scales reflect a strong orientation toward instrumental relationships; emphasis on occupying one's proper place and in engaging in appropriate action; avoidance of internal, external and inter-personal conflict; and adherence to norms and traditions [2].

Where this finding becomes of importance to our discussion is its link with the concept of guanxi. This describes the extensive penetration of business networks and the cooperative personal relationships and mutual obligations that arise as a result. A 2005 journal article explored this in some detail.

The rigid social hierarchy under the Confucian paradigm may also prevent fully autonomous and flexible teamwork. While creating and sustaining group attachment and conformity, the same elements of Chinese culture also create top-down control, which contradicts true teamwork norms of risk taking and responsibility ... The paradoxical feature of Confucianism may lead to risk aversion in the workforce, mistrust of co-workers and personalized favouritism [3, p. 319, 4].

and

Our analysis of literature revealed two interesting facts. First, as one of the most dominant ideologies in Chinese history, Confucianism has profoundly influenced management and HR practices in China in some paradoxical ways. The imprint of the Confucian legacy is still glaringly evident in modern Chinese organizations. Consequently, we posit that organization and man-agement practices in China can be partly understood through the examin-ation of Confucian values [3, p. 324].

Taken together, the emerging work on the Chinese personality characteristics and a consideration of the Confucian tradition, particularly guanxi, point in one direction. Interpersonal relationships among Chinese people in the workplace could develop in a different way to those that are evident in the West. However, this may not mean that they will necessarily learn in a different way. The operational question, of course, is: 'If so, in what way should the people development activities be conducted differently?'

The short answer to the question 'is learning in China different?' is that we do not know yet. There is insufficient evidence to date to suggest that 'inter–relatedness' will produce a different pattern of learning. However, we can offer a prognostica-tion based on the conclusions presented at the end of Chapter 13.

The problem, as and when it arises, will be dealt with by competent profes-sionals applying their skills to the situation that they face. The personal develop-ment professional will use his or her craft skills to adjust their approach accordingly.

Table 14.1 summarizes some views gained in the cause of interviews with training professionals employed by the different companies in the Jardine Matheson Group in Hong Kong. They indicate the set of adjustments that these development professionals think will be necessary to deploy training, learning and development in mainland China.

Such adjustments are already happening in respect of training, learning and development in China in respect of one feature of 'labour legacy'. It seems

Table 14.1 Some observations from Hong Kong

- There is a real eagerness to learn and a positive learning attitude from those I encounter in our management training. However, many of the participants have had little exposure to business elsewhere. They are therefore looking to the trainer to supply a lot of specific content and knowledge. They greatly value the learning provided by the company and see this as a form of personal value enhancement.

  Belinda Li, Dairy Farms
- The mainland Chinese I encounter are more enthusiastic learners.

  Joyce Chan, Gammon Construction
- As we develop our business in mainland China, there may be a need for more emphasis on detailed processes. Certainly, at present there is a different understanding of quality and of customer services. It will be easier for those who have had prior experience through working in multinational corporations.

  Catherine Chau, Hong Kong Land
- The same skills are required so we would use the same training techniques. However, on mainland China, interpersonal relationships are seen as very important – often more so than policies. Some practical issues will arise; first, there may be a need to seek other ways of getting things done rather than assuming procedural compliance. Secondly, there could be a requirement to spend a lot of time in selling the benefits of any training and learning interventions to functional managers before their support is secured and they use their network to the benefit of the organization.

  Ben Li, Jardine Aviation Services, Hong Kong International Airports
- In Hong Kong we require things yesterday, however, the pace of getting things done in mainland China could be more gradual. Working with management in China will take a longer time. The learners may be more reserved and less extrovert. While they look earnestly for opportunities to learn, some are less likely to come forward and request development; partly because they do not want to ask in case they are turned down; partly because they do not want to undermine the position of their boss.

  Alice Wong, Jardine Engineering Corporation

universally agreed that Chinese learners are relatively passive learners. This has emerged repeatedly in interviews with people development professionals and, as will be seen later, in case studies. This perspective was best expressed by William H. Mobley, the Group CEO & Managing Director of Mobley Group Pacific and a Professor at the China Europe International Business School. In an interview with the author, he offered the following thoughts based on both research and his business consultancy experience:

> *It may not be easy to create an environment with western trainers and Chinese learners where there is an interactive approach to learning. There is more need for context, structure and time must be taken to establish a relationship between trainer and learner. However, once that relationship is established, the interactive learning dynamic can be powerful.*
>
> *There are a number of factors at work. To an extent it is a product of the traditional Chinese educational system and participants feel: 'I'm the student, you're the teacher, so teach'. It is also about possible loss of face: participants may not speak up in case they get it wrong, or to embarrass the trainer with questions the trainer is not ready to answer.*
>
> *Language is also an issue. Where English is not the first language, the pace should be slower as participants need more time to process the information.*
>
> *Taken together, this may suggest an initially more passive learning style; that can become more interactive and dynamic with positive relationship and appropriate pace. Frequent use of metaphors, stories and concrete examples can help establish the context.*

The multinational interface

The case studies that follow next are drawn from two multinational companies who are concerned with developing a talent pool from China. The pragmatic but thoughtful approach needed to adjust global business ambitions to China is evident throughout. Similar case studies have been presented on Motorola University in Chapter 4 and Ingersoll-Rand in Chapter 12.

At Ciba (Case study 14.2), the aim is to create a common platform for learning. The emphasis is on appropriate local adaptations of global programmes.

TNT, the global logistics group has had a presence in China for 20 years and sees the country as offering major growth opportunities. It is currently establishing a China University; this and other initiatives are outlined in Case study 14.3.

⌐ **Case study 14.2 Implementing a global HRD strategy at local level: Ciba Specialty Chemicals**

Background

Ciba Specialty Chemicals is a global company (with headquarters in Basel, Switzerland) producing specialty chemicals which, added in small quantities, improve existing or add new qualities to materials at every stage of their production processes. As well as products, Ciba offers a wide range of knowledge-based services and expertise, providing customers with complete solutions to enhance their businesses. Ciba serves several major markets including the Automotive, Packaging, Home and Personal Care, Paper and Printing, Construction, Electronics, Water Treatment and Agriculture industries.

The company employs 15 000 people worldwide. Sales are well balanced between three major market areas: Europe, the Americas and the Asia-Pacific region. Manufacturing takes place in a number of countries with significant operations in Switzerland, the UK, the USA, France, Germany, Mexico and China – the subject of this case study.

The company employs some 900 people in mainland China, Hong Kong and Taiwan. There are a number of production facilities; they include production of antioxidants (for plastics industry), chemicals for water and paper treatment and pigments (for inks industry). About half of the 900 employees are in production, one quarter in sales and marketing and the others in research and development and support functions. All but 5% of the employees are Chinese nationals. The international employees and regionally seconded staff are working mainly in technical or management roles, with a number taking regional responsibilities.

The work of the competency centre

Ciba Specialty Chemicals coordinates and implements its people development policy through global and regional competency centres. Bob Morton, who is based in the UK, is Head of Competency Centre for Europe, Middle East and Africa. He works extensively across the regions in the OD field. In his view, developing programmes across different countries requires a carefully considered approach which takes full account of national cultures. He recognizes that there are differences between different countries in terms of their desire for and acceptance of experiential and instructional models; hence it is important to develop models that can be adapted to different contexts and to set up processes that 'ensure that this adaptation can take place'. The first question is 'what must be the same and what can be different?' The approach is to design courses and other activities and interventions using check-lists to ensure cultural compatibility and materials and activities that can be amended or customized at the local level. Where required new activities are designed on a local basis.

Germaine Tang, who has worked for Ciba Specialty Chemicals for nine years and comes originally from Singapore, is Head of Competency Centre, People Development for Asia Pacific. This extends across 13 countries with the largest numbers of employees located in China and India. She is based in Shanghai and describes her role as follows:

> *To ensure employees are equipped with the necessary skills and competencies to be effective in their roles and in developing a talent pool sufficient and ready for succession into key local or regional leadership positions.*

Current challenges

Germaine Tang has placed, and will continue to place, much of her energies across two distinct areas in China:

- general training for all staff
- development of leadership potential, especially local talents.

Ciba have a strong focus on people development and are prepared to commit resources to ensure that employees across all levels acquire a common language for skills. In Germaine Tang's view, this will create a common platform for learning. Accordingly, a range of courses aimed at the 'soft' skills of the employees has been developed and the intention is that all employees will attend this training over a period of time. These workshops are instructor-led; they are typically two to three days in duration with between 15 and 18 participants present. Topic areas include: personal effectiveness, working in teams, problem-solving, managing customer relationships, running a business etc. Most employees who have a development need will be given priority in attending these training courses.

The basic course design has been produced by Bob Morton's team. The Competency Centre People Development team in China 'ensure this translates' in the local context. This adaptation takes place at the design and the delivery stage. Content must be reviewed to ensure that it will be readily understood and seen as relevant.

The way in which courses need to be adjusted for the local learner can be very detailed and will only be understood by those with practical experience in this environment. A good example is the technique of 'visualization' as in:

> *'If you are uncomfortable giving presentations, imagine you are giving a successful presentation – focus on what is going well, enjoy the feeling of confidence, positive attention and approval from the audience'.*

In Germaine Tang's experience, some learners who have not undertaken a great deal of western soft skills training may find such a concept difficult to grasp.

Courses are mainly delivered by internal Ciba Specialty Chemicals' line managers and HR, who can be expected to understand the workforce, the employees that they face and the language that they use. However, the plan is to complement this by leveraging external providers into the training and development process to gain a broader perspective both internally and externally; this will need a different approach in customization at the delivery stage.

Germaine Tang's recent priority, which is growing in importance, concerns the development of leadership. This concerns the identification and development of high potentials for middle to senior positions in Asia. From a management development pool of about 400 people in the Asia Pacific region as a whole, some 20 high-potentials have been identified after discussions with senior managers and human resources. These 20 will be developed by a variety of means including: international secondments or transfers; participation in regional/global projects; provision of a mentor drawn for the senior regional leadership forum; participation in regional management programmes. A new management programme for the region is at the pilot stage. This will involve collaboration efforts from two very established business schools; the INSEAD (with a campus in Singapore) and the CEIBS (China Europe International Business School with a presence in China).

Some challenges

Inevitably, Germaine Tang feels that the resources at her disposal are often extremely stretched. She also admits to frustration when Ciba Specialty Chemicals have invested resources in developing and grooming people only to see them leave. However, she sees this as inevitable and that the strong company culture of people development will continue to have support from the top and companies with a good reputation for developing people have a better chance of attracting new talent.

Her views on Chinese learners are positive. She sees a real enthusiasm on the part of employees to learn. With exposure to different learning methods over time, they will become even more independent and self-directed learners:

Participants sometimes refer to me as 'teacher'. I will often tell them I'm not a teacher; my role is to facilitate your learning process.

However, as they become more exposed to management training and company practice, employees begin to feel more confident and will increasingly seek 'other ways' of doing things. This is seen as a general tendency in the business: not a particular issue for learning and development.

Overall, Germaine Tang feels:

> *In Ciba China we have made a good starting point. It is important to begin with developing this common management language across the businesses and at all levels of the organization. We will then go on to develop our line managers too. They play a pivotal role in the daily application of learning of their employees. By taking steps in ensuring that they give follow-up and support to the training and learning of their subordinates, then would the real transfer of learning take place back at the workplace.*

Case study 14.3 Aligning with business needs at TNT China

The business context

TNT has had a presence in China for nearly 20 years. This had originally taken the form of a joint venture company with a state-owned enterprise. Overseas owned companies entering the logistics sector in China then participated in this form of joint venture arrangement.

In tandem with China's entry into the World Trade Organization (WTO) in 2001, TNT's strategy in China was aligned to the new market opportunities which this created. In 2003, as TNT's joint venture tenure ended, TNT established its majority-owned entity in China. It currently has 2000 employees based in 25 branches across China and another 3000 in an automotive logistics joint venture. TNT has announced that it will divest the automotive logistics joint venture but will be greatly extending its scope and range of services in China by acquiring the Hoau networks and distribution group, a private company employing 12 000 people. Supported by some key expatriate expertise, the majority of the staff of the current and enlarged company after acquisition will be Chinese nationals.

TNT sees China as playing a crucial role in its business strategy. Based on market projection, as much as a third of world manufacturing capital could be located in China and, as a result, the logistics flow will be far higher. China could become TNT's second biggest market after Europe and this will require considerable commitment in management, physical and human resources.

Investing in people

Investors in People (IiP) is a UK-based standard of training effectiveness and, when this benchmark was applied outside the UK, TNT became one of the first companies to extend its range internationally. SiewKim Sim, who originates from Singapore, is the Human Resources Director for TNT Greater China. Previously based in TNT's Asia Regional Headquarters, she was responsible for ensuring that IiP certification was secured across all 11 countries in the region. Currently, given the huge organizational changes in training, formal IiP status is pending, but the principles are applied and application for accreditation is intended in the future. Indeed, SiewKim Sim says that a high proportion of the current employees in China know of IiP and its principles. What is beyond doubt is that they are aware of the TNT's view that the protection and development of its brand requires a commitment to investment in its people.

Over the last two years, TNT in China has trained about 2000 employees annually. The company delivered 14 000 days training each year, or an average of 7 days annual training per employee. Nearly all staff have participated in this training effort – from operatives and drivers upwards. Much of this training has concentrated on the systems and key processes needed to create business advantage for TNT – for example, operations, customer service and billings. Some have concentrated on the particular needs of the China market: TNT has introduced direct mail marketing to develop new business in China, a relatively novel marketing approach in the country. A growing proportion of the training has involved management and soft skills and the interpersonal skills involved in selling and leadership.

One consequence is that TNT's staff acquire capabilities which make them attractive to other employers. TNT's turnover rate of staff, at 12% annually, is much lower than the market norm; however, competition for scarce talents in this rapidly expanding market is exponentially accelerating. Although SiewKim Sim cited this as a key challenge, she emphasized that TNT's objectives are long term and:

TNT will continue to train, develop and build a career for our people.

As part of its strategic initiatives, TNT China established the TNT China University in September 2004. This was formed in cooperation partnership with the Shanghai Jiaotong University (SJU), one of the top three universities in China – with a strong reputation in both logistics and management education. SiewKim Sim sees the TNT China University as an essential element in developing a workforce with world-class competencies to deliver business goals. The University training programmes have mainly been delivered by a network of 80 in-house trainer-managers. They train as part of their professional responsibility and the process is cascaded downwards.

SJU intends to create one of the best logistics schools in the country and TNT will be able to call on a faculty of capable staff who understand the needs of their business. Topic areas to be developed include executive and certification programmes, leadership, e-learning, knowledge management and competency mapping.

Adapting to the Chinese market

SiewKim Sim emphasizes that:

Training strategy must be evolved in alignment with business strategy – that's the continuous challenge.

Business needs to drive the training requirements and TNT hopes to secure business advantage through the ability of their people to manage and deliver globally and locally using superior systems and processes. There are certain worldwide standards and best practices that are consistently deployed. Some may be adapted to the Chinese market – for example, a 'China Link' technology system was adapted from a global model and applied locally to accommodate business transactions in the Mandarin language. The sheer size and scale of the market is another factor – the newly announced acquisition Hoau has currently a physical presence in over 400 Chinese cities.

The Chinese employment market and labour demographics is of course a key feature of the adaptation required and has a major impact on training and learning. Government legislation is increasingly aimed at building and nurturing the labour force at this stage of economic transition. According to SiewKim Sim, the confluence of historical, economic, cultural and social developments and legacies have significant impact on workforce training needs in China. Hence, her strong belief that a consistent and long-term development strategy is critical to enable business to deliver targeted training results for business goals.

The problem of scale

In March 2001, the Chinese Government published its tenth five-year plan. This specifically addressed issues of quality and of weak competitiveness in world markets. It identified problems that were acting as barriers to productivity. Importantly, it called for the reform of the 'socialist market economic system' and the establishment of a modern enterprise system with clearly established ownership, well defined power and responsibility and separate enterprise management from government administration. Although the private sector is growing rapidly, the public sector will continue to play a dominant role.

The challenge involved in reforming the State Owned Enterprises (SOEs) is enormous. Visitors to China cannot fail to be impressed (indeed often overwhelmed) by the interest in western management methods. Indeed, at times, this seems to amount to an undue reverence reflecting the 'I'm the student you're the teacher' mind-set previously noted. What strikes any observer, however, is the sheer scale of the problem – there are huge numbers of supervisors, front-line and middle managers who need to be introduced to, what is for them, novel techniques. Consider the challenge facing Madam Xia Xiao Ling who produces a special feature on management skills for 'Workers' Daily'. Details are set out in Case study 14.4.

At times the approach may appear propagandist, or indeed simplistic. Case study 14.5 on the 'six-one' campaign at Nan Yang power could also be regarded in this way. This would be a mistake – concentrating on the underlying message rather than the means of expression reveals something important. There is a determination to get massive numbers of people into learning at work in the shortest possible time – using whatever methods seem appropriate.

Both the case 'The Sky for Supervisors' and 'Nan Yang Power' are case illustrations produced by Chinese development professionals. The reader is asked to excuse the imperfections in English, which arose from the need to compromise between the requirements of translation and elegance of expression.

What is beyond dispute is the desire to learn and apply the best techniques in the context in which Chinese business operates. This comes through clearly in Case study 14.6, which describes the work undertaken at the Electricity State Grid Advanced Training Centre.

Case study 14.4 The Sky for Supervisors

(The only special publication dealing with issues facing shop-floor workers and supervisors in China.)

Workers' Daily is affiliated to China Trade Union, a newspaper produced from Beijing and distributed throughout China to workers in state-owned enterprises. It has a daily print-run of over a million copies, which makes it the second biggest newspaper in the country (the first is People's Daily).

The purpose of the paper is to be the server to Trade Unions, factories and workers. In this purpose, a new special feature was introduced in 1987. This is entitled 'The Sky for Supervisors'. It is designed to explain the work and life reality of 150 million workers in China, to express their passion and voices. Especially to lead and encourage workers across China to enhance their workplace skills and role competition through self-development and team learning, promote the outstanding individual and team. The main target audience for this feature are the supervisors or 'cell leaders' (the lowest officers and highest soldiers in enterprises) and seven and a half million Trade Union leaders of more than 100 million cells in the state-owned enterprises.

These are the people the State has identified as the group needed to deliver operational plans at factory level and the pool from which the leaders of the future will be chosen. There is an urgent need to improve the comprehensive competency and especially management skills of this population.

Madam Xia Xiao Ling produced the special feature and is the editor in chief up to present. Her main message to her readers is:

If you want to survive you must learn.

Now, there is an all-round report on 'building learning cells, being a learning worker' initiative, not only to promote the successful experiences of state owned enterprises, individual and team, but also to urge the huge number of workers to learn and become more competitive. Recently, there was a major feature on 'worker's capability project' in a Shanghai Baogang steelworks, which is one of the 500 in the world, and 'Learning team building' in Shenyang Airplane corp. and get a great success. The special feature has introduced a competition for the most effective self-motivated learner, outstanding supervisors and holds an annual conference with 1000 chosen representatives, which focuses on improving skills at that level.

According to Madam Xia Xiao Ling, given the scale of the Chinese first line management population, the initial emphasis must be on individual self-development. The next stage is for the cells in the enterprises to work in groups locally to develop their skills. Only after that will it become possible to implement management training. To assist in this process of self-awareness and communication she has introduced a 'Windows on Education' column which contains suggestions for practical steps to training, ideology theory learning, operate skills, develop creativity, strengthen professional ethics and improve cell leaders skills – this was recently re-entitled Education Platform. Other regular features are: a special column on Innovation Presentation, Cell Leaders Management Skills Arena, State Owned Enterprise perspective, First Line Mirror to express the junior workers and cells. This has included a discussion on such practices as total quality management, production management, 'democratic management', managing small teams and people management – the last according to Madam Xia Xiao Ling is growing in importance in China and receiving greater priority in the newspaper.

All content is determined by the Publicity Department, which is a constituent part of the Communist Party as other national papers; National Trade Union is the administrative superior. Recently, a decision was made to widen the scope of the special by including ideas of success of cell management and worker growth from outside China – including management practice and skills and guest writers on cell management.

⌐ **Case study 14.5 'Six-One' at Nan Yang Power**

Background of the company

Nan Yang Power was founded in February 1969. Affiliated to State Grid, Henan Provincial power, Nan Yang Power is large-scale and responsible for power construction and management of power supply of many cities and designated to lead 11 county power companies.

Basic goal of the learning campaign – 'six-one'

In the last two years, Nan Yang Power has called for 'strive to mastery, pursue excellence' enterprise spirit according to 'building strong power net, with good assets, excellent service and performance', the purpose proposition of State Grid, promoting company competition and creativity by creating a learning corporate culture – people oriented, advocate learning, motivate and tap talent potential, explore a new field of corporate culture created by promoting 'six-one' campaign among the staff.

Content of 'six-one'

'Six-one' campaign, i.e. '*one book*: each person each year read a good book, *one article*: write a valuable theoretical essay or work experience, *one suggestion*: raise a suggestion for the improving of the work, *one project*: complete a project for the advertising of the company, *one piece* of experience: innovate an operation practice, *one sentence*: abstract a sentence as motto'.

'Six-one' campaign is a carrier to develop the staff to learn and read. 'Each person read a book' is the premise and foundation, the other five 'ones' are the heritage and development of the first, it is a system thinking and practice. 'Write a valuable theoretical essay or work experience' is an important step to strengthen the effect of learning and reading. 'Raise a suggestion for the improving of the work' is the sublimation of learning result. 'Complete a work for the advertising of the company' is a test criterion of the former three 'ones'. 'Innovate an operation practice' is a review and crystallization of the former four 'ones'. 'Abstract a sentence as motto' is a general advance of the former five 'ones'.

The linkage between 'six-one' and 'daily work'

'Six-one' campaign, which is around 'work in learning, learn in working', advocates a new learning concept in staff, promotes the merger of learn and work, learn and practice, business operation and corporate culture creating, forms a 'work process transfer to learn process, learn process transfer to work process' relationship chain.

Methods to make 'six-one' work

To make sure of the success of 'six-one' campaign, Nan Yang Power mainly makes great efforts as follows:

Establish a system, elaborately deploy. Nan Yang Power form a leadership team for the 'six-one' campaign, print and distribute the notice about promoting 'six-one' campaign, instruction about implementation of 'six-one', list 'six-one' campaign in annual measure objective, establish standardization activity and staff learning documents, settle a firm foundation for 'six-one' campaign.

Effectively operation, various practices. Nan Yang Power take 'six-one' in their annual working plan, identify the content, objective and purpose. Take advantage of the culture-art festival, corporate culture forum, sports activity, work contest and so on, lead the 'six-one' campaign to go deep.

Results and recognitions bought by this learning campaign

Nan Yang Power emerge a lot of technical master-hand and outstanding individual through this 'six-one' campaign. Managers write more than 300 theoretical essays and work experiences; staff write more than 600, raise more than 3600 pieces of suggestions, each them can read one or two books, 95% of staff can abstract one sentence as motto.

'Six-one' campaign drives the creating of corporate culture, builds high quality team, pours energy and vital force to the company, facilitates the success of Nan Yang Power. In the last two years, the volume of sales increase continually, get first in the contest of industry ethos among more than 60 organizations in Nan Yang and win 'May day labour medal' title.

Case study 14.6 Developing managers for the Chinese electricity industry: the State Grid Advanced Training Centre, Beijing

Background

The State Grid in China is responsible for the electricity transmission and distribution throughout the People's Republic of China. Its role is central to the progress of economic and social development. It is a state-owned enterprise with 1.5 million employees and is one of the largest organizations in the world. The China National Grid Advance Training Centre occupies a large site in the north of the city of Beijing. It has bedroom accommodation for 600 students at any one time and offers higher level management and technical training for the industry.

The challenges faced by the electricity industry are considerable. Much of the electricity production in China is located in the west of the country, while demand from the consumers is concentrated in the coastal regions and the east.

The State Grid is committed to the establishment of a 'hyper-grid' across the country to meet the future demands. Management capability must be improved at all levels and the industry must become more competitive in the way it delivers its service to customers. Expansion of the activities of the National Grid Advance Training Centre is an essential part of this transition.

The Centre's activities

The Centre delivers a programme of residential courses for Chinese managers from the national and provincial organizations, these are constituents of the State Grid organizations. The dominant approach is classroom instruction and courses can run from two to three months in duration to less than a week. The syllabus mainly concentrates on management training, though some technical subjects are included; class groups can comprise up to 100 participants, with 20–30 being the normal size. Classroom instructors are drawn from the industry, government, research departments and subject experts. Multimedia is used in the classroom. There is an increasing need for compliance and financial training and a growing interest in overseas practices. For some years, the most Senior Managers in the sector have received training overseas

Although some of the participants may have a degree which includes management science, for many it will be the first experience of management training. Attendance at the College can be linked with promotion on the return, so there is generally a high level of motivation on the part of learners.

Classroom training to learning

One of the challenges facing the College is the need to develop a range of approaches to learning. The Training Centre, together with a local consultancy firm, Alphasta Learning Solutions, has embarked on some research pilots to introduce different methods of learning through 'Leadership Transformation' learning projects. The methods included:

- *Leadership competency modelling and assessment by first line managers.* The leadership competency modelling and assessment has allowed each Manager to understand and establish clear job expectations, both for themselves as well as for their direct reports. This learning has become essential to support their role shift from 'planned' to 'market' economy. Once the gaps are discovered and agreed, the Managers are frequently encouraged to learn what is required through self-study.
- *Structured and guided business improvement projects by leadership coaching.* Coaching and managing continuous improvements capability of the Managers are developed through the introduction of the *Six Sigma* methodology to improve their project performance. This, coupled with a 'coaching skills' certification for the project team leaders, has allowed the managers to learn and acquire essential competencies to support their new role as a leaders practising 'democratic management'.
- *Managerial competency certification through a learning log process.* The Learning Log acts as a structured reflective learning tool-kit that allows the managers to codify their tacit knowledge, allowing them to confirm and share their learning. This practice has not only allowed the managers to align their learning to the organization but also to their personal needs.

Future challenges

The College has now produced its 11th five-year plan. This mainly focuses on the expansion of the facilities, from 600 residential places to 800. The volume requirements for trained managers dominate most of the other considerations but must take place alongside a transition agenda. The size and scale of the management challenge cannot be understated and must dominate thinking on future plans.

Moving forward

This brief overview of training, learning and development in China cannot claim to be more than a snapshot. At the current stage in the country's economic development, there is insufficient information available to do more than generalize or speculate. There are no worthwhile hard data on activities in the growing private sector – those organizations that are neither state-owned, subsidiaries of foreign organizations nor joint ventures. However, received wisdom in China is that such organizations currently undertake little people development since, at this stage, they can do little more than survive and hope to contain costs to grow. Given their ambitions to move into the higher value added products, it can be expected that the situation will change and they will, in time, adopt more progressive people management policies.

For the SOEs, however, the position is clear. They need to ensure that some basic processes are in place. They need to move rapidly into the formalized stage of people development outlined in Chapter 4 (p. 83) and developed in Chapter 11 (p. 212).

At this stage in their transition, it is suggested that they need three building blocks in place:

■ a basic understanding of fundamental management skills
■ a clearly understood set of skills or traits, best expressed as a set of competency frameworks
■ a process for individual development planning.

Together these constitute some of the human resource development processes described in Chapter 6. Many examples have all been included in case studies throughout this book: this serves to underline the fact that we are all facing similar issues wherever we are seeking to develop the capability of our workforce. Professionals will be applying their skills in demanding situations – as the final case study in the joint venture at Infinite Shanghai Communication Terminals illustrates. This is set out in Case study 14.7.

Case study 14.7 Creating and implementing a training plan at a Shanghai joint venture company

Background: the company

Infinite Shanghai Communication Terminals Limited is a joint venture between Viditec, an American company headquartered in Texas, and a Chinese State-owned enterprise, Shanghai Video and Audit. The company manufactures analogue telephone handsets and the founding overseas partner was the Siemens group, who sold their share holding to Viditec in 2001. Over 700 staff are employed in an assembly plant in a large industrial zone in Pudong, Shanghai. Some 500 of the employees are engaged in manufacturing operations and the overwhelming majority are female. Split shift working means that assembly can take place 12 hours a day. The company adopts the Working Hour System of Comprehensive Calculation in assembly plant, which means each operator works no more than 168 hours per month. The comprehensive calculation system must be registered and approved by the local government office according to the labour regulations. The other 200 employees work in research and development, quality control, logistics, sales and marketing and the support functions including human resources and finance.

Hui Qin Lu, known throughout the organization as Jingle Lu, started working for the company as a secretary and subsequently moved to a junior role in its human resource department. In 2005, she took a year out to gain a Masters Degree in Human Resource Management at Bournemouth University, returning in 2006 to take up the role of the Manager of the Human Resource and Administration Division. She has a staff of 10 reporting to her.

Much of the challenge of the job involves reconciling the western and Chinese approaches to human resources. The Chinese partners wish to see western management methods in place in the factory and the General Manager has years of management experience in European companies. However, the State Party Trade Union is the organ for workforce representation and Jingle Lu's job involves maintaining a delicate balance between the various stakeholders. Her main priorities across a wide range of responsibilities are training, developing better employee relations through joint agreement and cost control.

Planning training

One of Jingle Lu's main activities has been to introduce a more systematic approach to the identification of training needs and the management of training. She has prepared an annual training plan for the company based on detailed interviews with line managers and representative staff. This has led to the production of a training course catalogue which is made available as hard copy and on the company intranet. Nominations for participation in courses can be made electronically through the intranet.

The major initiative has been the introduction of a series of one-day courses held every Friday at the Dong Hua University premises. Between five and ten employees participate at a time and they can range from middle management down to factory operatives, depending on the subject under discussion. Typical topics would be communication skills, presentation skills and sales and marketing. The events are delivered by a firm of external consultants, Zhong-Ke consulting, who are Chinese nationals (instruction is in Mandarin Chinese), but who have experience in western teaching. Indeed, Jingle Lu has remarked that when she attended an early one-day event:

> *The instructor discussed the difference between human resource management and personnel management and it reminded me that the topic was covered in much the same way as my lectures at Bournemouth University.*

Generally, Jingle Lu sees little difference in terms of the content of the subject matter, but remarks, in common with others, that Chinese learners:

Are more used to instruction and are deferential to the instructor.

She is keen to promote more participative and active styles of learning. One initiative is to encourage those who have attended events to share their knowledge with colleagues in short workshops held on the company premises.

Operative work can be characterized as routine production. Training is on-the-job, is the responsibility of line managers and is monitored by senior production managers. There are three grades of payment for operative staff and they can only progress if they acquire and complete an assessment in the relevant skills. Jingle Lu therefore feels that the processes in place are effective.

The influence of the joint venture and the training delivered by the Zhong-Ke consultants, means that the line managers would understand the concept of coaching. However, pressures of time and the routine nature of the job means that, at present coaching is not given a high priority on the shop floor.

Reconciling individual and organizational objectives

Recently, one of the senior managers completed an MBA at Shanghai's Fu-Dan University. Although this was self-financed, it has led to an internal demand for company support for recognized qualifications. The ACCA accountancy qualification, for example, is highly regarded. While there is a willingness to encourage staff development, there is also a need to contain costs. The situation is made more difficult because there is currently draft human resource legislation from the Chinese Government which would limit the ability of companies to reclaim funding for the costs of external training for staff who leave. The draft law would appear to limit employee repayment to employers for employer-provided training of full-time, off-the-job technical training of six months or more. Changes under the draft law could result in fewer training and growth opportunities for the employee.

One practical step that Jingle Lu has taken is to introduce a mini-MBA training event. This will involve two days a week attendance over a four-month period. It will be delivered by the Zhong-Ke consultant and replicate, at a less intensive level, the essential theories, practices and techniques taught on the MBA. A certification will be issued, but it will not achieve formal accreditation within the University system.

The development challenge in China is of a scale that has never before been experienced. However, it is an exceptional case, not a special case. In this author's view, the same solutions will have been applied as elsewhere in the world. Their application may be quantitatively different but they will not be conceptually different.

References

[1]. Cheung, F.M. (2004) Use of Western and Indigenously Developed Personality Tests in Asia. Applied Psychology: An International Review, 53(2), 173–191.

[2]. Cheung, F.M., Leung, K., Fan, R., Song, et al. (1996) Development of the Chinese Personality Assessment Inventory (CPAI). Journal of Cross-Cultural Psychology, 27, 181–199, cited in Smith P.B., Bond, M.H. and Kagitcibasi, C. (2006) Understanding Social Psychology across Culture. London: Sage, p.140.

[3]. Wang, J., Wang, G.G., Ruona, W.E.A. and Rojewski, J.W. (2005) Confucian Values and the Implications for International HRD. Human Resource Development International, 8(3), 311–326.

[4]. Chen, X., Bishop J.W. and Scott, K.D. (2000) Teamwork in China: Where Reality Challenges Theory and Practice. In J.T. Lui, A.S. Tsui and E. Weldon (eds) Management and Organizations in the Chinese Context. New York: St Martin's Press.

15

Endnote – what does it all mean?

This review of learning, training and development has involved inputs and cases from people in some 19 countries. It is not claimed that this has produced a comprehensive view of what is going on in the world; it would be impossible to produce a robust summary at this stage in our global development. Instead, the book is written for practitioners and it shows that there is plenty of good practice taking place in all sorts of different organizations.

When I embarked on the project, I intended to highlight the way that different contexts would produce different ways of 'supporting, accelerating and directing' learning. In fact, the profession seems to have far more in common than divides it. It is true that different parts of the world are at different stages of sophistication in terms of their application of techniques. Further, most practitioners recognize that there are some prior experiences that the learner brings with them that require adjustments in delivery. By all means let's label this culture, but it is best seen as part of the wider context in which people learn. Today's development professionals act as intermediaries in the learning process and many of them are very good at their craft.

Let me now offer some personal observations on learning at work. I come from a part of the world which has prided itself on its strong educational values. My father was a teacher and ended his career as head of a school for educationally disadvantaged boys on a tough housing estate in Cardiff, Wales. I once asked him how he managed to keep 35 pupils at a time on track. 'Easy', he said, 'I tell them all to sit down, shut up and listen'. Having seen him in action I know that that was not his style at all. He put a lot of effort into developing their motivation through enhancing their self-esteem. His approach was based on delivering the right intervention at the right time. Commitment does matter – a key characteristic of a good trainer is enthusiasm for the job.

Most of the people interviewed, and all of those who provided case studies, thought that learning at work was a good thing. The acquisition of knowledge and skills gives people self-confidence in their immediate situation and makes them more positive about their ability to cope with future changes. We cannot wait for a 10-year academic study to investigate the validity of this belief – knowing that it would then come up with a definitive list of things that can't be said with any degree of certainty. We believe individual learning to be of value and set about our jobs with energy and commitment.

Moreover, in one important and under recognized respect, learning at work is different from learning within the education system. In 1976, the academic writer Fred Hirsch produced the hugely influential book with the title 'The Social Limits to Growth' [1]. He argued that we are approaching the limits to growth of our possessions and services, but that these are social limits. One idea that he articulated is of great relevance to our discussions here. He suggested that the economy is composed of two sectors: the material and the positional. The material sector encompasses the production of goods and services that can be increased without losses in quality. Positional goods are different. They are affected by social relationships – our enjoyment of these goals is affected by whether other people are consuming them too. Let's bring this complex but important idea to learning in the education and organizational settings.

Currently, learning in the education system, certainly for the abler, is displaying increasing characteristics of a positional good. Attendance at 'good schools' or 'ranked Universities' is seen as bestowing positional advantages at the expense of other students. Hence, access to these institutions becomes competitive and educational considerations are subordinate to desires for personal advantage.

Learning in organizations is not a positional good. True there are pressures on resources – learning takes time and this time must be found. However, for most organizations, the more people that can acquire work-related skills the better. Admittedly, there is a danger of trained labour going to work for the competition, but this does not seem to be a significant consideration, judging by the discussions and interviews undertaken in the course of the book. Indeed, I only once heard the argument advanced and that was by an individual at the Central Training Committee of the Chinese Communist Party!

By contrast, many leaders in many organizations see learning at work not only as a competitive weapon, but as something worthwhile in itself. My favourite illustration comes from Wales and is set out in Case study 15.1.

Case study 15.1 Learning in manufacturing in South Wales

The INA plant in Bynea, near Llanelli, South Wales employs some 280 people producing precision engineering components for the motor industry. It is part of Schaeffler (UK) which is a wholly owned subsidiary of a private company based in Germany. In the 1990s, the Llanelli plant enjoyed rapid growth; however, the factory experienced severe difficulties around the end of the decade as a result of the transfer of products to countries with lower labour costs. At one stage, it is fair to say that the workforce at Llanelli had given up. They saw products and machines leaving the plant with the associated loss of jobs and could see no end to this haemorrhaging.

Roger Evans was promoted internally to the post of Plant Director in 2001. He and his colleagues embarked on a successful and sustained management change process which has transformed the business. This programme has involved continuous improvement, training and flexible working; significantly these were linked by the statement: 'the rate of learning must be greater than the rate of change $(L > C)$'. Their investment in individual and team skills, which transformed the business, has led to wide recognition. The plant was Welsh People Development Company of the Year 2003, won the CIPD 'People Management' 2004 commendation for development activities, was regional winner of a National Training Award in 2004 and was awarded the Accelerate Wales Award for 'Best Improvement of a Lead Company, 2005'. Roger Evans was named Welsh Business Leader of the Year in 2006.

Roger Evans justifies the investment in people in the following terms:

In our business, people are the only differentiator. Plant and machinery are the same throughout the world. The challenge is to leverage the best out of people. This is about ensuring that they have the right skills and are orientated in the right direction. It is about building a capacity to understand and a sense of purpose.

In his field, competitors will always try to catch up, but they can only 'alter and adapt' not 'transpose and copy'. Success is achieved by understanding the people who comprise the workforce and their values. This requires determination but also humility.

You must be prepared to learn and adapt yourself at all times.

Poaching of trained employees by other organizations will always be an issue. The plant has lost good people who had featured in the succession plan. Roger Evans admits that it hurt at the time. However, such people will form part of an extended network (and could end up working for customers); it is therefore positive if they benefited from their time working at the Llanelli plant. Moreover, it is important that the company enriches the local community; developing people and giving them new skills is an important way of achieving this objective.

In short, a lot of people believe that learning is a good thing and will take the necessary steps to support it. Most professional developers, and certainly all that I have encountered in the course of this book, care about learning. We should be far less reticent in expressing this emotional commitment: there is nothing wrong in being emotionally committed to a good cause. The task now across the world is to model the behaviour we seek to promote in our organizations and to learn from each other. We must share information on good practices and be open and honest about our failures. In this modest way we might help to make the world a better place.

Reference

[1]. Hirsch, F. (1976) The Social Limits to Growth. London: Routledge.

Index